PRAISE FOR *NEW*

The prophet Isaiah spoke on behalf of God, "Behold I do a *new* thing!" I find great joy in watching the Spirit of God move in the lives of a new generation of Christian leaders. Watching Phil Baker grow as a man of God and vibrant leader has given me particular delight. I first met Phil as I taught him in a homiletics class at Houston Baptist University. Later, I saw how God used him as a gifted pastor. Through his writing in this book, I have come to know yet another dimension of his multi-faceted ministry. I commend this book to you wholeheartedly. You will profit greatly by reading it and taking the truth into your soul. In *NEW*, Phil demonstrates that the Spirit of our God is blowing with a new and fresh wind upon His church.

> Duane Brooks, PhD
> Pastor of Tallowood Baptist Church,
> Houston TX

Jesus delivered revolutionary teaching by asking great questions. In that same spirit, Phil is asking questions that modern Evangelicalism desperately needs to be asking. The beauty of *NEW* is that it takes us back to ideas that are very old, to bring biblical perspective to modern theological debates. It is refreshing to dive into the ancient Hebrew and Bible texts and also the writings of the earliest church fathers. Regardless of where you stand theologically, *NEW* is a helpful experience to process—not only what you believe, but why you believe it. As you dig in, you might find that familiar traditions and beliefs are actually old wineskins in need of bursting. *NEW* journeys through Phil's own questions of spirituality and faith, offering a refreshingly honest narrative of pursuing the fullness of Christ.

> Jason Bollinger
> CEO of Links International (USA)

Phil Baker's message through his first book, and his literary contribution to the world, is not success which is temporal, money which can distract, or the pursuit of mirages which are counterfeit locals of fulfillment. His message is the mandatory need for God and God alone. To ensure his readers get that truth, Baker shares a transparent pursuit of God as our utmost necessity in life now, and life eternal, illustrated by the many destructive personal lifestyles (wineskins), which prevent us from embracing Him as we could. Join Phil Baker on this pilgrimage to live for what matters most. You'll be glad you did.

Mike Satterfield
Teaching pastor, Fielder Church,
Arlington TX
Founder, Field of Grace Ministries

There are certain reminders believers need to hear again and again. One of the most important of these is to continue to check the filters through which we read and interpret Scripture. While this reminder predominates in seminary textbooks, Phil Baker demonstrates to a more popular audience the dangers of reading the Bible through the wrong lenses. Readers will enjoy the captivating topics and passages, and appreciate the pastoral tone in which Baker covers them.

Joey Dodson
Associate professor of biblical studies,
Ouachita Baptist University,
Arkadelphia AR

NEW

WINESKINS, AND THE SIMPLE WORDS OF CHRIST

PHIL BAKER

CONTENTS

For Daniel and Zeniah:

May you become mighty warriors for the kingdom of God who victoriously fight spiritual battles with spiritual weapons.

INTRODUCTION

Hi. My name is Phil Baker, and I can be a bit of a jerk. My wife, Stephanie, on the other hand, is an amazing woman. I knew she was a wonderful woman of God before we were married, but it's been over the roughly eight years we've been married that I've realized how truly amazing she is. Interestingly for me, this increasing awareness of the blessing I have in Stephanie has coincided with an increasing awareness of how much of a jerk I can be.

It started on our honeymoon. About five days into our adventure in Costa Rica, we came to the city of Arenal, where one can view a breathtakingly beautiful volcano and go on a zip-line through the rainforest. Being that Arenal is in a rainforest, there are several different types of primates wandering around that one would usually only be able to see firsthand at the zoo.

Now, you must know that we were married in the winter, and basketball season takes place during the thick of wintertime. I possess a slight addiction for all things NBA and especially the Houston Rockets, so being away from Internet access and American television for a few days during the season was sending me into the beginning stages of withdrawal. I know. I have a problem. You should pray for me.

Unfortunately, it gets worse. The first morning after breakfast, we were made aware that there were two computers in the main lobby that would be able to connect to the Internet. I was ecstatic! My prayers had been answered! Stephanie, not possessing the same perspective of God's benevolence, went outside with a few other travelers to look at the scenery.

After about fifteen minutes she hurried back inside, telling me there were howler monkeys in a tree a few yards away. She implored me to come outside and share that special moment with her. I assured her I would only be a few more minutes with Yao Ming and the Rockets, so she went back outside without me.

An additional fifteen minutes later, after the howler monkeys had disappeared into the forest, she dejectedly walked back in the lobby and found me still immersed in the nba.com website. And that, ladies and gentlemen, is how you make your brand-new bride cry on your honeymoon. I thought I messed up because I chose basketball over howler monkeys; she had to explain to me that I chose basketball over her.

I've found that marriage is often like having to take a prolonged, hard look in the mirror when you've just gotten up one morning hung-over, bloated, with bloodshot eyes and have nothing to fix yourself up with. Though some singles have done the hard work to develop remarkable self-awareness, being married forces us to confront dark, ugly truths about our character that, as single folks, we often spend a lot of time, money, and energy covering up and avoiding.

In the honeymoon phase of marriage we put our best foot forward and see each other through rose-colored glasses. However, suddenly the reality phase bursts on the scene, many expectations are proven fantasies, spouses' true natures are revealed, and conflicts ensue. The reality phase is the stage in marriage when the majority of affairs and divorces occur.[1] I believe one of the foundational reasons behind this heartbreaking fact is that during these years we come to see ourselves in an unfamiliar light that is at times overwhelming. Then, instead of doing the hard work of self-examination and repentance, we cast the spotlight onto our spouse, make him or her the villain, and look for a way out.

This same pattern began to rear its ugly head in me during the beginning of the reality phase of my relationship with Stephanie. I never considered having an affair or getting a divorce, but if my Savior had not mercifully intervened, I don't want to think what could have happened. In this window of time, Stephanie saw my inner-ugliness in ways no one else probably ever will. I'm so glad she loves Jesus more than she loves me, because it's her love for Jesus that caused her to continue loving this jerk.

One excruciatingly painful, but good thing, that Jesus began to show me during the reality phase was that I had entered marriage with a single-Phil mindset in many respects. I wanted to eat what I wanted to eat, when I wanted to eat it, without being questioned. I wanted to spend money how I wanted to spend money, when I wanted to spend money, without being questioned. I wanted to go wherever I wanted to go whenever I wanted to go there. I wanted to drive how I wanted to drive, watch what I wanted to watch, and listen to what I wanted to listen to at the volume I so desired (which, by the way, may be the reason my hearing has worsened over the last decade).

Without realizing it, I was trying to be married and single at the same time. I know that may sound like an awesome concept to some of you out there, but allow me to fill you in on a little secret: It doesn't work. Never will. What it produces is chaos. Mass-marital chaos. God began to show me again and again that if I wanted my marriage to be everything it is designed to be, single-Phil had to die.

Single-Phil didn't like hearing that at all. He put up quite a fight. In fact, I've realized that I've got to kill him every day for this to work, so that's something I'd love for you to pray for me about. And pray for Stephanie too, so that she will continue abiding in the Vine of Christ and manifest much fruit of patience toward the jerk she's married to.

This lesson about marriage is quite similar to an analogy Jesus told concerning how we are to receive Him and His teaching. He said in Matthew 9:16-17, "*But no one puts a patch of unshrunk cloth on an old garment; for the patch pulls away from the garment, and a worse tear results. Nor do people put new wine into old wineskins; otherwise the wineskins burst, and the wine pours out and the wineskins are ruined; but they put new wine into fresh wineskins, and both are preserved.*"

This is a book about Jesus and how His new wine systematically burst many of my old wineskins that I entered Christianity with, and also how He graciously helped me find new wineskins to receive Him correctly and live victoriously. Part one will cover the person and teaching of Jesus. Part two will pertain to the Holy Spirit and spiritual warfare. Part three will deal with how Jesus helps us to better understand the Old Testament. So, as you read this book, may you receive the new wine of Jesus Christ with new wineskins. And as you do, may the God of hope fill you with all joy and peace as you believe in Him so that you will overflow with hope by the power of the Holy Spirit.

PART 1

NEW WINESKINS OF JESUS AND HIS TEACHINGS

Chapter 1

TAKE ANOTHER LITTLE PIECE OF MY HEART, LORD JESUS

If you're reading this and you refereed any of my church-league basketball games when I was a kid, I need to ask your forgiveness. I'm sorry for cursing you out. I especially apologize to that referee in my senior year who threw me out of a game for dropping multiple f-bombs in his face, and then gave my team another technical foul due to me continuing to curse at him from the bleachers. I also apologize to my parents who witnessed those countless episodes of their Christ-professing youngest child letting a love for basketball dictate his approach toward Christianity rather than letting his love for Christ dictate his approach toward basketball.

God blessed me with a mother and father who loved Him and were committed to putting their children in an environment where they could learn to love Him as well. So, we went to our medium-sized, mostly white, Southern Baptist church in Houston, Texas, every Sunday. We were very active in the church. My parents taught well-attended Sunday school classes. My mom sang in the choir.

As a child, I was in Royal Ambassadors (Christianity's version of Boy Scouts), sang in the children's choir, and was also a faithful attender of Sunday school. I thought I was a pretty good kid. Yes, I was a bit hyperactive at times, especially when the Sunday school teachers foolishly brought donuts for us. And yes, one children's choir teacher promised me baseball cards each week if I'd stay calm, but at least I wasn't purposefully collapsing tables on other kids. I loved going to that church, and in some respects it still feels like home whenever I pop in.

My second grade Sunday school teachers were very compassionate people and very evangelistically minded. They had to be compassionate to voluntarily spend an hour with a room full of wild seven-year-olds every week. They quickly recognized in every one of us our need for a Savior and were committed to communicating that message to us each week. We were told that if we believed Jesus the Son of God is Lord, died for us on the cross for our sins, rose back to life on the third day, asked Him to forgive us for our sins, and invited Him into our hearts, then all the bad things we did would be forgiven, we could call ourselves Christians, and when we died we would get to go to heaven.

The next step was to go in front of the congregation, tell everybody what we've decided, and let them clap for us. The congregation would then form a huge line and come hug us. At the beginning of the service the next week, we'd go into this pool above where the choir sings, say "yes" to these same statements that we'd said we believed, get dunked, hear everybody clap again, and after the service get hugged and congratulated by a bunch of people once more. This all sounded like a good deal to me, and my friends had already done it.

I thought, *I believe God exists. I believe Jesus exists. I believe He died on the cross. I believe He rose again. I want to go to heaven. I want to be a Christian. Let's do this. Lord Jesus, please forgive me of my sins. I believe You died on the cross and rose from the dead. Please come into my heart.*

That may seem like a sweet, innocent little moment, but as I've reflected on that scene, there are some big problems going on. For one, since early childhood I was a jerk. What proved more detrimental to my relationships, though, was that I was absolutely oblivious to this truth. I definitely thought I was morally superior to my classmates, so when I was told that I needed Jesus to forgive me of my sins, I almost felt entitled to that forgiveness.

It's kind of like a student who gets the highest grade in the class on a test, maybe a 95, while the others fail miserably. With such a drastic discrepancy between the one student and all the others, the student with the 95 goes to the teacher and says, "I worked really hard, and it showed. Clearly I respect you and your class vastly more than the others. Will you please forgive my slight error and grant me five points of extra-credit?"

If one doesn't think there is much to be forgiven of, one won't think there are many changes needing to be made in one's character. I certainly didn't think I was evil, even though Jesus called His own disciples evil in Luke 11. In my mind, I was already a really good person, one of the best in my group, and now Jesus was going to be in my heart forever. Score one for Jesus!

"Invite Jesus into your heart." Interestingly, you'll never find that line in the Bible. It's not there. Have you ever seriously considered the implications of "asking Jesus into your heart" as it regards the issue of salvation?

Let me give you a few examples of what I'm getting at. Once or twice a month my wife and I host a small group from the church I pastor. When they arrive at our home, we invite them in. They are free to enjoy the AC, the couches, the food and drinks, the restroom, etc. We treat them like family. However, there are areas of the house that are closed off to them. There is also a time when they are welcome to arrive and a time when things need to wrap up and folks must go back to their homes. They are invited guests.

Twice during the time Stephanie and I have been married, we invited a college-age youth worker from our previous church that needed a place to live to stay with us. Each one was provided with a key to our house, access to our cars if needed, food if we cooked, their own room, their own bathroom, etc. However, even though they had their own room and even a key to the house, Stephanie and I owned the home. Though we loved having them stay with us and never had any reason to kick either of the youth workers out, we could have if we wanted to. The house belonged to us. They were merely invited to stay with us in a room of our house.

Are you starting to see where I'm going with this? Paul says in Romans 10:13, *"Everyone who calls upon the name of the Lord will be saved."* I believe that is true. But do you know what you're getting into when you call Jesus your Lord? The word "Lord" means "master." It implies ownership.

But who is the Lord? Is it Shiva? Is it Baal? No. When Jesus was born, an angel appeared to shepherds watching their flocks and said, *"Today in the city of David there has been born for you a Savior, who is Christ the Lord"* (Luke 2:11) Here we see that Jesus is called Savior, Christ, and Lord.

One chapter earlier, after Elizabeth, Mary's cousin, confirmed that Mary would give birth to Messiah Jesus, Mary replied, *"My soul exalts the Lord, and my spirit has rejoiced in God my Savior"* (Luke 1:46-47). Who was Luke saying is both Lord and Savior? Aren't they both God? Yes. Luke now connects the dots for us to show that Jesus is also God.[1]

There are so many examples in the Bible showing that Jesus is God, but for now I'll just give you one more in detail. In John 2, Jesus has just cleansed the Temple, and the religious leaders are infuriated. They ask Jesus what sign He will give to show He has the authority to do such a thing. He replies, *"Destroy this temple, and in three days I will raise it up"* (verse 19). John then states, *"But He was speaking of the temple of His body. So when He was raised from the dead, His disciples remembered that He said this"* (verses 21-22).

Okay, so who did Jesus say would raise Him up from the dead? He said He would raise Himself. Yet Paul wrote in Romans 10:9, *"If you confess with your mouth Jesus as Lord, and believe in your heart that God raised Him from the dead, you will be saved."* So, who raised Jesus from the dead, Jesus or God? The Bible teaches that Lord Jesus is God.

The speculation that Christians only began to teach the divinity of Jesus after the Council of Nicaea in 325 CE is simply untrue. Emperor Constantine didn't come up with that doctrine. From Genesis to Revelation, the Bible consistently affirms that Jesus is God. It is no wonder, then, that Ignatius, the Bishop of Antioch and disciple of the apostle John, wrote to the Trallian Christians in 105 CE, "Continue in intimate union with Jesus Christ our God."[2]

If Jesus is both Lord and God (see John 20:28); if the earth is the Lord's and all that is in it (see Psalm 24:1), which, by definition, includes our hearts, I'm not sure He will accept being merely a guest or even a renter. Jesus demands you sign over the title to the house. Take a look at just a few of Jesus's words concerning this matter:

> *Whoever wants to be My disciple must deny themselves and take up their cross and follow Me. For whoever wants to save their life will lose it, but whoever loses their life for Me and for the gospel will save it* (Mark 8:34-35).

> *What king, when he sets out to meet another king in battle, will not first sit down and consider whether he is strong enough with ten thousand men to encounter the one coming against him with twenty thousand? Or else, while the other is still far away, he sends a delegation and asks for terms of peace. So then, none of you can be My disciple who does not give up all his own possessions* (Luke 14:31-33).

> *Anyone who loves their life will lose it, while anyone who hates their life in this world will keep it for eternal life. Whoever serves Me must follow Me; and where I am, My servant also will be. My Father will honor the one who serves Me* (John 12:25-26).

These passages don't sound like your typical gospel presentations. You don't hear many evangelists using these verses before their altar calls, asking people to come give their lives away for Jesus. We read these words and want to say, "Take it easy, Jesus! No one's going to follow You if you keep on talking like that! You're being too extreme. Those words are not seeker-friendly. Do You even want any of these folks to come back next week?"

I'm going to be honest with you. As often as I teach from these verses and preach from them, a part of me cringes when I think about them. As I wrote in the introduction, I like doing what I want, when I want. I like shower-free Thursdays, even if Stephanie's not a fan of my post-Wednesday manly musk. I like eating mass quantities of fried okra and fried chicken until I'm agonizing with stomach pains on the bedroom floor, begging Stephanie to bring me some fiber pills and several large glasses of water. I like to watch Netflix or Sunday Night Football way past my bedtime, and then not be able to go to sleep and have to take an Ambien, only to wake up feeling like a zombie the next morning. I like doing me.

What I don't particularly enjoy is relinquishing control. However, when a controlling personality desires to enter into a relationship with the Lord of heaven and earth while remaining in control and reaping all of His benefits, what results is a big mess. And because I approached Jesus in this way for so long, I experienced mess after mess.

In Matthew 9, disciples of John the Baptist come to Jesus and ask why His disciples don't regularly fast like they and the Pharisees do. Setting aside two days a week to fast was a common practice of the Pharisees at that time.[3] Jesus responds by basically telling them that groomsmen preparing for a wedding don't fast while they still have the prospective groom in their company. But once the groom is married and taken away from them, they will get back to fasting.

There are several points our Lord is making here, but I believe the main thrust is that in the lives of His followers, who Jesus is, what He teaches, and what He has come to do takes precedence over everything else. He states, *"Neither do people pour new wine into old wineskins. If they do, the skins will burst; the wine will run out and the wineskins will be ruined. No, they pour new wine into new wineskins, and both are preserved"* (verse 17).

New wine expands as it ferments. New wineskins can handle new wine because new wineskins will expand with the fermenting new wine. However, old wineskins have already reached their capacity for expansion. So when new wine is poured into old wineskins, the new wine will literally cause the skins to burst, thus causing a huge mess and wasting both the new wine and old wineskins. My seven-year-old-self thought I could keep the old wineskins of being both self-righteous and self-governing while following Jesus. That's just not going to work.

It's kind of like the time my dad and I put together the basketball goal that's currently sitting in my driveway. Two grown men who've put many things together in the past don't need to completely depend on the instructions, right? Those instructions are just suggestions, aren't they? The instructions said the entire assembly would take around two hours. It took us two days. The reason? We did not get first things first and fully submit ourselves to the instructions.

Maybe you feel like you've tried the whole "Christian thing" and it didn't work for you. Let me ask you a question: Did you truly get first things first and submit yourself fully to the instructions? The instructions say Jesus must become your Lord. If you don't submit your entire self to Him as Lord, the whole "Christian thing" isn't going to work. God has only designed it to work according to the instructions. True Christianity isn't designed for Jesus to only have access to a piece of your heart; it is made for Him to own it all.

Jesus is more gracious, merciful, and patient than you can comprehend. He gave His entire life for you. When you repent of your sins and give your life to Him, He gives His life back into you through the Holy Spirit. As you walk with Him each day, He begins to transform you into a new person and make you more like Him.

This is what happened in my life. Jesus not only burst my early old wineskins but also several more as well, so that His new wine could take over fresh wineskins that would let Him be Himself in me. So much has changed since Jesus started helping me approach Him with new wineskins. I'm sure that referees throughout the Houston area are thankful.

In the next several chapters, I will cover several different aspects of Jesus and His teaching and the blessings of approaching Him with new wineskins. As you read the rest of this book, may the grace of the Lord Jesus Christ, the love of God the Father, and the fellowship of the Holy Spirit be with you in abundance.

Chapter 2

SEPIA JESUS

During my freshman year of college, some of my church buddies orchestrated a pickup game of basketball at the church gym. Unbeknownst to anyone, at some point that night a person dropped a melting piece of ice under my team's basket. I stole a pass on the opposite side of the court and headed down to my goal for an easy, uncontested layup. I decided to be slightly fancy and lay it up left-handed while slapping the backboard instead of just casually dropping the ball in with my right hand. I dribbled just to the left of the basket, planted with my right foot, and . . . tore my right anterior cruciate ligament.

The heart of man is prideful before a fall, and I crashed like Humpty Dumpty. Stupid ice cube. If you've ever had a major ACL repair, you know the rehab is excruciatingly painful to say the least. It's much more painful than the actual injury. There were days I was convinced my physical therapist was the antichrist, or at the least a sadist. However, I look back at it now and realize that if she hadn't forced me to develop full extension and flexion, I wouldn't be able to walk today. If she hadn't pushed me past the point my feelings told me was acceptable, I would have missed out on many things I enjoy and take for granted.

Once those several physical therapy sessions were over, it was up to me to put her expert strategies into practice and build strength into the muscles surrounding my right knee, which had atrophied significantly over the few months I was on crutches. Unfortunately, I trusted my feelings more than the expert's advice. I thought I could use basketball to strengthen my knee rather than the exercises recommended by the professional. Can you guess what happened?

About a year and a half after I tore my right ACL, I tore the meniscus in the same knee while playing basketball in the same gym. Have you heard about people getting their "ankles broken" on a crossover? Well, the youth minister of my church, Mike Satterfield, crossed me over and broke my knee.

It was kind of humorous, actually. One moment Mike was dribbling the ball and I was talking trash to him (something about taking the ball and his lunch money), and the next moment he shook me right out of the gym and into the hospital. Let that be a lesson to all of you out there. Don't ever talk trash to Mike Satterfield. You might embarrass and cripple yourself.

One of the main reasons I hurt my knee a second time, in conjunction with the root issue of pride, was that I had been filtering my physical therapist's counsel through the lens of my feelings and experiences. Her method of strengthening my knee was incredibly painful and not very exciting. Up until the ACL tear, I had built up quite strong legs, basically through playing basketball alone. Though it's not that big of a deal, as a 5'9" 18-year-old I could jump up and grab a ten-foot rim. Therefore, I reasoned that because basketball originally helped my legs become strong, and was far more enjoyable than the prescribed rehab, following my heart and using basketball as rehab was a better course of action than listening to the physical therapist.

Here are some questions to think about. What lens are you filtering Jesus and His teachings through? Is your understanding of Jesus and His teachings being passed through the lens of your experiences and feelings, the lens of your pastor's understanding of Jesus, or the lens of Saint Augustine, Martin Luther, John Calvin, or the popes? Like photographs with a brown filter, do you have a sepia Jesus? Or are you starting with Jesus and His teachings and then letting those filter your understanding of your feelings and experiences, your pastor's teachings, and the views of Jesus articulated by men such as Saint Augustine, Martin Luther, John Calvin, and the popes?

In Luke 6:40, Jesus says, "*The student is not above the teacher, but everyone who is fully trained will be like their teacher.*" In John 13:16, He states, "*No servant is greater than his master, nor is a messenger greater than the one who sent him.*" If Jesus is Lord and God, He is also the greatest teacher ever. If Jesus is Lord and God, He is also the master of all truth. Jesus isn't just the greatest teacher of truth and the master of all truth, for He said in John 14:6, "*I am the way, the truth, and the life.*" We can understand many truths and communicate many truths, but none of us can say with full integrity that we are the truth. These truths mean that I am not greater than Jesus, and neither are you. Saint Augustine wasn't greater than Jesus, and neither is Tim Keller. The apostle Paul wasn't greater than Jesus, and neither is John Piper.[1]

Martin Luther made wonderful contributions to Christendom. His 95 Theses helped reform Roman Catholicism, and he was the first to translate the Latin Bible into the German language. However, his translation was similar to many study Bibles of today, in that it came with introductions to each Testament and each book. Introductions in study Bibles are interesting because they often reveal the editor or commentator's slant or bias toward the text. They reveal his or her filter.

Before readers of the newly translated German Bible would even get to Matthew 1:1, they would see these words from Luther: "John's Gospel is the one, tender, true chief Gospel, far, far to be preferred to the other three and placed high above them. . . . So, too, the Epistles of St. Paul and St. Peter far surpass the other three Gospels—Matthew, Mark, and Luke. . . . In a word, St. John's Gospel and his first Epistle, St. Paul's Epistles—especially Romans, Galatians, and Ephesians—and St. Peter's first Epistle are the books that show you Christ and teach you all that it is necessary and good for you to know."[2]

Sepia Jesus. There were many good things that came about from the Protestant Reformation, but many sad and dangerous things as well. According to Luther, you don't actually need the Gospels of Matthew, Mark, or Luke to know who Jesus Christ is and what He requires. According to Luther, you don't actually need the Sermon on the Mount (Matthew 5–7) to understand the ethics that drive a life devoted to Jesus.

Unfortunately, that method of filtering Jesus and His teaching allowed Luther to feel at peace when ordering roughly 100,000 German peasants to be slaughtered by the nobility. He wrote, "I, Martin Luther slew all the peasants in the rebellion, for I said that they should be slain. All their blood is on my head, but I cast it upon the Lord God who commanded me to speak in this way."[3] Really? The Lord God commanded him to speak in that way?

Jesus said, *"So in everything, do to others what you would have them do to you, for this sums up the Law and the Prophets"* (Matthew 7:12). You might have heard something like that in elementary school. It's known as the Golden Rule. I have a hard time believing that Luther treated the German peasants the way he would've wanted to be treated by the Catholic Church, which persecuted him. Yet he clearly felt the Lord sanctioned those heinous actions. So what's going on?

What transpired with Luther is what goes on in all of us. I believe everyone that becomes a Christian enters that relationship with at least a few old wineskins. Like the Hebrews who were miraculously delivered out of slavery in Egypt, but within a few weeks of wandering in the wilderness were longing for the chains of Pharaoh once more, it is a much longer process to take Egypt out of us than to take us out of Egypt (see Exodus 16). Again, similar to the Hebrews in the desert, even after being redeemed we seem bent toward creating a Jesus that suits us, that is comfortable for us, that is okay with our vices, and so on. We tend to try to make a god in our own image.

We all come to the Bible with a filter; actually, we come with many filters. If you're like me, as a child you started learning about Jesus through the lens of your parents, Sunday school teachers, and pastors. Even my pastors were learning about Jesus through the filters of the commentaries on the Bible they read, the required reading in their seminary work, and the interpretation of Jesus and His teachings held by their seminary professors. The seminary professors were learning about Jesus through the filters of other professors and theologians, with certain denominational and hermeneutical slants and leanings.

Are we then left saying that everything is relative? Of course not. Am I now going to declare that I'm the only one with the corner on the truth? Not at all. I believe the original writings of the 66 books of the Bible are completely inspired by God. As such, I also believe that when Jesus said "*no servant is greater than his master*" (John 13:16), He called us to imitate His life of humility in all we do, even in the way we interpret Scripture.

Jesus is our master, so who are we to say Jesus didn't actually mean we are to treat others the way we want to be treated? Who are we to say Jesus didn't actually mean unless we forgive others their sins, our heavenly Father won't forgive us of our sins? Who are we to say Jesus didn't actually mean we are to love our enemies? Who are we to say Jesus didn't actually mean that not everyone who says to Him, "Lord, Lord," will enter the kingdom of heaven, but only the one who does the will of His Father who is in heaven?

These are such difficult teachings that when we read them, somewhere inside us a little evil voice says, "Did Jesus *really* mean that, though? Surely not! Think how much safer and fuller life would be if we disregarded those words." Sounds a little bit like Genesis 3:1, don't you think? So much heartache and destruction came into the world as a result of Adam and Eve not taking the Lord God at His word.

When Jesus began to challenge me to take His teachings at face value and filter everything else through them, a great crisis ensued in my heart. I was the worship leader and a small-group leader of a different Southern Baptist church in Texas at the time, and Jesus simply asked me, "If your traditions and doctrines don't line up with My life and teaching, which of those should be put out to pasture? New wine must be poured into new wineskins."

As Jesus said those words, I realized that if I began to teach that He meant exactly what He said, it might cost me my job in ministry. Losing my ministerial job would seriously affect my family's income and living situation, and I might be forced to get a "real" job or two. I might encounter a lot of persecution from my current church members, friends, family, and peers. Folks might label me as a heretic. I had to ask myself if knowing, teaching, and living the truth is worth it. Is Jesus worth it? It's easy to say yes, but when the things I just listed are actual possibilities, we find out if He actually is worth it to us.

Blaise Pascal once wrote, "Truth is so obscure in these times, and falsehood so established, that unless we love the truth, we cannot know it."[4] I realize what I'm asking you to do can be scary and difficult. Paradigm shifts usually are. Therefore, in the next chapter I'd like to begin to make what I believe is a historically valid case for us to take Jesus and His teaching at face value so that He truly becomes the lens by which we filter everything else. May you seek the truth, love the truth, know the truth, speak the truth, live the truth, continue in the truth, and be freed by the truth.

Chapter 3

JOHN WAYNE AND JESUS

There are several pictures of me as a child wearing a pseudo-buckskin jacket and pants with fringed edges and a coonskin cap. I didn't just admire Davy Crockett, the king of the wild frontier, I *was* Davy Crockett. I even tried to wear that silly costume to school. Fortunately, I wasn't allowed. Though that hurt my feelings at the time, someone in authority over me understood I didn't need to give my peers another reason to crack jokes on the short, stinky, sickly, skinny, hyperactive, slightly dyslexic pale kid with Napoleon Dynamite hair.

Davy Crockett became my hero after I saw John Wayne play him in the 1960 film *The Alamo,* where he swung his discharged rifle at approaching enemy soldiers as the screen faded to black. After seeing that movie I became fascinated with the story of the battle of the Alamo and the history of the Texas revolution. Over time, I began to realize there were several accounts of Crockett's death. Some portrayed him in an even larger-than-life light than John Wayne chose to, while others depicted scenes that were not too flattering. Honestly, seeing those varying accounts upset me. I was quite content with remembering Crockett going down like John Wayne did, and I desperately wanted the historical evidence to back up the tradition passed on to me. So, in a situation like this, how are we supposed to determine whose version is true? One step is to play the telephone game backward.

Do you remember this game from birthday parties when you were six to ten years old? Everyone sat in a circle, and an adult whispered a silly sentence to one of the kids, like, "Spray-painting hippos near the river with your wife isn't wise without a rifle." That kid would then try to remember the sentence correctly and whisper it into the ear of the person on his or her left. The process would go on until the message was communicated back to the first child. Inevitably, the last message would sound drastically different than the first, and everyone would have a good laugh. We would then trace the message backward and laugh even more when we determined who was responsible for distorting the interpretation, and, therefore, when those distortions occurred.

What I'm calling the telephone game is merely one of the basic filtering systems historians use to determine something's historical veracity. How about the doctrines of Christianity? Have you ever noticed that four theological experts can look at a simple passage like Matthew 5:44, where Jesus says, *"Love your enemies,"* and come away with four different interpretations? Which of the four has the right interpretation of the original message? If you were using the telephone game principle, where would you start to determine the original interpretation of the message?

You'd start at the original source and then hear the testimony of each successive person onward. You would start with studying how Jesus interpreted this command in His other words and also with His actions. Then, since no student is above his master, you would look at how the writings and actions of Jesus's apostles and disciples backed up the life and teaching of Jesus. Finally, if possible, you would look at the writings of the disciples of the apostles, the writings and accounts of the Early Church up to 313 CE, the time of Emperor Constantine's Treaty of Milan, and see if they both taught and lived out the same things Jesus and the apostles taught and lived out.

Let's look at some of the writings of Jesus and the apostles in the New Testament:

> *"You have heard that it was said, 'YOU SHALL LOVE YOUR NEIGHBOR and hate your enemy.' But I say to you, love your enemies and pray for those who persecute you, so that you may be sons of your Father who is in heaven. . . . For if you love those who love you, what reward do you have? Do not even the tax collectors do the same? If you greet only your brothers, what more are you doing than others? Do not even the Gentiles do the same? Therefore you are to be perfect, as your heavenly Father is perfect"* (Matthew 5:43-48).

> *Jesus [said], "Father, forgive them; for they do not know what they are doing"* (Luke 23:34).

> *Never pay back evil for evil to anyone. Respect what is right in the sight of all men. If possible, so far as it depends on you, be at peace with all men. Never take your own revenge, beloved, but leave room for the wrath of God, for it is written,*

"Vengeance is Mine, I will repay," says the Lord. . . . Do not be overcome by evil, but overcome evil with good (Romans 12:17-19, 21).

Christ Jesus came into the world to save sinners, among whom I am foremost of all. Yet for this reason I found mercy, so that in me as the foremost, Jesus Christ might demonstrate His perfect patience as an example for those who would believe in Him for eternal life (1 Timothy 1:15-16).

For you have been called for this purpose, since Christ also suffered for you, leaving you an example for you to follow in His steps, who committed no sin, nor was any deceit found in His mouth; and while being reviled, He did not revile in return; while suffering, He uttered no threats, but kept entrusting Himself to Him who judges righteously (1 Peter 2:21-23).

I am writing these things to you so that you may not sin. And if anyone sins, we have an Advocate with the Father, Jesus Christ the righteous; and He Himself is the propitiation for our sins; and not for ours only, but also for those of the whole world. By this we know that we have come to know Him, if we keep His commandments (1 John 2:1-3).

And now, testimony from the early Church:

The teaching [of the way of life] is this: Bless those who curse you and pray for your enemies. Fast for those who persecute you. For what reward is there, if you love only those who love you? Do not the Gentiles also do the same? Rather, love those who hate you, and you will not have an enemy (Didache, 80–140 CE).[1]

They comfort their oppressors and make them their friends. They do good to their enemies (Aristides, 125 CE).[2]

Now we pray for our enemies and try to win those who hate us unjustly so that they too may live in accordance with Christ's wonderful teachings, that they too may enter into the expectation, that they too may receive the same good things that we will receive from God, the ruler of the universe (Justin Martyr, 160 CE).[3]

"I say unto you, Love your enemies; bless them that curse you; pray for them that persecute you; that ye may be the sons of your Father who is in heaven, who causes His sun to rise on the evil and the good, and sends rain on the just and the unjust" (Athenagoras, 175 CE).[4]

Jesus commanded [His followers] not only not to hate men, but also to love their enemies. . . . He commanded not only not to injure their neighbors, nor to do them any evil, but also, when they are dealt with wickedly, to be long-suffering (Irenaeus, 180 CE).[5]

He bids us to love our enemies, bless them who curse us, and pray for those who despitefully use us. . . . An enemy must be aided, so that he may not continue as an enemy. For by help, good feeling is compacted and enmity dissolved (Clement of Alexandria, 195 CE).[6]

Do not willingly use force and do not return force when it is used against you (Commodianus, 240 CE).[7]

Christians do not attack their assailants in return, for it is not lawful for the innocent to kill even the guilty. . . . The hand must not be spotted with the sword and blood—not after the Eucharist is carried in it (Cyprian, 250 CE).[8]

Religion is to be defended – not by putting to death – but by dying. Not by cruelty, but by patient endurance. Not by guilt, but by good faith. For the former belongs to evil, but the latter to the good. . . . For if you wish to defend religion by bloodshed, tortures, and guilt, it will no longer be defended. Rather, it will be polluted and profaned (Lactantius, 304–313 CE).[9]

When I began reading these words for the first time, they were hard to swallow. Regardless of my feelings, here's the important question: do they line up with Jesus's life and teaching and the lives and teachings of the apostles? Clearly they do. And yes, I'm aware that the early Christian writers did make errors, and there are certain areas of doctrine where they are not all in agreement. However, the issue of nonresistance is one in which the early Church was completely united for the first 300 years of Christendom, despite facing intense persecution. Nonresistance was obviously the way of Jesus and the apostles in the New Testament.[10]

Perhaps one of the most beautiful descriptions of the early Christians is found in a document called *A Letter to Diognetus*, written sometime between 125 to 200 CE:

> Christians cannot be distinguished from the rest of human-kind by country, speech or customs. . . . They take part in everything as citizens and endure everything as aliens. Every foreign country is their homeland, and every homeland is a foreign country to them. . . . They live on earth, but their citizenship is in heaven. They obey the established laws, but through their life they surpass these laws. They love all people and are persecuted by all. Nobody knows them, and yet they are condemned. They are put to death, and just through this, they are brought to life. They are poor as beggars, and yet they make many rich. They lack everything, and yet they have everything in abundance. They are dishonored, and yet have their glory in this very dishonor. They are insulted, and just in this they are vindicated. They are abused, and yet they bless. They are assaulted, and yet it is they who show respect. Doing good, they are sentenced like evildoers. When punished with death, they rejoice in the certainty of being awakened to life. . . . In a word: what the soul is in the body, the Christians are in the world.[11]

What would cause Christians all over the earth to act this way, especially when it was so dangerous to be labeled a Christian? I believe the simple answer is that they took Jesus's words simply and seriously. Jesus knew that if He put His needs above ours and refused to die, we could not be saved, and He could not bear fruit for the kingdom of God. But if He put our needs above His, He could save and transform His enemies into sons and daughters of God that would bear much fruit for God's kingdom.

The early Christians recognized this simple example Christ set for us. They understood that when we put the needs of our enemies above ourselves, the power of the Gospel is unleashed. They can't help but see Jesus. And Jesus promised us that when He is lifted up, He will draw all people to Himself (see John 12:32). They also believed Lord Jesus when He said, *"If anyone serves Me, he must follow Me; and where I am, there My servant will be also; if anyone serves Me, the Father will honor him"* (verse 26). If we are really servants of the one we call our Lord, we must follow our Leader's example, and if we do, we will be where He is.

Whenever I start pontificating on such matters, someone always interjects the question, "But what would you do if someone broke into your house and wanted to hurt your wife?" Let me put it like this: I don't know what I would do, but I know what I should do. I know what I should do because I know what Jesus did do; He laid His life for everyone. He is the atoning sacrifice for our sins—and not just our sins, but the sins of the whole world. I don't want to be responsible for sending someone to hell that Jesus died to save.

However, I know I'm capable of snapping when people act in what I perceive is a threatening way toward my wife. When I was a youth minister, I had to apologize to a high school student for driving my knee into the kid's neck after he body-slammed my wife for mocking him after he made a foolish play in kickball. In situations like that my innate tendency has often been to act more like John Wayne than Jesus; to see Santa Anna's soldiers as the "bad guys" rather than people Jesus died to ransom.

Love has a strong desire to protect because, as Paul says, love always protects (see 1 Corinthians 13:7). The question I now need to ask myself is, *Who has Jesus called me to love?* First and foremost, He has called me to love Him with all my heart, soul, mind, and strength. I'm called to love my neighbors as myself. My brothers and sisters in Christ. My wife. My kids. My enemies.

Are not all Christians called to imitate Christ by demonstrating the love of God to all people? Are not all Christians, therefore, called to imitate Christ by seeking to protect the soul of every person on the planet from the deceit and ultimate destruction desired for them by our real enemies, the devil, and the spiritual forces of darkness? Are not all Christians called to fight spiritual battles with spiritual weapons rather than physical battles with physical weapons, and promised divine power to help us overcome our true adversaries (see 2 Corinthians 10:3-4)?

My boyhood hero, Davy Crockett, taught me that it was okay to kill as many people as necessary in order to protect one's land. But in Psalm 24:1-2, the true hero, God, gives us the correct perspective: *"The earth is the Lord's and all it contains, the world and those who dwell in it. For He has founded it upon the seas and established it upon the rivers.*" He is the Creator, so He owns creation. As Abraham Kuyper says, "There is not a square inch in the whole domain of our human existence over which Christ, who is Sovereign over all, does not cry, 'Mine!'"[12]

Yet some sick place in me prefers to say, "No. My rights as a Texan. My house. My stuff. My life." I know I have hurt so many people when my actions reflected a modified version of Jesus's words—a version that said, "Jesus is right in most situations, but there are practical exceptions where there is a better way." I have frequently been so selfish, and in those times demonstrated such a lack of trust in God. It seems that I often prefer the Davy Crockett kind of hero rather than the true hero God offers us in His Son, the Lord Jesus Christ, the radiance of His glory and the exact representation of His nature.

I'm not sure what happened to Davy Crockett in the end, but in Acts 7:55-56, we read how Stephen, one of the first deacons of the Church, was stoned to death by the members of the Sanhedrin for acting and speaking like Jesus. A young, zealous Pharisee named Saul looked on and approved of their actions. So, like his master, Jesus, Stephen chose to pray for their forgiveness. Then, "*being full of the Holy Spirit . . . [Stephen] gazed intently into heaven and saw the glory of God, and Jesus standing at the right hand of God; and he said, 'Behold, I see the heavens opened up and the Son of Man standing at the right hand of God.'*" Can you imagine being Stephen in that moment? I'm terrified and inspired at the thought. Surely the stones ceased to matter when Stephen's eyes met his Savior's.

Stephen's account demonstrates the veracity of Jesus's words in John 12:26: "*If anyone serves Me, he must follow Me; and where I am, there My servant will be also; if anyone serves Me, the Father will honor him.*" So may Jesus Christ be your true hero, and may you serve and follow Him no matter the cost. May you abide in Him, and let Him be Him in you. May you seek to love and protect the souls all of humanity from the snares of the devil. May your thoughts, words, and actions be full of peace. May you not be overcome by evil, but rather overcome evil with good. And may you be new wineskins for God to pour in the New Wine of Jesus Christ, that blessings would be unleashed into the world as you walk as Jesus walked by the power of the Holy Spirit.

Chapter 4

HYPERBOLIC JESUS

When I was in high school, a few friends and I skipped school one day and went to an understaffed electronics store. My friends had figured out how to remove the sensor from the CDs to prevent the store's alarm from tripping when they walked out with them under their jackets. The first time we went, I was terrified we would end up on the evening news. My conscience chided me for being an accomplice to theft and rebuked me for making fun of folks who experienced urinary incontinence in moments of duress.

I watched in disbelief as the whole process went down. One of my friends even picked up a CD for me, since I was the driver. The next time I went, I picked one up for myself. Then another. I think I stole about three CDs from that store that year. To some, my actions may not seem like a big deal; to others, the opposite may be true. What about Jesus? Does He have anything to say on the matter? Actually, He does.

> *"If your hand causes you to stumble, cut it off; it is better for you to enter life crippled, than, having your two hands, to go into hell. . . . If your foot causes you to stumble, cut it off; it is better for you to enter life lame, than, having your two feet, to be cast into hell. . . . If your eye causes you to stumble, throw it out; it is better for you to enter the kingdom of God with one eye, than, having two eyes, to be cast into hell"* (Mark 9:43-48).

Jesus says some harsh things in the Gospels, and these words are definitely near the top of the list. As we discussed in the last chapter, Jesus's command to love our enemies is not hyperbole or metaphor but literal. It would seem, then, that in this situation Jesus is commanding me to cut off my hand for stealing the CDs, and probably to pluck out one eye for coveting the CDs. Some Middle Eastern countries actually cut off the hands of thieves—and, not surprisingly, these places have quite low crime rates. So, is Jesus serious?

Clearly, He's serious about sin. But does He really want me to cut off my hand and pluck out my eye so I don't have to go to hell?

To answer these important questions, we need to ask some other important questions. First, are there examples in the Gospels of Jesus's disciples or potential disciples sinning with their eyes and hands in front of Jesus? Second, if there are examples, how did Jesus handle those situations? By analyzing those scenarios, we will be able to determine if Jesus literally calls us to cripple ourselves in order to avoid hell.

Jesus spent a significant amount of time talking about mankind's approach toward money. One of His most famous quotes comes from Matthew 6:22-24, where He explains how selfishness, materialism, greed, and even theft are all examples of eye-sins. He states, *"The eye is the lamp of the body; so then if your eye is clear, your whole body will be full of light. But if your eye is bad, your whole body will be full of darkness. If then the light that is in you is darkness, how great is the darkness! No one can serve two masters; for either he will hate the one and love the other, or he will be devoted to one and despise the other. You cannot serve God and wealth."* The "eye," what we value, will determine how we behave and how we treat people, things, and even God.

The Gospel writers depict Judas as having "bad eyes." Six days before Jesus is crucified, He is at the home of His cousin Lazarus, whom He previously raised from the dead. While Jesus is reclining at the table, Lazarus's sister Mary anoints Jesus's feet with a pound of pure nard to prepare Him for His upcoming burial. This perfume was valuable, and to use all of it on Jesus was generous and self-sacrificial. The bottle would have cost Mary around 11 months wages.[1]

Jesus commends Mary for her loving act, but Judas responds in a diametrically opposed manner. *"But Judas Iscariot, one of His disciples, who was intending to betray Him, said, 'Why was this perfume not sold for three hundred denarii and given to poor people?' Now he said this, not because he was concerned about the poor, but because he was a thief, and as he had the money box, he used to pilfer what was put into it"* (John 12:4-6). Jesus and Mary have good eyes and value the things God values. Judas's eyes, however, are corrupted. So Jesus rebukes Judas for rebuking Mary; but He doesn't ask for a spoon so Judas can pluck out his greedy eye. Interesting.

Later, when Jesus and His disciples are eating the Passover meal on the night He will be arrested, Jesus tells them one of them will betray Him. The disciples begin discussing who would do such a horrible thing, and then— can you believe it?—an argument breaks out concerning which one of them is the greatest. Try to imagine that conversation. As the grim reality of Jesus's impending betrayal, abandonment, denial, torture, and crucifixion begin to cause Him great distress, John cries out, "I'm His favorite!" Matthew replies, "I threw a huge party for Jesus with my money when I left my tax collecting booth!" Peter shouts, "I walked on water while all you cowards stayed on the boat!" Talk about awkward moments.

A few moments later, Jesus says to the group, *"Simon, Simon, behold, Satan has demanded permission to sift you like wheat; but I have prayed for you, that your faith may not fail. . . . When I sent you out without money belt and bag and sandals, you did not lack anything. . . . But now, whoever has a money belt is to take it along, likewise also a bag, and whoever has no sword is to sell his coat and buy one. For I tell you that this which is written must be fulfilled in Me, 'AND HE WAS NUMBERED WITH TRANSGRESSORS'; FOR THAT WHICH REFERS TO ME HAS ITS FULFILLMENT"* (Luke 22:31, 35-37).

Strange, isn't it, that throughout Jesus's ministry He has commanded His disciples to love their enemies and their neighbors as themselves, yet now He seems to be advocating the use of violence. Notice how Jesus reminds the disciples of their commissioning in Luke 9 and how they went out preaching the Gospel against all odds. They depended on God to meet even their most basic needs, and through the power of the Holy Spirit they healed people everywhere. Now Jesus tells the disciples that because He is about to be betrayed, they should sell their coats for swords. When the disciples bring to His attention they have two swords, Jesus tells them that is enough (see Luke 22:38).

Wait a minute. Two swords are enough for the revolution? Is it possible Jesus has not, in fact, changed His stance on violence but is rather choosing to make the most of a teachable moment, even at this tremendously stressful hour of His life? Why are the disciples supposed to sell their coats to buy swords? According to Jesus, the remaining disciples needed to have swords for the moment He would be betrayed so He would be numbered among transgressors, as the prophecy in Isaiah 53:12 declared. Therefore, we now ask the question, *Did any transgressions committed with swords occur among any of the 11 disciples in the Garden of Gethsemane during Jesus's arrest?*

We will begin by examining Mark's account of the incident:

> *Immediately while He was still speaking, Judas, one of the twelve, came up accompanied by a crowd with swords and clubs, who were from the chief priests and the scribes and the elders. Now he who was betraying Him had given them a*

signal, saying, "Whomever I kiss, He is the one; seize Him and lead Him away under guard." After coming, Judas immediately went to Him, saying, "Rabbi!" and kissed Him. They laid hands on Him and seized Him. But one of those who stood by drew his sword, and struck the slave of the high priest and cut off his ear. And Jesus said to them, "Have you come out with swords and clubs to arrest Me, as you would against a robber? Every day I was with you in the temple teaching, and you did not seize Me; but this has taken place to fulfill the Scriptures." And they all left Him and fled (Mark 14:43-50).

In Mark's account, Jesus lives out His own command to not resist the evil person (see verse 39), and then rebukes His captors for bringing swords and clubs to apprehend Him. Strange, considering a little while ago Jesus gave His disciples permission to bring two swords to the scene. Jesus concludes His rebuke by informing them that their sinful actions have just fulfilled ancient prophecies concerning the Messiah. Mark's account was most likely the earliest of the four Gospels.[2] His is also the most concise. Matthew's account, also under the inspiration of the Holy Spirit, sheds more light on this defining moment in history.

Matthew reveals in his account, told in Matthew 26:47-56, a level of compassion in Jesus that seems otherworldly. Not only does Jesus practice His message of nonviolent resistance toward His betrayer, Judas, and the arresting mob, but He also does good to those who hate Him and is merciful as His heavenly Father is merciful (see Luke 6:27-36). Earlier in His three-year ministry, Jesus had warned Judas that one of the disciples would betray Him. Now, instead of destroying him there on the spot, Jesus calls Judas a friend and allows him to go through with this villainous deed in order to fulfill the Scriptures.

In Mark's account, it is at this point that one of the disciples slices off an ear of the slave of the high priest (see 14:47). Jesus then rebukes the mob for coming to arrest Him with swords and clubs, as if He were a bandit. Matthew, however, reveals that before Jesus rebukes the mob, He rebukes the disciple for living by the sword and commands him to put the sword back in its place (see 26:52-54). He then calls the disciple to think rationally. If He truly is the Messiah, as the disciple professes He is, then He has "twelve legions of angels" at His command (verse 53). In biblical times, a legion was said to consist of around 6,000 Roman soldiers.[3] So at any particular moment, Jesus could summon 72,000 angels to go to war for Him. The Lord Jesus doesn't need worldly weapons to fight His battles.

What about Luke? What jewels does he uncover at the scene of the crime in his account, told in Luke 22:47-53? First, Luke lets us know that when the disciples saw Jesus was about to be arrested, they asked if they should attack with the two swords He told them to bring. From the earlier verses, where Jesus told them to sell their coats for swords, we might expect to hear Jesus yell, "Yes! Now! Attack!" But Jesus remains silent. Why does Jesus not tell them to resist the evildoers? Why does He not give the okay to harm His betrayer and arrestors? Why does He not tell them to wage war with worldly weapons? If there was ever a time for a just war, this is it. Yet Jesus doesn't give the go-ahead.

Jesus is not a hypocrite. He is not going to contradict Himself, even when His back is against the wall. Jesus is going to walk the talk and practice what He preaches—and He expects His followers to do the same. Therefore, when His disciple cuts off the right ear of the slave, Jesus tells him, "*Stop! No more of this!*" (verse 51). Then, continuing to practice what He preaches, Jesus blesses His persecutors by healing the ear of the slave. Jesus didn't utter empty words. When He called His disciples to follow Him, He meant it. Jesus is the way that we are to follow.

John wrote the last Gospel, most likely between 90–100 CE.[4] His account of the incident is not dissimilar from the other Gospels, but the details he adds bear tremendous significance on this story. In his account, Jesus and His disciples weren't merely up against a ragtag mob sent by the chief priests and Pharisees. Rather, they were up against a Roman cohort and officers from the chief priests and Pharisees (see verse 3). History tells us a Roman cohort is a battalion of soldiers numbering around 600 soldiers.[5] Needless to say, the Jewish authorities were planning on making the most of this opportunity. In their minds, there was no way they were going to let Jesus avoid capture again, as He had every time before. Just in case of a power play, the chief priest and Pharisees brought in the big guns to subdue this supposed troubler of Israel and the world.

> *Judas then, having received the Roman cohort and officers from the chief priests and the Pharisees, came there with lanterns and torches and weapons. So Jesus, knowing all the things that were coming upon Him, went forth and said to them, "Whom do you seek?" They answered Him, "Jesus the*

Nazarene." He said to them, "I am He." And Judas also, who was betraying Him, was standing with them. So when He said to them, "I am He," they drew back and fell to the ground. Therefore He again asked them, "Whom do you seek?" And they said, "Jesus the Nazarene." Jesus answered, "I told you that I am He; so if you seek Me, let these go their way," to fulfill the word which He spoke, "Of those whom You have given Me I lost not one." Simon Peter then, having a sword, drew it and struck the high priest's slave, and cut off his right ear; and the slave's name was Malchus. So Jesus said to Peter, "Put the sword into the sheath; the cup which the Father has given Me, shall I not drink it?" (John 18:3-11).

As it turns out a power play did ensue, and what it reveals is astonishing. Jesus walks right up to the Roman soldiers and Jewish officers and asks them whom they are seeking. They answer *"Jesus the Nazarene,"* to which Jesus replies, *"I am He."* Interestingly, the translators added the word "He" into the text for grammatical reasons. What Jesus actually says is, *"I am."* At these words, the entire army of arrestors, including Judas, draws back and falls to the ground. Then Jesus tells them if they have come to arrest Him, they should let the others go. At this point they still haven't moved. Imagine hundreds of trained soldiers and officers on the ground, only listening to Jesus.

I've never seen anything like this in my near three-and-a-half decades. All the crazy arrests I've seen on *Cops*, the evening news reports, and even YouTube pale in comparison to what happened in the Garden of Gethsemane that night. When Jesus said, *"I am,"* He was quoting Exodus 3, where the Lord God appears to Moses in a burning bush and tells His plan for Moses to lead the Hebrews out of bondage. In verse 13, a curious, yet terrified, Moses says to the Almighty God, *"Behold, I am going to the sons of Israel, and I will say to them, 'The God of your fathers has sent me to you.' Now they may say to me, 'What is His name?' What shall I say to them?"* God replies, *"I AM WHO I AM . . . thus you shall say to the sons of Israel, 'I AM has sent me to you'"* (verse 14).

When Jesus tells His arrestors *"I am,"* He is teaching them a powerful lesson. He is not only the Messiah but also the One who spoke to Moses out of the burning bush. He is the Lord God; and if He is the Lord God, He is the source of all power. No human army can stop Him. He calls the shots. All He has to do is peel back the curtain a tad and show folks a bit of His divinity, and we would all be forced to acknowledge He is God.

Chuck Swindoll writes of John's account, "Jesus again employed the highly significant self-designation, *ego eimi*, 'I AM'. . . . John rarely includes details unless they have theological significance. The enemies of God shrank before the presence of the Almighty, foreshadowing their posture at the end of time."[6] If Jesus of Nazareth, the Lord God, gave each of these men what they deserved, they would all be annihilated. But Jesus didn't do anything different than what He had been doing the last three years of His ministry. He did not come to lord His power over people but to serve God by serving us all.

John informs us that Malchus is the name of the high priest's slave who was assaulted by the disciple wielding his sword. John also clues us in that Peter, the disciple who a few hours ago brashly boasted of his greatness and faithfulness to Jesus, is the very one who again is not pursuing God's interests, but man's, by attacking the subdued Malchus. Why does John pause to give us the name of the man whose ear Jesus healed?

Malchus's name means "kingly one."[7] This detail begs the question as to who acts more like King Jesus in this scene—Judas, Peter, or Malchus? Jesus had commanded His followers, *"You have heard that it was said, 'An eye for an eye, and a tooth for a tooth.' But I say to you, do not resist an evil person; but whoever slaps you on your right cheek, turn the other to him also"* (Matthew 5:38-39).

Malchus left quite a testimony. All four Gospel writers remain silent about his actions after the assault. The most logical explanation for this omission is that neither Jesus nor anyone else had to break up a brawl between Peter and Malchus in order for Jesus to heal his ear. Malchus was not even a follower of Jesus, yet he, rather than Judas and Peter, seems to be the one most imitating the meekness of the King.

None of the Gospel writers record any retaliatory words or actions by Malchus. Similarly, Isaiah prophesied that the Messiah, Jesus, the suffering Servant and true King of Israel, while meekly and quietly taking the people's sin on Himself, would not do any violence (see Isaiah 53:9). The meek inherit the earth; they don't betray, bully, and hurt others to obtain it for themselves. Meek Malchus left room for the wrath of God; he left room for God to repay. In doing so, he became the recipient of a blatant miraculous demonstration of God's love, compassion, and healing power.

In Malchus's testimony, I recognize that my actions don't reflect the actions of my King as consistently or purely as they should. In fact, as someone who identifies himself as a Christian, my portrayal of Christ to the world is often skewed with hypocrisy. My eyes and hands have willfully engaged in sin more times than I can imagine. I've valued countless things above Him and hurt countless others for the sake of those idols. My eyes deserve to be plucked out and my hands cut off.

Though Jesus doesn't demand either of Judas, Peter, or us, His earlier words in Mark 9 and His actions here demonstrate how serious He is about sin. In one sense, Jesus wasn't using hyperbole. It actually would be better for Judas, Peter, Malchus, or any of us to enter life crippled rather than having two eyes or two hands and go into the unquenchable fire of hell. Part of the good news is that because Jesus absorbed all our sin on Himself on the cross and then victoriously rose from the dead on the third day, those who put their faith entirely in Him and follow His way will be completely and permanently healed in the end, even if their bodies are killed by their persecutors.

But what about Judas? If it was prophesied he would betray Jesus, did he really have a shot at having faith in Jesus and receiving eternal life? If not, what does that say about God, who supposedly so loves the world? We will look at these questions and more in the next chapter. As you continue reading, may you grow in the grace and knowledge of the Lord Jesus Christ.

Chapter 5

JUDAS AND JESUS

Imagine one day an eleven-year-old quadriplegic boy and his father came home from the store with $120 worth of groceries. As the dad lifted his boy out of the car, he turned to his son and said, "Son, I love you and I've got confidence in you. I'm going inside to wash up. Have all the groceries inside by the time I come out of the restroom. If you obey me, you can have two scoops of ice cream after dinner. But if you disobey me . . . just remember what happened the last time you disobeyed me. Okay, buddy?"

The child, not wanting to disappoint His father, drove his own smaller motorized vehicle around to the back of the car to begin what seemed like the impossible. He leaned his head over into the trunk to take hold of the bag containing the milk, gripping the handles with his teeth. Unfortunately, as he slowly pulled the milk toward him, it toppled to the ground, spilling everywhere. At that moment his father burst out of the back door to see the sea of milk covering the driveway. The boy cried and apologized, but to no avail. The enraged father grabbed his paralyzed son and proceeded to beat and berate the boy.[1]

I realize this hypothetical situation is extreme. It almost feels like a modern form of slavery. An incredibly cruel master toys with a young slave by promising rewards if certain tasks are performed, but then manipulates those scenarios so failure is always ensured. But what about Judas? Was he a slave? In the biblical accounts, he appears to be living with the same opportunities to enter the kingdom of God as the other disciples. But was that really the case? Did he ever have a chance at redemption?

It had been prophesied hundreds of years before Judas's lifetime that someone close to the Messiah would betray the innocent Anointed One, do it for 30 pieces of silver, and that money would be used to buy a potter's field. So did Judas ever have a chance at eternal life? Did he have the ability to choose to love and follow Jesus, or was he set up and forced, like a slave, to become the Messiah's betrayer? What do those answers say about God?

Before going any further, I must admit that many people much more intelligent and educated than me have written lengthy books on the issues of God's sovereignty and mankind's free will. So as I give my thoughts on these weighty matters in one chapter, please know that we are merely dipping our toes into the ocean. Also, I'd like you to consider how you formed your beliefs on this matter. Did they come from reading the Scriptures, your pastor's teachings, your parents' convictions, or a professor's instructions?

In some of my undergraduate classes in my Christianity major, I was basically taught to understand the issues of sovereignty and free will first through the lens of John Calvin's beliefs, and then through certain words of the apostle Paul that corresponded with Calvin's teachings, and then the other Scriptures. I must say I am thankful for the education I received, and I wouldn't be where I am today if not for the good seed that was sown into me while in college. However, looking back, I can see the filter through which I was being taught to understand the Scriptures.

What I would like you to do now is prayerfully put your preconceptions of these topics aside. Instead of beginning with sixteenth-century writings, we will again play the game of telephone. We will look at several Scriptures and early Christian quotes that deal with the topic of God's sovereignty. Then we will do the same with the subject of mankind's free will. After examining all these weighty words, we will be able to give a sound reply to the questions concerning Judas. Are you ready? We will begin with what the Scripture says about God's sovereignty:

> *The Lord kills and makes alive; He brings down to Sheol and raises up. The Lord makes poor and rich; He brings low, He also exalts. He raises the poor from the dust, He lifts the needy from the ash heap to make them sit with nobles, and inherit a seat of honor; for the pillars of the earth are the Lord's, and He set the world on them. He keeps the feet of His godly ones, but the wicked ones are silenced in darkness; for not by might shall a man prevail. Those who contend with the Lord will be shattered* (1 Samuel 2:6-10).

> *The lovingkindness of the Lord is from everlasting to everlasting on those who fear Him, and His righteousness to children's children, to those who keep His covenant and remember His precepts to do them. The Lord has established His throne in the heavens, and His sovereignty rules over all* (Psalm 103:17-19).

Remember the former things long past, for I am God, and there is no other; I am God, and there is no one like Me, declaring the end from the beginning, and from ancient times things which have not been done, saying, "My purpose will be established, and I will accomplish all My good pleasure" (Isaiah 46:9-10).

And we know that God causes all things to work together for good to those who love God, to those who are called according to His purpose. For those whom He foreknew, He also predestined to become conformed to the image of His Son, so that He would be the firstborn among many brethren; and these whom He predestined, He also called; and these whom He called, He also justified; and these whom He justified, He also glorified (Romans 8:28-30).

I charge you in the presence of God, who gives life to all things, and of Christ Jesus, who testified the good confession before Pontius Pilate, that you keep the commandment without stain or reproach until the appearing of our Lord Jesus Christ, which He will bring about at the proper time—He who is the blessed and only Sovereign, the King of kings and Lord of lords (1 Timothy 6:13-15).

Peter, an apostle of Jesus Christ, to those . . . who are chosen according to the foreknowledge of God the Father, by the sanctifying work of the Spirit, to obey Jesus Christ and be sprinkled with His blood: May grace and peace be yours in the fullest measure (1 Peter 1:1-2).

Now, here is some testimony from the early Church on God's sovereignty:

To her who has found mercy in the greatness of the All-Highest Father, and Jesus Christ His only Son; to the church beloved and enlightened in her love to our God Jesus Christ by the will of Him who wills all things (Ignatius, 105 CE).[2]

They were convinced that they should call the Maker of this universe the Father, for He exercises a providence over all things and arranges the affairs of our world (Irenaeus, 180 CE).[3]

Nothing happens without the will of the Lord of the universe. It remains to say that such things happen without the prevention of God. For this alone saves both the providence and the goodness of God. We must not, therefore, think that He actively produces afflictions. . . . Rather, we must be persuaded that He does not prevent those beings who cause them. Yet, He overrules for good the crimes of His enemies (Clement of Alexandria, 195 CE).[4]

Kings are not appointed by the son of Saturn . . . but by God, who governs all things and who wisely arranges whatever belongs to the appointment of kings (Origen, 248 CE).[5]

"And allow us not to be led into temptation." In these words, it is shown that the adversary can do nothing against us unless God has first permitted it. So all of our fear, devotion, and obedience should be turned toward God. For in our temptations, nothing is permitted to do evil unless power is given from Him (Cyprian, 250 CE).[6]

From these Scriptures and commentaries by the early Christians, we see that God is absolutely sovereign and the ultimate ruler of all. He created all things and reigns over all things. Nothing happens that He is not aware of, that He does allow, or that He will not use to accomplish His good, pleasing, and perfect will. Because He exists outside of time, He is able to see and know everyone who will eventually end up with Him in the new heavens and new earth, and who will burn in the lake of fire. But what does Scripture say about our free will as it relates to God's sovereignty?

So it came about in the course of time that Cain brought an offering to the Lord of the fruit of the ground. Abel, on his part also brought of the firstlings of his flock and of their fat portions. And the Lord had regard for Abel and for his offering; but for Cain and for his offering He had no regard. So Cain became very angry and his countenance fell. Then the Lord said to Cain, "Why are you angry? And why has your countenance fallen? If you do well, will not your countenance be lifted up? And if you do not do well, sin is crouching at the door; and its desire is for you, but you must master it" (Genesis 4:3-7).

For this commandment which I command you today is not too difficult for you, nor is it out of reach. It is not in heaven, that you should say, "Who will go up to heaven for us to get it for us and make us hear it, that we may observe it?" Nor is it beyond the sea, that you should say, "Who will cross the sea for us to get it for us and make us hear it, that we may observe it?" But the word is very near you, in your mouth and in your heart, that you may observe it. . . . I call heaven and earth to witness against you today, that I have set before you life and death, the blessing and the curse. So choose life in order that you may live, you and your descendants, by loving the Lord your God, by obeying His voice, and by holding fast to Him (Deuteronomy 30:11-14, 19-20).

"Woe to the rebellious children," declares the Lord, "Who execute a plan, but not Mine, and make an alliance, but not of My Spirit, in order to add sin to sin; who proceed down to Egypt without consulting Me, to take refuge in the safety of Pharaoh and to seek shelter in the shadow of Egypt!" . . . For thus the Lord God, the Holy One of Israel, has said, "In repentance and rest you will be saved, in quietness and trust is your strength." But you were not willing (Isaiah 30:1-2, 15).

Jerusalem, Jerusalem, who kills the prophets and stones those who are sent to her! How often I wanted to gather your children together, the way a hen gathers her chicks under her wings, and you were unwilling (Matthew 23:37).

As He was setting out on a journey, a man ran up to Him and knelt before Him, and asked Him, "Good Teacher, what shall I do to inherit eternal life?" And Jesus said to him, "Why do you call Me good? No one is good except God alone. You know the commandments, 'Do not murder, Do not commit adultery, Do not steal, Do not bear false witness, Do not defraud, Honor your father and mother.'" And he said to Him, "Teacher, I have kept all these things from my youth up." Looking at him, Jesus felt a love for him and said to him, "One thing you lack: go and sell all you possess and give to the poor, and you will have treasure in heaven;

and come, follow Me." But at these words he was saddened,
and he went away grieving, for he was one who owned much
property (Mark 10:17-22).

"I say to you, among those born of women there is no one
greater than John; yet he who is least in the kingdom of God
is greater than he." When all the people and the tax collec-
tors heard this, they acknowledged God's justice, having been
baptized with the baptism of John. But the Pharisees and the
lawyers rejected God's purpose for themselves, not having been
baptized by John (Luke 7:28-30).

Here is some testimony from the early Church on our free will:

When you are desirous to do well, God is also ready to assist
you (Ignatius, 105 CE).[7]

We have learned from the prophets, and we hold it to be true,
that punishments, chastisements, and good rewards are rendered according to the merit of each man's actions. Now, if
this is not so, but all things happen by fate, then neither is
anything at all in our own power. For if it is predetermined
that this man will be good, and this other man will be evil,
neither is the first one meritorious nor the latter man to be
blamed. And again, unless the human race has the power of
avoiding evil and choosing good by free choice, they are not
accountable for their actions. . . . We maintain that each man
acts rightly or sins by his free choice (Justin Martyr, 160 CE).[8]

But man, being endowed with reason, and in this respect
similar to God, having been made free in his will, and with
power over himself, is himself his own cause that sometimes
he becomes wheat, and sometimes chaff (Irenaeus, 180 CE).[9]

Christ passed through every stage in life in order that He
Himself could serve as a law for persons of every age, and
that, by being present among us, He could demonstrate His
own manhood as a model for all men. Furthermore, through
Himself He could prove that God made nothing evil and
that man possesses the capacity of self-determination. For

man is able to both will and not to will. He is endowed with power to do both (Hippolytus, 225 CE).[10]

Since we consider God to be both good and just, let us see how the good and just God could harden the heart of Pharaoh. . . . If the sun had a voice, it might say, "I both liquefy and dry up." Although liquefying and drying are opposite things, the sun would not speak falsely on this point. For wax is melted and mud is dried up by the same heat. In the same way, the operation performed through the instrumentality of Moses, on the one hand, hardened Pharaoh (because of his own wickedness), and it softened the mixed Egyptian multitude, who departed with the Hebrews (Origen, 225 CE).[11]

I do not think that God urges man to obey His commandments, but then deprives him of the power to obey or disobey. . . . He does not give a command in order to take away the power that He has given. Rather, He gives it in order to bestow a better gift . . . in return for his having rendered obedience to God. . . . I say that man was made with free will (Methodius, 290 CE).[12]

These Scriptures and commentaries reveal that God, in His sovereignty, has given all mankind the free will to accept or reject Him by His grace through faith. He does not dole out rewards or punishments if the recipients are incapable of completing the prescribed tasks. Therefore, He does not arbitrarily select some people for salvation and some for damnation, but based on His foreknowledge of those who will choose to receive Him, He sets in motion a process by which they are conformed to the image of His Son. However, as with Jesus and the rich young ruler in Mark 10, God still compassionately reaches out to those who will reject Him, showing that His grace is resistible.

The story of the rich young ruler also demonstrates the truth of Ezekiel 33:12-13—that though unregenerate people are capable of doing good things, those good things cannot save them.[13] Jesus affirmed the rich young ruler had kept many of God's commands, yet he failed in at least one area, which put him in dire need of a Savior. We know from James 2:10 that even if we stumble in keeping one point of the Law we are guilty of violating it all, and Jesus tells us the whole Law is summed up in the commandment that we are to love our neighbor as ourselves. Therefore, it is quite easy to understand why Jesus told the man, *"No one is good except God alone."* No one has ever loved their neighbors as themselves throughout their whole life. No one, that is, except Jesus.

Paul writes in Romans 6 that people who have not yet been born again are slaves to sin. However, the Bible clearly demonstrates that while disobedience is the norm for unregenerate people, God has given everyone the grace to do good things.[14] So, what does it mean that we are slaves to sin?

Paul writes in Titus 3:3, *"For we also once were foolish ourselves, disobedient, deceived, enslaved to various lusts and pleasures, spending our life in malice and envy, hateful, hating one another."* The word translated "enslaved" is *douleuontes*, and it is found two other times in Scripture (Romans 12:11 and Ephesians 6:7). Each time, Paul uses the word to mean rendering service to either God or people.[15] Each time, he calls people to do this volitionally, without being forced by an outside or inside entity.[16] Paul wrote in Titus 3 that humans were habitually and volitionally presenting themselves to their lusts and pleasures to render them service. At the same time, as Deuteronomy 30:11 reminds us, God's commands were neither too difficult for humans nor out of their reach.

In Romans 6:16, Paul writes, *"Do you not know that when you present yourselves to someone as slaves for obedience, you are slaves of the one whom you obey, either of sin resulting in death, or of obedience resulting in righteousness?"* In Genesis 3, Adam and Eve were presented with a choice as to which voice they would obey. They chose to obey Satan, and when they did they transferred their allegiance to him. I will discuss this subject more in a later chapter, but for now consider these Scriptures:

> *Truly, truly, I say to you, everyone who commits sin is the slave of sin. The slave does not remain in the house forever; the son does remain forever. So if the Son makes you free, you will be free indeed* (John 8:34-36).

> *For He rescued us from the domain of darkness, and transferred us to the kingdom of His beloved Son, in whom we have redemption, the forgiveness of sins* (Colossians 1:13-14).

> *The Lord's bond-servant must not be quarrelsome, but be kind to all, able to teach, patient when wronged, with*

gentleness correcting those who are in opposition, if perhaps God may grant them repentance leading to the knowledge of the truth, and they may come to their senses and escape from the snare of the devil, having been held captive by him to do his will (2 Timothy 2:24-26).

We know that we are of God, and that the whole world lies in the power of the evil one (1 John 5:19).

Basically, we are born with natures that are corrupt but not totally depraved. Once we knowingly sin, we become slaves of Satan's kingdom and need a Redeemer to save us by grace through faith.[17] C.S. Lewis described this truth in his book *The Lion, the Witch and the Wardrobe*. In the story, Peter, Susan, Edmund, and Lucy discovered a wardrobe that led them into a new world named Narnia. While there, Edmund met the evil White Witch, who befriended him and offered him Turkish delight if he brought his siblings back to her. She also promised Edmund that if he accomplished that task, he would rule over his siblings. Edmund went back to his siblings, lied to them, and manipulated them, but he didn't succeed in convincing them to follow him.

So Edmund left them and went back to the White Witch. However, according to the rules of Narnia, all traitors belong to the White Witch. He now became her slave. Eventually, the children met Aslan the lion, the king of Narnia, and formed an army to fight the army of the White Witch. But before the battle, the Witch went to Aslan's tent and reminded him of the rules. He couldn't just take Edmund back, for she had the right to execute every traitor. Aslan persuaded her to renounce her claim on Edmund's life by bargaining to exchange his life for Edmund's. Aslan was tortured that night and finally executed so Edmund could be set free. But in the morning, Aslan was resurrected![18]

This is a beautiful depiction of the Gospel. We are all like Edmund, for when we sin, we choose Satan as our master—and nothing in our power can free us from his grasp. Only by the blood of Jesus can we be ransomed, redeemed, and born again into the kingdom of God. However, Edmund could disobey the Witch even when he was in her custody. Also, even after Aslan did all that was necessary for Edmund's redemption, he didn't force Edmund to choose life. By Jesus's work on the cross and through His resurrection, the doors of Satan's kingdom are now wide open for anyone on spiritual death row to go free. But they must choose to give their lives to Jesus by grace through faith in Him.

So, how does all this relate to our original questions concerning Judas? Perhaps the best way to answer is to consider Peter, the other disciple who failed Jesus on His last night. Toward the end of Peter's life, he wrote two letters that are preserved in the New Testament. In 2 Peter 3:7-9, he writes of the synergy of God's sovereignty and man's free will: "*But by His word the present heavens and earth are being reserved for fire, kept for the day of judgment and destruction of ungodly men. But do not let this one fact escape your notice, beloved, that with the Lord one day is like a thousand years, and a thousand years like one day. The Lord is not slow about His promise, as some count slowness, but is patient toward you, not wishing for any to perish but for all to come to repentance.*"

Now consider the remarks of Clement of Alexandria, which also convey this synergy: "A man by himself working and toiling at freedom from passion achieves nothing. But if he plainly shows himself very desirous and earnest about this, he attains it by the addition of the power of God. For God conspires with willing souls. But if they abandon their eagerness, the Spirit who is bestowed by God is also restrained. For to save the unwilling is the part of the one exercising compulsion. But to save the willing is that of one showing grace."[19]

How do these passages pertain to the life of Judas as recorded in Scripture? Both Judas and Peter spent a lot of time with the best Teacher who ever lived. Both received amazing insights about the Scriptures. Both proclaimed the kingdom of God, cast out demons, and healed the sick. Both blew it at various times. Though Jesus had incredible patience with each, both Peter and Judas utterly failed the Lord on His last night on earth.

I don't think it's out of the realm of possibility that Judas, at some point after his betrayal of Jesus, started to put some prophecy puzzle pieces together. Then, overwhelmed with a worldly sorrow, he again took matters into his own hands instead of trusting in the Lord—and the way that seemed right to him ended in death. He was unwilling to do the hard work that constituted full repentance and ended up hanging himself in the purchased field. Peter, however, didn't take himself out of the game. Even when he was overwhelmed with depression and doubt and wanted to quit, he was willing to follow Jesus's voice (see John 21).

There is one more passage we need to consider that seems to settle the matter against Judas having free will. In John 6:64-65, 70-71, we read, "*Jesus knew from the beginning who they were who did not believe, and who it was that would betray Him. And He was saying, 'For this reason I have said to you,*

that no one can come to Me unless it has been granted him from the Father. . . .
Did I Myself not choose you, the twelve, and yet one of you is a devil?' Now He
meant Judas the son of Simon Iscariot, for he, one of the twelve, was going to
betray Him." Seems like a slam dunk, right?

Jesus knew who would betray Him. He told the disciples one of them would betray Him. He said no one can come to Him unless God grants it. Bada-bing, bada-boom—Judas must not have had free will. The only problems are that (1) the rest of Scripture testifies that humans have free will, and (2) all the early Church writers of the first three centuries affirm humanity possessing free will. Consider these words on the subject in a defense of Christianity against the harsh criticisms of a Platonist named Celsus:

> Celsus imagines that an event, predicted through foreknowledge, comes to pass because it was predicted; but we do not grant this, maintaining that he who foretold it was not the cause of its happening, because he foretold it would happen; but the future event itself, which would have taken place though not predicted, afforded the occasion to him, who was endowed with foreknowledge, of foretelling its occurrence. . . . And that this may be seen, I shall take from the Scriptures the predictions regarding Judas, or the foreknowledge of our Savior regarding him as the traitor. . . .
>
> Judas is spoken of by the mouth of the Savior . . . as it was foreknown that he would betray the Savior, so also was he considered to be himself the cause of the betrayal, and deserving, on account of his wickedness. . . . It was possible for him to show mercy, and not to persecute him whom he did persecute. But although he might have done these things, he did not do them, but carried out the act of treason, so as to merit the curses pronounced against him in the prophecy.[20]

Prophecy, God's sovereignty, and free will all work together when we consider God's foreknowledge. God could ask prophets hundreds of years before Judas's time to write that someone close to the Messiah would betray Him, do it for 30 pieces of silver, use that money to buy a potter's field—and yet not force anyone to fulfill those prophecies, simply because He exists outside of time and can see the end from the beginning.

God is not a wicked slave master who toys with His slaves by offering them liberation while knowing they are incapable of achieving it. He does not delight in punishing them when they fail with extreme tortures that would put our world's cruelest sadists to shame. God is love, and love can only thrive where there is the opportunity for it to be either chosen or rejected. Love requires free will.

When my wife and I adopted our two beautiful African American children, the last step was for the family to stand before a judge and be questioned. Our prospective son and daughter could not have made it through that step if we had not first drawn them to ourselves. By the time of the court hearing, they had lived in our house for six months and were every bit a part of our family. However, at the courthouse that December morning, the judge gave them the opportunity to say they wanted to go back into foster care with a different family. We had already chosen them, and I'm so glad they chose us back.

Mankind was created by God with free will. The greatest command Judas was given is the same command all of us have been given. We must choose to love the Lord our God with all our heart, with all our soul, with all our mind, and with all our strength, and choose to love our neighbors as ourselves. Like Jesus, we must choose to rely on God's power and choose His choices.

Jesus graciously tried to the end to demonstrate God's love to Judas—to give him one last opportunity to see the truth before he committed his act of betrayal. On His last night on earth, the Lord of heaven and earth took the position of the lowest servant of the house and washed the dirty, grimy, filthy feet of the one plotting His arrest (see John 13:1-5). The life of Judas shows a God who will go to incredible lengths of grace to demonstrate His love to even those He knows will betray and reject Him. It shows that God loves and respects us so much that He will let us choose whether or not we will embrace by faith the life that He extends to each of us today. It reveals a God who loves us enough to give us both free will and all the grace we need to have the faith to choose to follow Him.

So, what has God been calling you to do lately? And what are you going to choose to do about that? As written in the Epistle of Barnabas (70–130 CE), "May the God and Lord of all the world grant you wisdom, understanding, and knowledge, together with true comprehension of His ordinances and the gift of perseverance. Take God for your teacher, and study to learn what the Lord requires of you; then do it, and you will find yourselves accepted at the Day of Judgment."[21]

Chapter 6

IF/THEN JESUS

I remember the night I discovered Santa Claus wasn't real. During my third grade year, my friends at school planted what I thought were vicious anti-Christian rumors in my head that the large, jolly, bearded white man in the red suit was a myth. So I stayed up late that Christmas Eve and hid behind the couch to see if the allegations were true. Sure enough, around 9:45 PM, I saw my mother begin to fill our stockings, which were hung by the chimney with care. What a downer. After all those years and presents, my annual benefactor was all a lie. Christmas wineskins ruined.

I wonder how long I would have believed that lie if no one had told me differently or I hadn't sought the truth out for myself. Relatives still give me presents from this Santa fellow, even though I'm 35 as I write these words. But this is certainly not the only kind of myth passed down through the generations—there are many other strange claims surrounding people, ideas, and events in history. When we take a hard look at the facts, we can easily be shocked and appalled at what the masses have been convinced is truth.

Remember, as Pascal said, "Truth is so obscure in these times, and falsehood so established, that unless we love the truth, we cannot know it."[1] I want to know, live, and communicate the truth, especially concerning the fundamental matters of Scripture. In the God-breathed, authoritative Scriptures, Jesus said we are truly His disciples if we continue in His word, and as we do that, we will know the truth and be set free (see John 8:31-32).

So let me provide some historical truths for you. I'm going to present to you facts concerning two doctrines that have been taught throughout Church history. I will call them Doctrine A and Doctrine B. As I present them, I want you to consider which of the two you would bet your life savings on if you were forced to do so. In other words, if you were backed into a dark alley by Grotto and his thugs, and he made you put all your life savings, your house, and your car on one doctrine or the other, which would you choose?

I'll start with Doctrine A. The early Church writers believed Doctrine A from the beginning of Christendom through the beginning of the fifth century. Some of these writers include Clement of Rome, a disciple of the apostles Paul and Peter; Ignatius, a disciple of the apostle John; and Polycarp, also a disciple of the apostle John. Only the Gnostics denied Doctrine A during this time. The apostle John said the teaching of these Gnostics was inspired by *"the spirit of the antichrist"* (1 John 4:2-3).[2]

Now on to Doctrine B. Only the Gnostics believed Doctrine B during the first four centuries, and the early Church writers labled it a heresy. The doctrine first gained acceptance in the Church due to the writings of the fifth-century theologian St. Augustine, who was born into a Gnostic home and chose to convert to Christianity after Emperor Theodosius 1 made Christianity the official religion of the Roman Empire in 380 CE. Doctrine B only began to receive mass appeal in Christendom during the sixteenth century due to the writings of John Calvin, who frequently leaned on the works of Augustine.[3]

Based on those facts, if you had to bet your life savings on one of those beliefs, which would you go "all in" on? I'm guessing it wouldn't be Doctrine B. I was taught this doctrine from childhood through my undergraduate and seminary studies. It is known as the doctrine of "unconditional security"—that once you are saved you are always saved, and not even an act of God Himself can jeopardize that security.

As a side note, for the first 300 years of Christendom, every Christian who wrote on the subject of God's sovereignty wrote that God is the ultimate sovereign ruler who has given mankind free will. The only folks during that time who said mankind was totally depraved, did not have free will, and that God arbitrarily selects some people for salvation and some for damnation were . . . the Gnostics.[4] Keep that in mind as you continue reading.

Inevitably, during the 30 or so years I spent in my previous denomination, I came across a multitude of passages that sharply contrasted the interpretations of the vast majority of my teachers on the subject. Usually, these conditional sentences came in the form of if/then statements: "If you do this, then that will happen." I found that though there were many verses in the New Testament that could lead brilliant teachers like Augustine and Calvin to believe in unconditional security, there were a multitude of conditional statements in the New Testament regarding the security of the Christian.

Honestly, to think Christians could lose their salvation was a scary proposition. So for many years I simply accepted my spiritual leaders' explanations of those conditional passages and put my questions to bed. However, in the spring of 2011 all those questions were forced back to the surface when I began to research the Ante-Nicene Christian writings. It became difficult for me to accept that the apostles John, Peter, and Paul could have been so poor at discipling and communicating the fundamental truths of the faith that their disciples misinterpreted the matter of conditional versus unconditional security.

It was equally concerning for me to realize that if my spiritual leaders were right in their interpretations, it meant the Gnostics had interpreted the Scripture correctly and all the Christians of the known world were not teaching orthodoxy for the first 300 years of our faith.[5] It seemed odd that those whom John said had the spirit of the antichrist would get this crucial matter of salvation right and the Christians, those with the Holy Spirit, would get it wrong. I had a hard time buying into that line of reasoning. Let's take a look at some of those early Christian writings.

> The Lord made it plain that, while He never forsakes those who place their hopes in Him, He visits pains and penalties on the rebellious; and as a sign of this, Lot's wife, who had accompanied him in his flight, but later changed her mind and fell out with him, was turned into a pillar of salt to this day. That was to let all men see how doubt and distrust of God's power bring a judgment upon themselves, and become a warning to future generations (Clement of Rome, 96 CE).[6]

> A tree is made manifest by its fruit. So those who profess themselves to be Christians will be recognized by their conduct (Ignatius, 105 CE).[7]

> Into this joy, many persons desire to enter. They know that, "By grace you are saved, not of works," but by the will of God through Jesus Christ. . . . But He who raised Him up from the dead will raise up us also—if we do His will, and walk in His commandments, and love what He loved, keeping ourselves from all unrighteousness (Polycarp, 135 CE).[8]

> Let us therefore repent with the whole heart, so that none of us perish by the way. . . . Let us then practice righteousness so that we may be saved to the end (Second Clement, 150 CE).[9]

Let those who are not found living as He taught, be understood not to be Christians, even though they profess with the lips the teachings of Christ. For it is not those who make profession, but those who do the works, who will be saved. . . . The Son of God has promised again to deliver us with prepared garments—if we do His commandments (Justin Martyr, 160 CE).[10]

With respect to obedience and doctrine, we are not all the sons of God. Rather, it is only those who truly believe in Him and do His will. . . . Those who do not obey Him, being disinherited by Him, have ceased to be His sons (Irenaeus, 180 CE).[11]

It is neither the faith, nor the love, nor the hope, nor the endurance of one day; rather, "He that endures to the end will be saved" (Clement of Alexandria, 195 CE).[12]

Hoodwinking multitudes, [Marcus, the heretic] deceived many persons of this description who had become his disciples. He taught them that they were prone, no doubt, to sin. However, he said that they were beyond the reach of danger because they belonged to the perfect Power (Hippolytus, 225 CE).[13]

Certain ones of those [heretics] who hold different opinions misuse these passages. They essentially destroy free will by introducing ruined natures incapable of salvation and by introducing others as being saved in such a way that they cannot be lost (Origen, 225 CE).[14]

To put on the name of Christ, and yet not to go in the way of Christ—what else is this but a mockery of the divine name! It is a desertion of the way of salvation. For He Himself teaches and says that the persons who keep His commandments will come into life (Cyprian, 250 CE).[15]

A son . . . who deserts his father in order not to pay him obedience is considered deserving of being disinherited and of having his name removed forever from his family. How much more so does a person deserve to be disinherited who

forsakes God—in who the two names meet that are entitled
to equal reverence: Lord and Father? . . . Of what punishments, therefore, is he deserving who forsakes Him who is
both the true Master and Father? (Lactantius, 304 CE).[16]

It was difficult for me to read these words without getting defensive.
Soon, I had to put them down and grab my Bible so I could convince myself
the New Testament writers clearly and undisputedly countered these early
interpretations. However, as I began to scour the Scriptures, God directed me
to an overwhelming number of passages that supported the early Christians'
writings. It was a difficult few days, to say the least. Here are merely a handful
of those passages on conditional security.

*Therefore everyone who confesses Me before men, I will also
confess him before My Father who is in heaven. But whoever
denies Me before men, I will also deny him before My Father
who is in heaven* (Matthew 10:32-33).

*You will be hated by all because of My name, but the one who
endures to the end, he will be saved* (Mark 13:13).

*Abide in Me, and I in you. As the branch cannot bear fruit
of itself unless it abides in the vine, so neither can you unless
you abide in Me. I am the vine, you are the branches; he who
abides in Me and I in him, he bears much fruit, for apart from
Me you can do nothing. If anyone does not abide in Me, he is
thrown away as a branch and dries up; and they gather them,
and cast them into the fire and they are burned. If you abide in
Me, and My words abide in you, ask whatever you wish, and
it will be done for you. My Father is glorified by this, that you
bear much fruit, and so prove to be My disciples. Just as the
Father has loved Me, I have also loved you; abide in My love. If
you keep My commandments, you will abide in My love; just
as I have kept My Father's commandments and abide in His
love* (John 15:4-10).

*But if some of the branches were broken off, and you, being a
wild olive, were grafted in among them and became partaker
with them of the rich root of the olive tree, do not be arrogant*

toward the branches; but if you are arrogant, remember that it is not you who supports the root, but the root supports you. You will say then, "Branches were broken off so that I might be grafted in." Quite right, they were broken off for their unbelief, but you stand by your faith. Do not be conceited, but fear; for if God did not spare the natural branches, He will not spare you, either. Behold then the kindness and severity of God; to those who fell, severity, but to you, God's kindness, if you continue in His kindness; otherwise you also will be cut off (Romans 11:17-22).

And although you were formerly alienated and hostile in mind, engaged in evil deeds, yet He has now reconciled you in His fleshly body through death, in order to present you before Him holy and blameless and beyond reproach—if indeed you continue in the faith firmly established and steadfast, and not moved away from the hope of the gospel that you have heard, which was proclaimed in all creation under heaven, and of which I, Paul, was made a minister (Colossians 1:21-23).

Take care, brethren, that there not be in any one of you an evil, unbelieving heart that falls away from the living God. But encourage one another day after day, as long as it is still called "Today," so that none of you will be hardened by the deceitfulness of sin. For we have become partakers of Christ, if we hold fast the beginning of our assurance firm until the end, while it is said, "Today if you hear His voice, do not harden your hearts, as when they provoked Me." For who provoked Him when they had heard? Indeed, did not all those who came out of Egypt led by Moses? And with whom was He angry for forty years? Was it not with those who sinned, whose bodies fell in the wilderness? And to whom did He swear that they would not enter His rest, but to those who were disobedient? So we see that they were not able to enter because of unbelief (Hebrews 3:12-19).

My brethren, if any among you strays from the truth and one turns him back, let him know that he who turns a sinner from

*the error of his way will save his soul from death and will
cover a multitude of sins* (James 5:19-20).

*But false prophets also arose among the people, just as there
will also be false teachers among you, who will secretly intro-
duce destructive heresies, even denying the Master who bought
them, bringing swift destruction upon themselves. Many will
follow their sensuality, and because of them the way of the
truth will be maligned; and in their greed they will exploit you
with false words; their judgment from long ago is not idle, and
their destruction is not asleep. . . . These are springs without
water and mists driven by a storm, for whom the black darkness has been reserved. For speaking out arrogant words of
vanity they entice by fleshly desires, by sensuality, those who
barely escape from the ones who live in error, promising them
freedom while they themselves are slaves of corruption; for by
what a man is overcome, by this he is enslaved. For if, after they
have escaped the defilements of the world by the knowledge of
the Lord and Savior Jesus Christ, they are again entangled in
them and are overcome, the last state has become worse for
them than the first. For it would be better for them not to have
known the way of righteousness, than having known it, to
turn away from the holy commandment handed on to them.
It has happened to them according to the true proverb, "A dog
returns to its own vomit," and, "A sow, after washing, returns
to wallowing in the mire"* (2 Peter 2:1-3, 17-22).

*Beloved, while I was making every effort to write you about our
common salvation, I felt the necessity to write to you appealing that you contend earnestly for the faith which was once for
all handed down to the saints. For certain persons have crept
in unnoticed, those who were long beforehand marked out for
this condemnation, ungodly persons who turn the grace of our
God into licentiousness and deny our only Master and Lord,
Jesus Christ. Now I desire to remind you, though you know all
things once for all, that the Lord, after saving a people out of
the land of Egypt, subsequently destroyed those who did not
believe* (Jude 3-5).

> *I testify to everyone who hears the words of the prophecy of this book: if anyone adds to them, God will add to him the plagues which are written in this book; and if anyone takes away from the words of the book of this prophecy, God will take away his part from the tree of life and from the holy city, which are written in this book* (Revelation 22:18-19).

For me, it was extremely difficult to change such a fundamental belief. It was almost like a grieving process. Naturally, when I have presented this material to solid Bible-believing people since that time, some have accepted it, while others have not.[17] Of those who have had a hard time with it, the main verse they quote in response is John 3:16: "*For God so loved the world, that He gave His only begotten Son, that whoever believes in Him shall not perish, but have eternal life.*" Like them, I completely believe this verse, because I also completely believe in the authority of the Scriptures.

But when you take a closer look at the Greek word translated "believe" in this verse (*pisteuon*), you find it is a present active participle, which means a current, active believing state.[18] Therefore, a more helpful rendering of the sentence could be, "*Whoever, believing in Him, shall not perish, but have eternal life.*" This corroborates Jesus's statement in Luke 8:13, in the parable of the soils: "*Those on the rocky soil are those who, when they hear, receive the word with joy; and these have no firm root; they believe for a while, and in time of temptation fall away.*"

The people represented by rocky soil held a true but shallow faith in God, but when they stopped actively believing, they fell away and became apostates. To commit apostasy literally means to depart or fall away from a previous place of standing.[19] Given this, it stands to reason that you can neither depart nor fall away from a place you've never been. Paul clearly says in 1 Timothy 4:1 and 2 Thessalonians 2:3 that some Christians will commit apostasy when they truly leave the faith.

Other folks I have spoken with insist the early Christians must have been preaching a doctrine of works-based salvation. This is simply not true. The early Christians believed we receive new birth and initial salvation by repenting of our sins and trusting in the life, way, and saving work of the Lord Jesus Christ alone by grace though faith. We then stay on the Vine of Christ and maintain our salvation by grace through an obedient, repentant, love/faith relationship with Him. Active believers in Christ then have security of their salvation.[20]

Second Peter 1:1-11 summarizes how these beliefs can be understood as salvation by grace through faith:

> *Simon Peter, a bond-servant and apostle of Jesus Christ, to those who have received a faith of the same kind as ours, by the righteousness of our God and Savior, Jesus Christ: Grace and peace be multiplied to you in the knowledge of God and of Jesus our Lord; seeing that His divine power has granted to us everything pertaining to life and godliness, through the true knowledge of Him who called us by His own glory and excellence. For by these He has granted to us His precious and magnificent promises, so that by them you may become partakers of the divine nature, having escaped the corruption that is in the world by lust.*
>
> *Now for this very reason also, applying all diligence, in your faith supply moral excellence, and in your moral excellence, knowledge, and in your knowledge, self-control, and in your self-control, perseverance, and in your perseverance, godliness, and in your godliness, brotherly kindness, and in your brotherly kindness, love. For if these qualities are yours and are increasing, they render you neither useless nor unfruitful in the true knowledge of our Lord Jesus Christ. For he who lacks these qualities is blind or short-sighted, having forgotten his purification from his former sins. Therefore, brethren, be all the more diligent to make certain about His calling and choosing you; for as long as you practice these things, you will never stumble; for in this way the entrance into the eternal kingdom of our Lord and Savior Jesus Christ will be abundantly supplied to you.*

Peter informs us that salvation and security will never be Jesus + something else—it is always by grace through faith in Him alone. Jesus's grace gives us the ability to grow in His likeness, to repent, to forgive, to love, to serve others, to humble ourselves, to walk with the Spirit, and to endure to the end. And it is His grace that lovingly gives us the ability to make the choice to either accept the promptings of His Spirit, believe in Him, and rely on His abundant provision of grace, or to continually reject Him and fall away in unbelief.

The early Christians held a childlike faith in their reading and love-driven application of the Scriptures, so they did not live in uncertainty and fear of losing their salvation. In many ways, it's similar to the way healthy married couples don't live in uncertainty and fear of getting a divorce. It is quite interesting, then, that Paul says in Ephesians 5:21-32 that God created marriage to demonstrate the Gospel to the world. Paul states that from the beginning God designed marriage to be one man and one woman together forever.

Jesus affirmed these same words and preached against divorce throughout His ministry. However, He did give one (and only one) reason why divorce is acceptable in God's eyes: marital unfaithfulness. Take a moment and read Matthew 19:1-9. To Jesus, marriage was to be the most secure and binding of human relationships, yet not even marriage was an unconditional covenant.

This analogy of marriage helps us understand Paul's words in 2 Timothy 2:11-13: *"It is a trustworthy statement: For if we died with Him, we will also live with Him; if we endure, we will also reign with Him; if we deny Him, He also will deny us; if we are faithless, He remains faithful, for He cannot deny Himself."* God will never be the adulterer in the relationship, for if He sinned the world would end. But He will let us disown Him in unbelief.

So, where does that leave us? It leaves us with a choice similar to the one Pascal put before many folks in his day. He basically said that if there is no God, we do not stand to lose anything but a small amount of fun for upholding a strict moral standard. However, if there is a God, we stand to gain everything if we adhere to His revelation—and we stand to lose everything if we behave otherwise.

To put it another way, if we lead our lives believing our faithfulness to Jesus and His teaching affects our eternal destiny, and we find out our actions didn't matter in the end, we will probably have helped a lot more people than we would have otherwise. However, if we lead our lives believing our faithfulness to Jesus and His teachings on being born again do not have any bearing on our eternal destiny, and we find out it mattered tremendously, we will be in a lot of trouble.

I don't claim to have the corner on the truth, and I am quite fallible (just ask my wife). However, I do claim the Scriptures have the corner on the truth and that Jesus is truth. So when I read in Matthew 28:18-20 that before Jesus ascended into heaven, He told His disciples to make disciples of all people groups, baptizing them and teaching them to obey everything He had commanded them during His ministry, I believe it means *everything*. What Jesus says in the Great Commission is so plain it takes an elementary school education to understand and a seminary degree to confuse. Jesus actually expects His followers to obey *all* His commands, because that's what followers of Jesus do.

I'm aware my finite brain can't have a perfect understanding of the Scriptures. Yet I am 100 percent convinced that when Jesus returns, our partial understanding will be done away with and we who are in Him will know fully even as we are fully known (see 1 Corinthians 13:9-12). Until then, I believe the historical facts and Scriptures I have presented to you are worth betting your life on. Whether you realize it or not, you are already gambling. So may you be filled with humility, godly wisdom, and an all-consuming love for Jesus that enables you to persevere in genuine belief and love for Him to the end.

Chapter 7

DADDY ISSUES AND JESUS

One of the earliest memories I have of my dad is of him reading me a bedtime story when I was four or five years old. After finishing the story and tucking me in, snug as a bug in a rug with only my head exposed, he kissed me on the forehead and passed gas. At the time, I was disgusted. However, as an adult, I think it's absolutely hilarious. Back then, I swore I would never do such a thing to my children. But now, since Stephanie and I have adopted two beautiful siblings, I can totally see myself following in my father's footsteps. You know, starting a Baker family tradition. Stephanie thinks you should pray for me. She is clearly the better half in this relationship.

Times were not always rosy in my house as a child. Like most families, we had some good times, but we also had some pretty difficult times. Unfortunately, my parents separated when I was in the ninth grade. I still remember my reaction on hearing the news. I asked my brother, who is two years older than me, "What's going to happen at Christmas? Are we still going to get presents?" Ah, the self-centered mind of an adolescent.

I wasn't completely sure why they separated, but in my mind I placed the blame on my father. Up until that point in my life, my main coping strategy had been to sleep. But then something more insidious began to emerge. Within that year, I began to skip school and get drunk regularly. By age 16, I was smoking cigarettes and marijuana as well. Basically, I exchanged one socially acceptable coping strategy (sleep) for several socially unacceptable strategies. Needless to say, none of them helped heal the anger I felt toward my father. They actually served to create more problems that I wanted to escape from.

By the summer following my sophomore year of high school, I was well aware of my corrupted nature. Though I had been breaking God's moral law since childhood, I was now getting drunk on a semi-regular basis, and I had come dangerously close to needing my stomach pumped. Then, during a Young Life camp that summer, I heard the Gospel message as if for the first time. I confessed and repented of my sins, believing Jesus—my Lord and Savior, the Son of God who came in the flesh—was crucified and rose from the dead on the third day.

On September 15, 1996, I was rebaptized at my church. Today I'm grateful for the abundance of believers there who impacted my life in a positive way, and I know the new leadership is doing wonderful things for the kingdom of God. Unfortunately, though, at that time there were no discipleship or mentoring programs in place to help people like me with this critical life transition. The new wine of Christ was poured into several of my old wineskins, and a great mess ensued. With no one to teach me how to follow Jesus, I soon fell back into destructive practices. After graduating high school, I fell into a deep depression and drug addiction.

By the time I was 19, I was a total pothead. I wasted what should have been my sophomore year of college smoking marijuana every day, all day, instead of going to class. My GPA was completely in the toilet. Also, I'm an asthmatic who shouldn't have been around smoke every day. I frequently had bouts of bronchitis, but I kept smoking even when the mucous I was coughing up was black and I was laboring to take a breath.

I hated my life. I felt like a complete failure. I didn't think I was good at anything. I was constantly comparing myself to my brother and felt stupid, ugly, friendless, rejected by girls, talentless, and futureless. I wanted to die. So I began to plan my suicide—another act of escapism that doesn't achieve one's goal.

Fortunately, God set up a divine appointment between me and the new youth minister at my church. He asked if I wanted to help lead worship for the youth praise band, even though I didn't know what that meant or entailed. I had been playing music in bars with my brother since I was 16, but I didn't understand the worship-leading concept. Mike, my youth minister, began mentoring and teaching me what it meant to be a follower of Jesus. However, I was still secretly struggling with hatred toward my father and my marijuana use.

Eventually, a friend directed me to an intercessory prayer ministry at a different church, and they prayed for me for about an hour. I went there because I wanted prayer to help me stop smoking weed. I felt that was my main problem. But about 45 minutes into the prayer time, one of the believers asked if I hated my father. I was shocked and told her I did. She gave me an analogy of a tree. She asked if I were going to kill a tree, would I merely cut off the tree's branches? Of course not. I must go after the trunk. She then said I should think of my drug issue as a branch and my hatred of my father as the trunk.

She told me that Jesus said if we forgive other people their sins, our heavenly Father will forgive us our sins. But if we don't forgive other people's sins, our heavenly Father won't forgive our sins. They prayed for about 10 to 15 more minutes and asked me to forgive my father. I played along, but in my heart I refused. And I went home and kept smoking weed. Then I got sick again. So I set up another intercessory prayer meeting the next month. During that meeting, I asked God to forgive me of my hatred of my father. I committed to apologize to him the next time I saw him and forgive him from my heart.

So I called my dad and asked if we could get together for lunch. He came over to pick me up, and before we drove to the restaurant, I asked if I could tell him a few things. I began by apologizing for harboring bitterness toward him, for saying so many rude things to him and behind his back, for being disobedient, and for the general disrespect and ingratitude I had shown him throughout my life. Then I forgave him for general ways I felt I had been wronged by him. It was the hardest conversation of my life, but all the bitterness left. We have since had lunch every Thursday. It is truly my favorite time of the week.

My reconciliation with my father marked the beginning of my healing from addiction and birthed significant life change in me. As a side note, my parents, who never divorced throughout those years, ended up reconciling and moving back in together. What a testimony of God's faithfulness!

The prayer ministry also helped me see that my perception of my father had been shaping my perception of God. For more than two decades, I had perceived my father in a negative light, and that had led me to engage in behavior that was displeasing to my heavenly Father. Basically, I was imposing the trust issues I had with my earthly father on my heavenly Father. I was filtering God through the lens of my perception of my dad. What I needed to determine was whether those feelings and filters were justifiable.

The first passage of Scripture that helped burst the old wineskins I had concerning God as my heavenly Father was James 1:16-17: *"Do not be deceived, my beloved brethren. Every good thing given and every perfect gift is from above, coming down from the Father of lights, with whom there is no variation or shifting shadow."* This simple passage was quite profound. I realized every good thing in my life was a gift from God the Father. My abilities to hear, see, smell, touch, and taste were all gifts from God. The breath I just took, and that one, and that one, were all gifts from God. The cognitive ability to understand this passage was a gift from God. The ability to make the money to afford a house with functioning air conditioning and heating systems, clean running water, electricity, and a non-leaking roof were gifts from my heavenly Father. The ability to know and love God was a gift from God, as was the free will to reject Him.

It's a difficult adjustment when one day you feel God has been holding out on you and the next day you realize you're a spoiled brat. When I was a kid, I thought we were poor because I was comparing my family to the more wealthy families at my schools, and especially to celebrities on television. So, going to Swaziland, Africa, in 2004 and seeing real poverty was eye-opening for me. At that time, Swaziland had the highest percentage of citizens living with AIDS in the world. Yet I encountered so many people who possessed grateful hearts. Their unshakable attitude of thanksgiving constantly rebuked my perception of the hand I had been dealt. It would prove to be the best month of my life.

The week before I left for Swaziland, I agreed to take a job as a student minister at a small Baptist church in a wealthy area of town. I would make $25,000 a year, which, compared to my peers, and with an undergraduate degree, was a small salary. However, compared to the rest of the world, I was living like a king.[1] I remember hearing at that time that the $25,000 I was making a year put me among the top 10 percent richest people in the world.[2] If I were making that same amount now, I would be among the top two percent richest people in the world. How are your wineskins holding up?

Looking back, I realized my skewed perception of reality had produced an ungrateful heart that had led me to selfish ambitions and using others to help me feel better about myself. I hadn't realized how much my heavenly Father had blessed me, how He was going above and beyond in meeting my needs, and how much He loved me. As a result, there was a strong, self-centered, how-can-you-benefit me attitude in virtually all my relationships.

I hypocritically gave away my virginity, which God had mercifully helped me keep into my early twenties, to a good girl who was not the right match for me. In committing that act, I not only sinned against God but also against her, her future husband, and my future wife. As Paul writes in 1 Thessalonians 4:1-8, I defrauded by brother (her future husband) by taking from him what, in God's eyes, belonged to him alone. In doing so, I was not treating her the way I would have wanted any man to treat my future wife, Stephanie, before she and I met. Like a jerk, I didn't love my neighbors as myself.

During that relationship, I also alienated myself from my best friend, who, like my family, could see the red flags I was unwilling to acknowledge. He was the best friend I've ever had, and the best friend I've ever lost. Interestingly, if you'd asked me during any of these times if I believed in God, I would have said I did. However, I had significant trust issues, because if I had truly trusted God, I would have obeyed His voice rather than my own impulsive, egocentric thoughts. God desires that we not only profess belief in Him with our lips but also demonstrate it with our lives.

Thankfully, God has gone far beyond saying that He is good (see Psalm 119:68); that He is just, faithful, and does no wrong (see Deuteronomy 32:4); and that He is love (see 1 John 4:8). Our heavenly Father realized lessons are more often caught than taught, so before the foundation of the world He demonstrated His fullness to us in the only way possible for Him to tabernacle with us. In 1 Timothy 6, we read that God the Father dwells in unapproachable light, and in Exodus 33 we find that no one can see His face and live. However, God desires communion with us and longs for us to experience His fullness. Therefore, God the Father sent His only begotten Son, the Anointed One, the Messiah, the Christ, the Word become flesh, so we could better understand who He is and trust Him.

Read these Scriptures pertaining to Jesus's relationship with the Father:

> In the beginning was the Word, and the Word was with God, and the Word was God. He was in the beginning with God. All things came into being through Him, and apart from Him nothing came into being that has come into being. . . . And the Word became flesh, and dwelt among us, and we saw His glory, glory as of the only begotten from the Father, full of grace and truth (John 1:1-3, 14).

> For God so loved the world, that He gave His only begotten Son, that whoever believes in Him shall not perish, but have eternal life. . . . He who believes in Him is not judged; he who does not believe has been judged already, because he has not believed in the name of the only begotten Son of God (John 3:16, 18).

> If you had known Me, you would have known My Father also; from now on you know Him, and have seen Him. . . . Have I been so long with you, and yet you have not come to know Me,

Philip? He who has seen Me has seen the Father; how can you say, "Show us the Father"? Do you not believe that I am in the Father, and the Father is in Me? The words that I say to you I do not speak on My own initiative, but the Father abiding in Me does His works. . . . If you loved Me, you would have rejoiced because I go to the Father, for the Father is greater than I (John 14:7, 9-10, 28).

God . . . in these last days has spoken to us in His Son, whom He appointed heir of all things, through whom also He made the world. And He is the radiance of His glory and the exact representation of His nature (Hebrews 1:1-3).

"Begotten" is an interesting word we do not often hear in our culture. Some translations explain the word by saying, "One and only Son," but that honestly does not help much. To begin to understand what it means that Jesus is the only begotten Son of God, let me explain by using an analogy from the early Church (remembering, of course, that all analogies will fall short at some point).

For this analogy, the sun will represent God the Father, and its light will represent Jesus, the only begotten Son of God. As long as the sun has been around, its light has emanated from it. The light of the sun is not greater than the sun itself, but it is co-existent with the sun. The light is not the source of the sun; rather, the sun is the source of the light. Neither is the light of the sun created by the sun, but rather begotten of the sun. Jesus is the light, and that light reveals, or glorifies, the sun. This is why the writer of Hebrews says that Jesus is the radiance of God's glory and the exact representation of His nature.[3]

Jesus, the Word who was God and was with God from the beginning, was never created, for by Him *all* things were created. The eternally existing *Logos* of God was not created but begotten.[4] He is very God of the eternal one true God, and God is one. All these truths reveal why Jesus could say to Philip, *"Have I been so long with you, and yet you have not come to know Me, Philip? He who has seen Me has seen the Father"* (John 14:9). Those words can be life-changing for people like me who have grown up with trust issues.

Maybe you've been hurt by a parent, so it's hard for you to trust in a God who calls Himself a heavenly Father. Maybe you've been hurt by Christians who call God their heavenly Father, so it's difficult for you to become part of what you consider a dysfunctional family. Maybe you've read sections of the Old Testament where you see God making laws or doing things that appear to be contradictory to One who calls Himself slow to anger and abounding in steadfast love.

Whatever the case, wherever you are, these passages you've just read call you to look at Jesus before you analyze God the Father. These passages state that if you want to understand what God the Father is like, you should study Jesus. So let me ask you: *How do you feel about Jesus? Is He someone you feel you can trust?* Personally, I can't think of anyone more trustworthy, and He is the exact representation of the Father's nature.

The apostle Paul wrote, *"For while we were still helpless, at the right time Christ died for the ungodly. For one will hardly die for a righteous man; though perhaps for the good man someone would dare even to die. But God demonstrates His own love toward us, in that while we were yet sinners, Christ died for us"* (Romans 5:6-8). This passage does not imply that God forced Christ to die for us, but that Jesus willingly engaged in this selfless act.

In fact, Hebrews 12:2 tells us to fix our eyes on Jesus, *"who for the joy set before Him endured the cross."* His joy was not found in experiencing the agony, but in what would be accomplished through His humiliation—our reconciliation. Our deliverance from the domain of darkness brought Jesus Christ joy as He contemplated and endured the physical and spiritual torture of the cross. We fix our eyes on Jesus because He shows us God the Father.

For nearly two decades, I believed I had a terrible earthly father, and thus a sketchy heavenly one. But how many people can say they had fathers who constantly told them they loved them? Or had fathers who always provided new clothes for school? Or had fathers who came to virtually all their sporting and musical events? Or had fathers who played sports with them, even if they did not particularly enjoy those sports? Or had fathers who were separated from their mothers but still managed to keep doing these things?

I could go on, but you get the idea. Perception is not always reality. The reality is I am blessed to have the father I do, and I had a much better upbringing than millions of other people. Likewise, though I thought my heavenly Father was untrustworthy, nothing could be further from the truth. Jesus Christ, the image of God, has demonstrated to us the complete character of God the Father, and He is good. He is worthy of us laying down our lives for

Him, because He has already laid down His life for us. He is worthy of us surrendering all for, because He has already surrendered all for us.

So may you trust in Father God with all of your heart and not lean on your own perception. May you believe in the name of His only begotten Son, Jesus Christ, and obey Him out of a deep love and respect for all He has already done for you.

PART 2

NEW WINESKINS OF THE HOLY SPIRIT AND SPIRITUAL WARFARE

Chapter 8

WDJD? (WHAT DID JESUS DO?)

I was given several unfortunate nicknames as a kid. I was called "Peanut" after I got a buzz cut the summer following eighth grade and everyone found out I had misshapen head. One other nickname that stuck was "Casper"—as in Casper the friendly ghost. You see, I am what politically correct people call "pigmently challenged." Okay, I'm pale. Folks like me don't tan—we're either porcelain white or we're burned.

One summer day when I was 10, I went to Water World and "forgot" to bring sunscreen. I came home quite red and received a tongue-lashing from my mother. Of course, later that evening I was complaining about the terrible pain I felt from the second-degree burns I had incurred. Though my mom was disappointed by my actions, she was always quick to do whatever she could to help her children.

She heard that Noxzema was an effective ointment on sunburns, so she rubbed a decent amount over my scorched back. I felt some relief, so we continued the process for a few days. On day five I was still in excruciating pain, so I asked my mom to anoint me with more Noxema. Within fifteen minutes I began to have an anaphylactic allergic reaction in which the airways in my throat began to constrict. My mom told one of my family members to call 911, and an ambulance was sent to our house.

Just as the emergency phone call was being made, my devoted Southern Baptist mother heard a voice in her head telling her to wash off the Noxzema. She had never experienced anything like that before, but she was obedient and cleaned me up. Before the paramedics could arrive, I was running around the house, playing with my toys, and breathing like a champ, as if nothing out of the ordinary had happened.

In our church at that time, much was spoken about God the Father and Jesus the Son, but the Holy Spirit was almost never mentioned. Sure, every once in a while we would hear how the Holy Spirit seals us for the day of redemption, guides us into all truth, is a wonderful Counselor, and convicts the world of sin, righteousness, and judgment—but that was pretty much where the teaching stopped. However, at some point I do remember being taught that many of the gifts of the Holy Spirit were not available today. This raises two important questions regarding this mysterious third member of the Trinity: (1) who is the Holy Spirit, and (2) what is His main purpose in our lives?

To answer the first question, who is the Holy Spirit, we must begin with Matthew 28:19-20, where Jesus tells His disciples, "*Go therefore and make disciples of all the nations, baptizing them in the name of the Father and the Son and the Holy Spirit, teaching them to observe all that I commanded you; and lo, I am with you always, even to the end of the age.*" At this point, Jesus was resurrected and about to ascend back to God the Father. With these final instructions, He tells the disciples to make disciples of all people, teach them to obey all His commands, and baptize them in the name (singular), of the Father, Son, and Holy Spirit. Grammatically, this sentence doesn't make sense. The name (singular) of three beings? Why not the names (plural) of three beings?

One of the points Jesus is making is that the Father, Son, and Holy Spirit are, in some mysterious way, one. Remember the analogy of the sun representing God and its light representing Jesus? Let's apply that same analogy to the Holy Spirit and say He represents the heat of the sun. As long as the sun has been around, light and heat have emanated from it. Neither the light nor the heat are greater than the sun, but both are co-existent with it. Neither the light nor the heat are the source of the sun; rather, the sun is the source of both the light and the heat. Both the light and the heat of the sun glorify, or reveal, things about the nature of the sun.

While this analogy doesn't fully explain the Trinity, it does an adequate job of describing the eternal three-in-oneness that still has its origin in God the Father. Scriptures such as John 14 can futher help us dig into just who this mysterious Holy Spirit is. In this passage, Jesus is speaking to His disciples the night before He is crucified and is telling them He must leave them to go to His Father. When the disciples begin to freak out, Jesus gives them these promises: "*I will ask the Father, and He will give you another Helper, that He may be with you forever; that is the Spirit of truth, whom the world cannot receive, because it does not see Him or know Him, but you know Him because He abides with you and will be in you. . . . But the Helper, the Holy Spirit, whom the Father will send in My name, He will teach you all things, and bring to your remembrance all that I said to you*" (16-17, 26).

The key words in this passage are "another Helper." In the original language, the word "another" means "another of the same kind; another of similar type."[1] So Jesus was telling His disciples that when He left, God the Father would send another Helper who was of the same kind as Him. Jesus then calls this Helper, who is of the same kind as Himself, the "Spirit of truth" and "the Holy Spirit."

Later, in Acts 16:6-10, we read about Paul and his companions at the beginning of his second major missionary journey. *"They passed through the Phrygian and Galatian region, having been forbidden by the Holy Spirit to speak the word in Asia; and after they came to Mysia, they were trying to go into Bithynia, and the Spirit of Jesus did not permit them; and passing by Mysia, they came down to Troas. A vision appeared to Paul in the night: a man of Macedonia was standing and appealing to him, and saying, 'Come over to Macedonia and help us.' When he had seen the vision, immediately we sought to go into Macedonia, concluding that God had called us to preach the gospel to them."*

Who forbade Paul to preach in Asia or go into Bithynia? Who gave Paul the vision of the Macedonian man pleading for him to come there instead? Luke, the writer of Acts, is teaching us much doctrine in this historical account, for it appears he is informing us the Holy Spirit, in some mysterious way, is the Spirit of Jesus, who, in some mysterious way, is God. Was Jesus hinting at this truth in John 14 when He told the disciples the Holy Spirit, who was of the same kind as Himself, would come to be their divine Helper? Was he hinting at this truth in Matthew 28 in the singularity of the name of the Trinity and when He told the disciples that though He was going away, He would be with them always?

We've already established that Jesus Christ is the Lord. However, just for further clarification, let's look at 1 Corinthians 8:6. Paul writes, *"For us there is but one God, the Father, from whom are all things and we exist for Him; and one Lord, Jesus Christ, by whom are all things, and we exist through Him."* Clearly, as Paul states here, Jesus Christ is the Lord, and there is only one Lord. Therefore, it is quite remarkable that Paul writes in 2 Corinthians 3:17-18, *"Now the Lord is the Spirit, and where the Spirit of the Lord is, there is liberty. But we all, with unveiled face, beholding as in a mirror the glory of the Lord, are being transformed into the same image from glory to glory, just as from the Lord, the Spirit."*

The Lord is the Spirit, and Jesus Christ is the Lord. The Holy Spirit is the Spirit of Jesus, and Jesus is the radiance of God the Father's glory and the exact representation of His nature. He is the image of the invisible God. Paul's words in 2 Corinthians 3:17-18 are profound on several levels. Not only do they demonstrate who the Holy Spirit is, but they reveal His main purpose in our lives. The main reason God has given us the precious gift of the Holy Spirit is to help us become more like Jesus, both inwardly and outwardly. To be sure this is a process, but if the Holy Spirit is truly inside us, it's inevitable that we will eventually become like Jesus. Consider these other passages:

> *Truly, truly, I say to you, he who believes in Me, the works that I do, he will do also; and greater works than these he will do; because I go to the Father* (John 14:12).

> *And we know that God causes all things to work together for good to those who love God, to those who are called according to His purpose. For those whom He foreknew, He also predestined to become conformed to the image of His Son, so that He would be the firstborn among many brethren; and these whom He predestined, He also called; and these whom He called, He also justified; and these whom He justified, He also glorified* (Romans 8:28-30).

> *But the fruit of the Spirit is love, joy, peace, patience, kindness, goodness, faithfulness, gentleness, self-control; against such things there is no law* (Galatians 5:22-23).

> *For our citizenship is in heaven, from which also we eagerly wait for a Savior, the Lord Jesus Christ; who will transform the body of our humble state into conformity with the body of His glory, by the exertion of the power that He has even to subject all things to Himself* (Philippians 3:20-21).

These passages reveal the process of being conformed to the likeness of Jesus is both "yet" and "not yet." It is happening now but will be completed after our physical deaths. In the meantime, we should focus on two aspects of the Holy Spirit.

The first is found in Galatians 5:22-23, where Paul highlights the fruit of the Spirit, and thus the character of Jesus. If we have the Holy Spirit within us, we should be growing in each of these areas. Are we struggling with apathy or bitterness, or are we growing in joy? Do we have control or worry issues, or are we growing in peace? Do we respond with anger when we feel disrespected or threatened, or are we growing in gentleness? Do we find ourselves justifying our failures or broken commitments, or are we growing in faithfulness? Do we treat others poorly, or are we growing in love? As people who have been rescued out of the domain of darkness by the grace, mercy, and sacrifice of Jesus, how many disciples have we made during the span of our lives?

The second aspect of the Holy Spirit, found in John 14:12, is more controversial. Here, Jesus says, *"Truly, truly, I say to you, he who believes in Me, the works that I do, he will do also; and greater works than these he will do; because I go to the Father."* The main issue is derived from the phrase "greater works," but I believe Jesus is making more important points in this passage. First, Jesus says this promise is for whoever will believe in Him. *Whoever.* That included His disciples, but it also includes us. Second, Jesus says whoever believes in Him will do the same works He does, because He is going to the Father. *The same works.* Just dwell on that fact for a moment. Jesus said that if we believe in Him, we will be able to do the same works He did through the power of the Holy Spirit.

Now, if we really want to know God's purpose for our lives, or what we should do in any situation, we should look at what Jesus did. Instead of wristbands with WWJD (What Would Jesus Do?), maybe we should make some saying WDJD (What *Did* Jesus Do). This is the real question we should be asking, for we are called to walk as Jesus walked by the power of the Holy Spirit. So, what works did Jesus do? He loved His enemies. Healed the sick. Blessed His persecutors. Expelled demons. Turned the other cheek. Raised the dead. Extended forgiveness to undeserving sinners. Loosed the chains of injustice. Defended the powerless. Proclaimed the good news of the kingdom of God. Prophesied. Walked humbly with God. Called for racial reconciliation. Prayed. Memorized Scripture. Performed various miracles. Fasted. Resisted the devil. Made disciples who made disciples.

You get the point. And if you don't think these things are possible for us, or that Jesus doesn't expect us to do them, just read the book of Acts. It is filled with fantastic encouragement for believers because it proves that Jesus kept His promise from John 14:12, and His promise is still valid today. Whoever believes in Jesus can be like Him and do what He did through the gift of the Holy Spirit. So, the real question is how determined you are to be like Him and do what He did.

Bible teacher Ray Vander Laan, in his message *The Dust of the Rabbi*, explains what Jesus's followers understood Him to be saying when He called them to be disciples who made more disciples: "A disciple is not someone who wants to know what the teacher knows. . . .[or] even someone who wants to know what God knows. . . . A disciple is someone who, more than anything else in the whole world, wants to be what the teacher is. . . . How badly do you want to be like Jesus?"[2]

One of my character flaws, of which Stephanie has recently made me aware, is that I'm not a good gift receiver. For example, as an anniversary gift, she recently bought me a nice black leather jacket. How did I respond? I smiled and said "thank you," but then explained how I already had a nice black leather jacket. Yes, it was given to me when I was in high school in the '90s, but it still fits. '90s stuff is retro, right? Maybe you're thinking a better term would be "antiquated."

Surely you feel sorry for both Stephanie and me right now, but your feelings of pity are most likely present for different reasons. You may pity me because I am completely out of touch with fashion reality, but you probably feel sorry for Stephanie because I did not respond anywhere close to appropriately when she gave me an amazing gift. It was almost as if I had rejected her loving gesture.

When Peter preached his first sermon on Pentecost, he concluded by saying, *"Therefore let all the house of Israel know for certain that God has made Him both Lord and Christ—this Jesus whom you crucified."* The people who heard his message were pierced to the heart and said, *"Brethren, what shall we do?"* Peter answered, *"Repent, and each of you be baptized in the name of Jesus Christ for the forgiveness of your sins; and you will receive the gift of the Holy Spirit"* (Acts 2:36-38).

God the Father sent His Son, Jesus Christ, not just so we could avoid the eternal fires of hell but so we could be transformed into the image of Christ through the gift of the Holy Spirit. How have you been responding to this gift? Who had more joy than Jesus? Who had more peace? Who loved and helped more people than He did? Don't you want to be like Him? Who knows, if you fully embrace the gift of the Holy Spirit, you might start earning the nickname "Christian" like His disciples in Acts 11.

So may you earnestly ask God for a fresh outpouring and infilling of the Holy Spirit. And may you joyfully receive Him so that you may do the works that Jesus did and radiate the warmth of His glory to the world.

Chapter 9

SEEING THINGS FOR THE FIRST TIME

Have you ever had your worldview turned upside down? It's a bit unsettling. When I arrived in Swaziland in 2004, one of the men who was part of the mission I was entering took my bag with one hand, grabbed my hand with the other, and started walking me down the road where we would be staying. We walked about a quarter of a mile holding hands and talking like an old married couple.

Honestly I was a bit creeped out, but his actions were totally normal there. In fact, the man was being welcoming and hospitable. It took a while for me to get adjusted to that culture, because something I used to feel was wrong was now viewed as pure. When we become born again into Jesus's kingdom, it can also feel like He is turning our worldview upside down.[1] However, it's crucial to remember we all enter life with an inverted perspective of reality. Jesus is actually helping to set everything right side up again.

Most of us were born into a democracy. A democracy is extremely different than a kingdom. In a democracy, if we don't like our leaders, we can vote them out of office. If we don't like our laws, we can vote in different laws. In a democracy, the majority usually gets its way. If you are like me, you were born again into the kingdom of God with a democratic mindset. You have been pouring new wine into old wineskins, and as a result you have repeatedly been making messes.

All kingdoms have a king, a domain, laws and values, and subjects. The kingdom of God is no different, and yet, because it is from heaven, it is completely different than all the kingdoms of the earth. The kingdom of God has no earthly king. Jesus is its king, He will never stop being king, and no one has the right to change His laws. The kingdom of God has no geographic borders; it exists through whomever Jesus's Spirit has free reign. Excluding the realm of heaven or His eventual millennial earthly reign, this is King Jesus's domain.

Therefore, it is important for us to remember that no one is born into the kingdom of God. King Jesus Himself said in John 3:3, *"Truly, truly, I say to you, unless one is born again he cannot see the kingdom of God."* How does this work? As I stated in chapter one, Jesus gave His entire life for us. If we repent of our sins and give our entire lives back to Him, He gives His life back into us through the Holy Spirit and begins to transform us to become like Him. We are born *again* into His kingdom. When this happens, as Paul writes in Colossians 1:13, we get rescued out of the domain of darkness and transferred (or translated) into Jesus's kingdom.

The laws of the kingdom of God are first and foremost the commands of Jesus Christ. Many of these are found in King Jesus's inaugural address in Matthew 5–7, which is also known as the Sermon on the Mount. Jesus's life illustrates the values of the kingdom of God—the way He treated those inside the kingdom, those outside the kingdom, and the things of this world. The subjects of the kingdom of God are those who have entered into a covenantal relationship with the King and love Him, obey Him, and reflect His nature to the world. We must remember that Jesus said to the Jews who longed for God's kingdom to come on earth, but refused to follow Him, *"The kingdom of God will be taken away from you and given to a people who will produce its fruit"* (Matthew 21:43).

Pause for a moment and reflect on where laws and values come from. Don't they derive from the worldview of those making them? King Jesus's values and laws are expressions of His worldview. If you are a subject of God's kingdom, it is assumed you will reflect the values of your King out of love for Him. Therefore, it is important to understand Jesus' worldview. The Gospel of Mark gives us a crash course.

There is no birth narrative in Mark's account. Jesus comes on the scene as a 30-year-old man ready to begin His ministry. Mark writes, *"Jesus came into Galilee, preaching the gospel of God, and saying, 'The time is fulfilled, and the kingdom of God is at hand; repent and believe in the gospel'"* (Mark 1:14-15). Jesus's declaration to the people of Galilee that *"the kingdom of God is at hand"* meant God's sovereign, dynamic rule had come to them.

Jesus didn't then give lengthy expository messages or a weekend self-help seminar to encourage people to think more positive thoughts. Instead, He embarked on a cosmic showdown and brought drastic life-change. Seven times in the first chapter of Mark, the words "unclean spirit" or "demon" are used, and Jesus drives them all out.

Keep in mind that Galilee was one of the most religious areas in the world at that time.[2] These were God-loving, church-going people—and they were demonized. Mark could have just told one story and used one word, but instead he used the phrases seven times and alluded to many stories. First chapters are important in setting the foundation for a book. What do you think Mark was trying to reveal about Jesus's worldview?

I believe Mark was communicating the same worldview the apostle John reinforced to the readers of his first letter when he wrote, "*We know that we are of God, and that the whole world lies in the power of the evil one*" (1 John 5:19). Earlier in that same letter, he wrote, "*The Son of God appeared for this purpose, to destroy the works of the devil*" (3:8). John conveyed the same worldview Paul had communicated to the Ephesians a few decades earlier when he wrote, "*Put on the full armor of God, so that you will be able to stand firm against the schemes of the devil. For our struggle is not against flesh and blood, but against the rulers, against the powers, against the world forces of this darkness, against the spiritual forces of wickedness in the heavenly places*" (Ephesians 6:11-12).

When Adam and Eve obeyed Satan rather than God, they made him their master. God had instructed them to rule over the earth and steward it. So, by transferring their allegiance to Satan, he became the *de facto* ruler of the earth, even though God was the ultimate ruler of everything (see Luke 4:5-8). When Adam and Eve rebelled against God, they rebelled against the Source of all life—and as goes mankind, so goes the earth. Death and decay entered the world and trickled down to all aspects of the earth.

Surprisingly, for Jesus the Gospel of the kingdom was not so much about taking people from earth to heaven but about bringing a foretaste of the kingdom of heaven to people. Jesus came to show us how to again become pure, God-glorifying image-bearers. The Gospel of the kingdom means an eventual holistic reversal of the devil's works introduced after the Fall. For this reason, to Jesus the good news of the kingdom necessarily involves demonstrations to Satan that his time is short and that all who follow him will one day be vanquished. To Jesus, the good news of the kingdom began with His arrival and will be brought to fulfillment after He comes back.

In what is called The Lord's Prayer, Jesus told us to pray, "*Our Father who is in heaven, hallowed be Your name. Your kingdom come. Your will be done, on earth as it is in heaven*" (Matthew 6:9-10). Clearly, then, there are beings who are not doing His will; otherwise He would not ask us to pray that His will would be done. Also, according to Jesus's words, there are areas on earth where His kingdom is not reigning. Therefore He commands us to pray that both these things will take place on earth as they do in heaven.

So, how will we know when the kingdom of God has come on earth? King Jesus said, *"If I cast out demons by the finger of God, then the kingdom of God has come upon you"* (Luke 11:20). In Matthew 4:23-24, we read, *"Jesus was going throughout all Galilee, teaching in their synagogues and proclaiming the gospel of the kingdom, and healing every kind of disease and every kind of sickness among the people. The news about Him spread throughout all Syria; and they brought to Him all who were ill, those suffering with various diseases and pains, demoniacs, epileptics, paralytics; and He healed them."*

Some people believe the disciples stopped preaching the Gospel of the kingdom after Pentecost. That is simply inaccurate. In Acts 8 we read, *"Philip went down to the city of Samaria and began proclaiming Christ to them. The crowds . . . heard and saw the signs which he was performing. For in the case of many who had unclean spirits, they were coming out of them shouting with a loud voice; and many who had been paralyzed and lame were healed. So there was much rejoicing in that city. . . . They believed Philip preaching the good news about the kingdom of God and the name of Jesus Christ"* (verses 5-8, 12).

What about Paul? Did he carry on Jesus's mission of preaching the kingdom of God? Did that message go out with a demonstration of power? In Acts 19:8, 10-12, we see how God used Paul to start the church at Ephesus: *"He entered the synagogue and continued speaking out boldly for three months, reasoning and persuading them about the kingdom of God. . . . This took place for two years, so that all who lived in Asia heard the word of the Lord, both Jews and Greeks. God was performing extraordinary miracles by the hands of Paul, so that handkerchiefs or aprons were even carried from his body to the sick, and the diseases left them and the evil spirits went out."*

Jesus spoke about the kingdom of God more than 100 times, and His disciples continued to practice what He had started. Just as Jesus's message did not simply come with words but with a demonstration of the power of God, so the disciples' did as well. They definitely needed God's power to help them as they came up against the forces of darkness.

I was in Swaziland the first time I saw a demon come out of someone. It may surprise you, but the person the demon came out of was not a local SiSwati but a professing Christian from America taking part in the mission trip. I will call him "Bob" as I share the entry from my journal that night.

My friend Bob, who is a Christian, has suffered from schizophrenia for six years. He has shared that when under stress or anxiety, will hear audible voices that will berate him in cruel ways. Because of this condition, Bob is on medications that cause him to have a difficult time finding the words he desires to say and hinder his ability to remember things.

About a week ago, I began to feel that God was going to heal Bob, and he wanted my friend Jaco and I to be present. I waited and waited for God to confirm the promptings He seemed to be putting on my heart. Then tonight, while most of our group was watching a movie, Bob showed up at my door.

Eventually, our conversation shifted to the power of God and how everything done through the disciples in the Gospels and Acts can be done now because we have the same Holy Spirit living inside us as they did. I felt God prompting me to say something about how I felt God wanted to heal him. Bob told me that before he came to Africa, his mom told him that she believed God was going to heal him during the trip.

Bob told me he had a dream that the leader of our trip came into his room while he was sleeping and touched his head and stomach. He became stiff and then felt relaxed. Bob told me he believed God could heal him. He went back to his room to pray and read Luke 10, and I went to get Jaco.

As Jaco and I stood outside of Bob's room, we felt God wanted us to cleanse our hearts. So we asked God to remove any sin from us and fill us with His Holy Spirit. When we went into Bob's room, he told Jaco he believed that a demon was inside of him causing him to hear the voices. Jaco placed his hand on Bob's head, and I put my hands on Bob's stomach and back. Then we began to pray.

For five minutes Jaco asked Jesus to bring Bob total healing in the name of Jesus, but nothing happened. Suddenly, I began to feel the demon inside of Bob was laughing at us. A chill shot up my spine. But then I heard a different voice; calm, yet stern. God told me I must open my mouth and, through the power of the Holy Spirit, cast the demon out in the name of Jesus. If I did not open my mouth, the demon would stay.

So I began to pray out loud. As I began to say the simple words the Holy Spirit gave me, Bob began to breathe heavily, and then he became tense and stiff. Different areas of his back started to pulsate. The Spirit enabled me to speak more boldly and rebuke the demon in the name of Jesus, casting it out of Bob, never to return. As I was saying those words, a long, bellowing, gurgling growl began to proceed out of Bob's mouth. It was by far the craziest noise I've ever heard come out of a human. It was not of this world.

Bob began to cough up fluid for about three to four minutes. Then he went totally limp. At that moment, Jaco said the demon was completely gone. I felt God telling me to pray for His Holy Spirit to fill Bob. As we prayed, Bob stood up, looked at us, and said, "I feel different. I've never felt like this before!" It was amazing! It was totally God! I have been praying for God to do something like this in my life for the past seven months or so. All I can do is praise and thank God as I stand in complete awe of His power and grace.

Now, I realize that for some of you, at least part of this story caused you trouble. How could a Christian have a demon? If we are bought with a price, owned by God, and the temple of the Holy Spirit, how could we also be possessed by a demon? I agree that can't be possible. But don't jump to the conclusion that Bob wasn't a Christian, because I believe he was. The issue lies in in the word many Bibles translate as "demon possessed."

All Greek words have a lexical range, which means they can have multiple meanings and usages. *Strong's Concordance* defines *daimonizomai* as, "I am possessed, am under the power of an evil-spirit or demon." Strictly speaking, the word means "demonized."[3] Derek Prince, in his book *They Shall Expel Demons*, states, "To be 'possessed'—by a devil or demon—implies that a person is 'owned' by a devil or demon. But there is no basis for this in the Greek word *daimonizo*, which conveys no suggestion of ownership, but means merely 'to subject to demonic influence.'"[4]

In my opinion, if a person is not born again, he or she is subject to both demonic oppression and possession. Also, Scripture provides for the possibility that Christians can be demonized, or tormented by demons, as I will discuss in a later chapter. Because evil spirits exist throughout the world, and our struggle is with them and not with other humans, it makes sense that a value of the kingdom of God is to not commit acts of violence toward others. Such actions do nothing to deter or defeat the real enemy and only serve to reinforce and perpetuate the values of Satan's kingdom.

I realize it can be scary when your worldview is shaken. But do not be afraid, for God does not give us a spirit of fear. Also, know that King Jesus has not come to turn your world upside down but to turn things right side up again. Remember the encouraging words Paul wrote in 2 Corinthians 10:3-4: "*For though we walk in the flesh, we do not war according to the flesh, for the weapons of our warfare are not of the flesh, but divinely powerful for the destruction of fortresses.*"

If you are in Christ, there are spiritual weapons at your disposal that have divine power to demolish demonic strongholds. So may you be a mighty warrior for the kingdom of God and fight spiritual battles with spiritual weapons. May you be strong and courageous, resist the devil, and watch him flee from you. May you draw near to God and see Him draw near to you. May God's kingdom come and His will be done in your life, as it is in heaven.

Chapter 10

TRAILERS FOR THE MAIN ATTRACTION

In late October 2012, Stephanie and I started New Beginnings Bible Church out of our house. It has produced some of the most rewarding and challenging moments of my life, and I wouldn't trade it for the world. One of those rewarding moments occurred during the church's early stages as a small group of us gathered in my house one Saturday morning before heading out to do door-to-door prayer ministry in my neighborhood.

I gave a short devotional from the book of Acts, and we began to pray for God's guidance and infilling of His Spirit. During that time of prayer, the Holy Spirit directed us to pray for one of our deacons, Terry, a middle-aged African American man, who was having a difficult time with his back. Terry has had back problems for more than two decades, but a recent re-inuring of that area had left him grimacing with the slightest of movements and unable to concentrate on much of anything other than the pain. Terry said that on a pain scale of one to 10, with 10 being the worst, his pain was around a nine.

Deborah, a middle-aged Caucasian woman, had brought her five-year-old granddaughter that day. We'll call her "Sandra." We asked Sandra if she would ask Jesus to heal Terry's back. She said, "Okay, but I don't know what to say." We encouraged her to tell Jesus what she wanted Him to do for Terry. She agreed, put her hand on Terry's back, and prayed, "Jesus please heal Terry's back. In Jesus's name, amen."

We asked Terry where he was on the pain scale. He said he was better; maybe at a six, but he was still in discomfort. Perhaps Terry was being overly nice at this point for the kiddo's sake. He's a really good guy, you know?

I felt led to try a different strategy. I asked Terry when was the last time he was able to touch his toes while keeping his knees straight. He said it was more than 20 years ago. I asked him to stand up and try it. He gave it a shot but couldn't reach his kneecaps. So I asked Sandra if she would pray for Terry once more, asking Jesus to heal him. She obliged, Terry was able to extend about halfway down his shins, and his pain lowered to a two on the scale. We asked Sandra to pray one final time for Jesus to heal Terry completely. She did, and Terry touched the floor with no pain.

Terry, Deborah, and Sandra then went out as a group to do the door-to-door prayer ministry and saw God reach many people with the testimony of what had just transpired. A Hispanic middle-aged woman broke down in tears as they prayed for her and thanked them for being the exact help she needed at the right time. What an awesome picture of the Gospel of the kingdom of God and how the power of God can bring people together!

In light of this story, I need to address some questions about the gifts of the Holy Spirit. *What are the gifts of the Holy Spirit? What is the nature of the gifts? What are the purposes of the gifts? What is the duration of the gifts? Can people only have one gift? How can we discover our gifts?*

We will begin with a listing of the gifts of the Holy Spirit found in three of Paul's letters. (Note there is some overlap of gifts in the passages). First, Romans 12:6-8 lists these gifts: *prophecy, service, teaching,* **encouraging** (or *exhortation*), *giving, leading,* and *mercy.* In 1 Corinthians 12:4-11, 27-31, we find these gifts: *word of wisdom, word of knowledge, faith, healing, effecting of miracles, prophecy, distinguishing* (or *discerning*) *of spirits, speaking in tongues, interpretation of tongues, helps,* and *administrations.* Finally, in Ephesians 4:11-13, we find the gifts of *apostle, prophet, evangelist, pastor, and teacher.*

As you read these lists, you may have felt one of your personal gifts was left out. Why wasn't *musician, handyman, painter, athlete,* or *writer* on the list? The answer to that question is found in the second question we posed: *What is the nature of the gifts?* Paul writes in 1 Corinthians 12:4-7, "*Now there are varieties of gifts, but the same Spirit. And there are varieties of ministries, and the same Lord. There are varieties of effects, but the same God who works all things in all persons. But to each one is given the manifestation of the Spirit for the common good.*" So, the simple answer is there is a difference between the physical gifts God gives to all people at their birth and the supernatural gifts of the Holy Spirit that He gives to those who receive His Son by grace.

So, what are the purposes of the Spiritual gifts? In Ephesians 4:12-13, Paul says they are "*for the building up of the body of Christ; until we all attain to the unity of the faith, and of the knowledge of the Son of God, to a mature man, to the measure of the stature which belongs to the fullness of Christ.*" This means God has given several of the gifts for the purpose of helping grow the Church to become more like Christ.

But that is not all. In 1 Corinthians 12:7 Paul also wrote, "*To each one is given the manifestation of the Spirit for the common good.*" The "common good" means the welfare of everyone in the world, not just Christians. There-fore, spiritual gifts are not only given to build up the Church but also to impact the world in a positive way for the glory of God. Let me give you an example.

A few years ago, a college group I was leading felt led to do a water bottle ministry every Saturday at a large park in our hometown. The park was filled with thousands of walkers and joggers every day, but especially on Saturdays. We would bring about 100 iced-down water bottles in coolers and ask pass-ers by if they would like a free bottle of water. If they agreed, we would come alongside them, hand them the water, and ask if there was anything we could pray for them about.

If they declined prayer, we would say, "God bless you," and go back to passing out water. If they asked for prayer, we would ask if we could pray for them right then. They could continue to walk, jog, or stop. We would pray with them however they felt comfortable; they didn't even have to close their eyes. Then we would begin to pray as God led. God did many miraculous things through that ministry, and we established some good relationships with both Christians and non-Christians.

Before we would go out, we would meet at church for a brief devotional and prayer time. During one of those times, as we were praying for the folks we would encounter, a picture suddenly flashed into my mind. I saw a fit, blonde woman in blue athletic attire who had body image issues—and then the picture was gone. I shared the vision with the others, and we asked God to bless the woman and demonstrate His love to her.

We arrived at the park, and God blessed many people. However, after an hour of passing out water and praying for folks, no blonde woman in blue had come my way. I was starting to become downcast, as there was only one bottle of water left. But just then, seemingly out of nowhere, the woman came walking right toward me.

I asked if she'd like some water, and she gladly accepted. Then I asked if there was anything I could pray for her about. She looked me in the eye, then looked away and said, "Peace." I asked, "Would it be okay if I prayed for you right now?" She agreed. I thanked God for His great love for her, for His faithfulness to His Word, and that He is near to the humble. I thanked Him that she was humbling herself right then and believing in the power of prayer. I then asked God to demonstrate His nearness to her.

I asked that she would stop trying to find peace in things of this world, like beauty, wealth, and human approval. I asked that she would be healed from the fear that people would reject her. I asked that she would come to believe in the depths of her soul that the One who truly sees her as she is— the One who knows her best, loves her most, and demonstrated that love by sending His Son to die and rise again for her. I prayed that the Lord of peace would give her His peace at all times and in every way.

When I closed the prayer, she was in tears but was smiling. She asked how I knew to pray that. I told her that God knew her completely and was giving her a sign that His way for her was the best, that he would be with her through whatever changes He was calling her to make, and that He was giving her a sign to believe in Jesus. She walked away overjoyed, knowing the Lord of heaven and earth cared immensely about her and loved her more than she had ever realized.

So far we've address what are the gifts of the Holy Spirit, what is the nature of the gifts, and what are the purposes of the gifts. To some the next question may seem unnecessary, but to others it may be critical: *What is the duration of the gifts?* Did some of them cease with the death of the first 12 apostles, or do they continue to this day? Let's begin with a passage in Acts 2:

> *When the day of Pentecost had come, they were all together in one place. And suddenly there came from heaven a noise like a violent rushing wind, and it filled the whole house where they were sitting. And there appeared to them tongues as of fire distributing themselves, and they rested on each one of them. And they were all filled with the Holy Spirit and began to speak with other tongues, as the Spirit was giving them utterance.*
>
> Now there were Jews living in Jerusalem, devout men from every nation under heaven. And when this sound occurred, the crowd came together, and were bewildered because each one of them was hearing them speak in his own language. . . . But Peter, taking his stand with the eleven, raised his voice and declared to them. . . . "This is what was spoken of through the prophet Joel: 'AND IT SHALL BE IN THE LAST DAYS,' GOD SAYS, 'THAT I WILL POUR FORTH OF MY SPIRIT ON ALL MANKIND; AND YOUR SONS AND YOUR DAUGHTERS SHALL PROPHESY, AND YOUR YOUNG MEN SHALL SEE VISIONS, AND YOUR OLD MEN SHALL DREAM DREAMS; EVEN ON MY BONDSLAVES, BOTH

MEN AND WOMEN, I WILL IN THOSE DAYS POUR FORTH OF MY
SPIRIT and they shall prophesy'" (verses 1-6, 14, 16-18).

Peter quotes a prophecy from Joel that says all flesh—all who are born-again—will experience the outpouring of the Holy Spirit in the last days. He says those days have now arrived. In Hebrews 1:2, the author backs up Peter's words when he writes that God, *"In these last days has spoken to us in His Son, whom He appointed heir of all things, through whom also He made the world."* The apostle John takes things a step further when he writes, *"Children, it is the last hour; and just as you heard that antichrist is coming, even now many antichrists have appeared; from this we know that it is the last hour"* (1 John 2:18).

Peter says the outpouring of the Holy Spirit is for the last days, and the writer of Hebrews says we are in the last days. John says we're in the last hour. It seems logical, therefore, to deduce that the gifts of the Holy Spirit are for today. However, there is an even better scriptural argument showing the gifts of the Holy Spirit continue to this day.

One of the main texts people use to show the gifts have ceased is 1 Corinthians 13.. This is the famous "love chapter" often used at weddings. Interestingly, if you read the chapter in context with chapters 12 and 14, it really isn't about marriage but the practice of spiritual gifts. Also, about half of the chapter itself deals with those gifts. Let's take a look at the section of this chapter that causes the controversy:

> *Love never fails; but if there are gifts of prophecy, they will be done away; if there are tongues, they will cease; if there is knowledge, it will be done away. For we know in part and we prophesy in part; but when the perfect comes, the partial will be done away* (1 Corinthians 13:8-10).

Clearly, Paul is saying gifts will cease, but the issues are when they will cease and why they will cease. Some think several of the major gifts were just for the original 12 apostles and ceased when they died. Some think they ceased because the Church put together the canon of Scripture. They say that when the Bible was put together, the "perfect" came, so there was no need for many of the spiritual gifts.

Of course, the New Testament records deacons such as Stephen and Philip doing signs, wonders, and healings through the enabling of the Holy

Spirit (see Acts 6:8; 8:6-7). Furthermore, for those who believe the "perfect" Paul referred to is the Bible, it's clear that even though the Bible is totally inspired by God, all its prophecies have not yet been fulfilled. It clearly points to a day when all things *will* be perfected.

Think of it this way. When we have been given our new, incorruptible bodies and God has wiped away every tear from our eyes, a gift of healing will no longer serve a purpose. When we can worship God around His throne in one holy language, the gifts of tongues and interpretation of tongues will no longer serve a purpose. When we can commune with God face to face and know fully even as we are fully known, the gift of a word of knowledge will no longer serve a purpose. Likewise, the gift of effecting of miracles, such as the casting out of demons, will have no purpose when Satan and his demons have been thrown into the lake of fire.

Spiritual gifts are sort of like watching a trailer to a movie. A trailer is only a couple of minutes long and only gives you a taste of what the upcoming movie is about. You can only know in part and see in part. But when the movie finally comes out, you are able to know and see fully. After Jesus comes back, the partial will be done away with.

The early Christians wrote extensively about the gifts of the Spirit and were united in declaring they had not ceased. Irenaeus, a disciple of Polycarp, wrote this in 180 CE:

> The Lord raised the dead, and the apostles did so by the means of prayer, and this has been frequently done in the brotherhood on account of some necessity. When the entire church in that particular locality entreated God with much fasting and prayer, the spirit of the dead man has returned, and he has been bestowed in answer to the prayers of the saints. . . . Those who are truly His disciples, receiving grace from Him . . . perform [works] in His name, in order to promote the welfare of others, according to the gift that each one has received from Him.
>
> Some truly and certainly cast out devils. The result is that those who have been cleansed from evil spirits frequently both believe and join themselves to the church. Others have foreknowledge of things to come. They see visions, and they utter prophetic expressions. Still others heal the sick by

laying their hands upon them, and the sick are made whole. What is more, as I have said, even the dead have been raised up and remained among us for many years.

What more can I say? It is not possible to name the number of the gifts which the church throughout the whole world has received from God, in the name of Jesus Christ, who was crucified under Pontius Pilate, and which she exerts day by day for the benefit of the Gentiles, neither practicing deception upon any, nor taking any reward from them. For, just as she has received without charge from God, so does she minister without charge. . . . Calling upon the name of our Lord Jesus Christ, she has worked miracles for the benefit of mankind, and not to lead them into error. The name of our Lord Jesus Christ even now confers benefits. It cures thoroughly and effectively all who anywhere believe on Him.[1]

Remember that in Ephesians 4:12-13, Paul said God gave the gifts to build up the body of Christ "*until we all attain to the unity of the faith, and of the knowledge of the Son of God, to a mature man, to the measure of the stature which belongs to the fullness of Christ.*" Has the entire Church around the world reached unity and maturity in Christ? If not, the gifts haven't ceased.

Now, what about the question as to whether we can only have one gift? Remember in 1 Corinthians 12:4-6 that Paul says, "*Now there are varieties of gifts, but the same Spirit. And there are varieties of ministries, and the same Lord. There are varieties of effects, but the same God who works all things in all persons.*" Evidently, the Holy Spirit can work any of the spiritual gifts in anyone at any time. However, Paul does later write in verses 29-30 that not everyone has the same gifts. Therefore, we can glean from this instruction that not everyone will see all the gifts working in his or her life at the same time.

I encourage you to do a study on the manifestations of the spiritual gifts in the life of Paul. I have, and there is only one gift I don't see occurring in Paul's life: interpretation of tongues. For the others, I can make a case there was at least one occurrence—though many are demonstrated multiple times throughout his life. Believers in Jesus are capable of possessing multiple spiritual gifts, which is why Paul would write in 1 Corinthians 12:31 that we are to "*earnestly desire the greater gifts.*"

Finally, if multiple spiritual gifts are available to us, how do we discover those gifts? In Luke 9, Jesus sent out His 12 disciples into various cities to proclaim the kingdom of God, heal the sick, and cast out demons. They followed His orders and had tremendous success. Later, in Luke 10, Jesus called 72 other disciples and gave them similar instructions; yet He said nothing about casting out demons. Like the 12, these were just ordinary people who were intent on following and being like Jesus. This is what happened:

> The seventy returned with joy, saying, "Lord, even the demons are subject to us in Your name." And He said to them, "I was watching Satan fall from heaven like lightning. Behold, I have given you authority to tread on serpents and scorpions, and over all the power of the enemy, and nothing will injure you. Nevertheless do not rejoice in this, that the spirits are subject to you, but rejoice that your names are recorded in heaven" (verses 17-20).

Jesus had told them in advance they would at least be blessed with the spiritual gift of healing (see verse 9). However, as they went out in faith for the sake of the kingdom of God, they discovered they had been blessed with the spiritual gift of the effecting of miracles. They were able to cast out demons in the authority and power of Jesus's name. The same principle is true for us. As we take risks for the kingdom of God and live by faith in situations where we must depend on God's power, He empowers us through His Spirit to accomplish the tasks laid out for us.[2]

I'd like to share one more story to bring this point home. Mary and John are incredibly faithful members of my church, and John is also my father-in-law. They were partners one Saturday on one of our door-to-door prayer outreaches. That morning we had our usual devotion and prayer time before going out. We prayed that God would manifest Himself to the people we would encounter so they would know He is real, He loves them, His Gospel is true, and they can trust Him in making whatever changes He is calling them to make.

One of the first houses Mary and John came to was owned by a Spanish-speaking woman who didn't know any English. Although Mary is Hispanic, she only speaks and understands a little Spanish. However, as the woman spoke, she began to understand her perfectly and was able to communicate fluently in Spanish with her. The woman invited Mary and John inside and told them she hadn't spoken with her adult son in several years. She asked if they would pray for her and for her son. They knelt with the woman and prayed for the woman and her son, with Mary still speaking completely in Spanish.

The woman thanked Mary and John for the prayers, and they left to continue going door to door. About five minutes later, the woman drove up beside them in her car, waving her cellphone and shouting with a huge smile on her face. Almost immediately after Mary and John had left the woman's house, her son had called and they had begun to reconcile. I'm not sure if Mary has spoken or been able to interpret an unknown tongue since, but as she went out to work for the kingdom of God, He gifted her to accomplish His assignment.

It's true that spiritual gifts are only the partial and not the full. They are the trailer, not the movie. A healed person will eventually get sick again. Even Lazarus, who Jesus raised from the dead, eventually died again. Therefore, we should take Jesus's advice not to rejoice in the spiritual gifts in and of themselves, but rather in what Jesus did to make us sons and daughters of the King of kings.

One final point we must not miss is that when Jesus saw His disciples doing the works He did, He was overwhelmed with joy. "*He rejoiced greatly in the Holy Spirit, and said, 'I praise You, O Father, Lord of heaven and earth, that You have hidden these things from the wise and intelligent and have revealed them to infants. Yes, Father, for this way was well-pleasing in Your sight'*" (Luke 10:21). Don't you want to make Jesus rejoice today?

May you be like those 72 disciples and have the faith of a child, believing that everything Jesus and the apostles did is what Jesus wants to do through you. May you take great risks of faith for the kingdom of God, discover many spiritual gifts, and play an active role in destroying the works of the devil. May you, through the Holy Spirit, be a light to the nations, open blind eyes, and bring out those who dwell in darkness from the prison.

Chapter 11

GIVING KEYS TO THIEVES

A journal entry dated June 19, 2004, when I was in Swaziland, Africa:

A lady named Becky came to Jaco last night and asked if he and I would pray for her the next morning. Earlier in her life she was heavily involved with the occult and Jainism, the religion of her family, but converted to Christianity as a teenager. A few years ago she began to have severe panic and anxiety attacks, along with frequent nightmares and evil visions during the daytime. She would sometimes be sitting in class at her university and the walls would suddenly turn to blood and demonic-looking spiders would crawl toward her.

It was around this time that she married her husband, Doug. Becky and Doug had several ministries pray for her spiritual healing, but nothing positive ever came from those encounters. In fact, things only became worse. However, just before they came to Swaziland, Becky felt that God wanted to heal her during the trip. Doug is a Christian, but he had been struggling in his faith and wrestling with a substantial amount of doubt. I had a strong feeling going into the prayer room this morning that God wanted to do something special in Doug, but I wasn't sure exactly what.

Becky sat in a chair in the middle of the prayer room while Doug leaned up against a wall about 10 to 15 feet away. Jaco and I placed our hands Becky's head and back and began to pray, Jaco first. He began to rebuke any demons or evil spirits in Jesus's name and by His blood, but nothing seemed to happen. After about five minutes I began to pray out loud, yet still nothing happened. That was the point I began to realize God's purpose for Doug. He was standing behind us watching everything and hadn't said a word for about 10 minutes.

God showed me that if he did not open his mouth and begin to intercede for his wife, similar to my situation with Bob, Becky would not be set free. My purpose in that moment was not to cast out any demons; that was Doug's job. My purpose was to intercede for Doug. So I prayed out loud that Doug would cry out to the Lord for his wife. Then Doug slowly came forward, tears flowing from his eyes, and started to intercede for his wife. With ever-increasing boldness and compassion, Doug pleaded for God to set Becky free.

The Holy Spirit began to fill us, and the evil spirits began to leave Becky. Becky's stomach began to heave, and she leaned forward and repetedly coughed up a clear fluid to the ground. There was a lull, and we continued to silently pray for her. My hand suddenly felt the muscles in her back pulsating. I realized there was at least one more evil spirit inside her.

God told me to encourage Doug to keep praying out loud, and Becky said we needed to pray against the spirit of anxiety. Doug prayed for her with even more compassion and faith, and she began heaving and coughing again, with more fluid coming out. Once again, after several minutes there was a lull. Then, after a minute or two, I felt her back pulsating, and Becky told us we now needed to pray against the spirit that was causing the evil day-visions and nightmares. So we did, with Doug mostly leading the way.

For the last 30 minutes or so as Doug had been praying, I had one hand on Becky's back and one on Doug's. As Doug was casting out the third evil spirit, I felt him shaking and growing weak. It seemed like the evil spirit Doug was casting out of his wife was trying to enter him. I intensely prayed for God to protect Doug and place the full armor of God on us all. Soon, Doug straightened up and got back to interceding for his wife, who once again began coughing out the same liquid substance as before.

About 45 to 50 minutes had passed since we began praying for Becky, and finally she said she felt at peace. We then asked the Holy Spirit to fill her completely, remove anything unclean in her, and not allow those things to ever return. After about three minutes, she had one small spasm in her back and one last cough, expelling the last of the fluid. It was over. As Doug walked with the Spirit through that scary situation, not only did God set his wife free, but He also set Doug free from the doubts that had been plaguing him.

I'm not sure why Becky was still being tormented and oppressed by evil spirits after becoming born again and receiving Jesus as her Lord and Savior. And I say with confidence she was born again due to the fact the spiritual gift of discerning of spirits was present in her to assist us in casting out the evil spirits in her. Jesus Himself tells us Satan doesn't cast out Satan (see Mark 3:20-27). What, then, are some reasons why Christians can be oppressed by demons and evil spirits while still having the Holy Spirit in them?

To tackle this issue, I will again turn to Derek Prince, the Scriptures, and the early Church writings. First, leaning on Exodus 20:3-5, Prince states a person's family background in false religions can lead to demonic oppression even after that person receives Christ.[1] He writes, "God warns against all forms of idolatry or other involvement with false 'gods.' The evil consequences of these particular sins can extend to four generations. . . . I have discovered that such babies are often demonized before they emerge from the womb. This is particularly true of people with backgrounds in Eastern religions such as Hinduism or Buddhism, or false religions such as Freemasonry or Mormonism."[2]

Yoga is sweeping the West. Many Christians practice yoga for supposed health reasons and even take part in yoga classes at their churches. But is Christian yoga even possible? Subhas R. Tiwari, a professor at the Hindu University of America, writes, "The simple, immutable fact is that yoga originated from the Vedic or Hindu culture. . . . The effort to separate yoga from Hinduism must be challenged because it runs counter to the fundamental principles upon which yoga itself is premised. . . . Efforts to separate yoga from its spiritual center reveal ignorance of the goal of yoga."[3]

Dave Hunt writes that Hindus believe "yoga was introduced by Lord Krishna in the *Bhagavad Gita* as the sure way to Hindu heaven; and Shiva (one of the most feared Hindu deities, known as "The Destroyer") is addressed as *Yogeshwara*, Lord of Yoga. One of the most authoritative Hatha Yoga texts, the fifteenth-century *Hathayoga-Pradipika* by Svatmarama, lists Lord Shiva as the first Hatha Yoga teacher."[4]

Jesus says He is the only way to the Father (see John 14:6), but in Hinduism Lord Krishna says yoga is the sure way to Hindu heaven.[5] Jesus says He has come to give us life to the fullest but that the thief has come to steal, kill, and destroy (see John 10:10). And the Hindu god known as The Destroyer is the first yoga teacher. Hmm.

Hunt continues, "The goal of all yoga is to obtain oneness with the universe. That's also known as the process of enlightenment, or union with the Brahman (Hinduism's highest god). The word 'yoga' means 'union' or 'to yoke.'"[6] If Hinduism is a pantheistic religion and Christianity is monotheistic, can there possibly be union between the two? Also, yoga is designed to yoke an individual to the Brahman. What do the Scriptures say about that?

Paul writes, "*Stop becoming unevenly yoked with unbelievers. What partnership can righteousness have with lawlessness? What fellowship can light have with darkness? What harmony exists between the Messiah and Beliar, or what do a believer and an unbeliever have in common? What agreement can a temple of God make with idols? For we are the temple of the living God* (2 Corinthians 6:14-16 ISV)." God will not be yoked with a false deity, and therefore, neither should His people.

Unfortunately, it gets more serious. In Deuteronomy 32:15-18, Moses warns the Hebrew people against the idolatrous yoking practices of their forefathers. "*But Jeshurun . . . forsook God who made him, and scorned the Rock of his salvation. They made Him jealous with strange gods; with abominations they provoked Him to anger. They sacrificed to demons who were not God, to gods whom they have not known, new gods who came lately, whom your fathers did not dread.*" The people were worshiping demons, though most likely they were unaware of it. But God was aware, and it was an abomination in His eyes.

Paul comments on this passage in 1 Corinthians 10:14-22 when he writes, "*Therefore, my beloved, flee from idolatry. I speak as to wise men; you judge what I say. Is not the cup of blessing which we bless a sharing in the blood of Christ? Is not the bread which we break a sharing in the body of Christ? Since there is one bread, we who are many are one body; for we all partake of the one bread. Look at the nation Israel; are not those who eat the sacrifices sharers in the altar? What do I mean then? That a thing sacrificed to idols is anything, or*

that an idol is anything? No, but I say that the things which the Gentiles sacri-
fice, they sacrifice to demons and not to God; and I do not want you to become
sharers in demons. You cannot drink the cup of the Lord and the cup of demons;
you cannot partake of the table of the Lord and the table of demons."

Shiva, the Hindu destroyer god, taught people through yoga to yoke themselves to the Brahman in order to achieve enlightenment and become one with the universe. Paul wrote that when we partake in idolatry, we can become a sharer in demons. Literally, he says that when we engage in these idolatrous practices, we can fellowship with demons.[7] Shiva isn't being completely forthright with us, is he? Jesus said whenever Satan speaks a lie, he speaks from his own nature, for he is a liar and the father of lies (see John 8:44). Peter taught that our adversary, the devil, prowls around like a roaring lion looking for someone to devour (see 1 Peter 5:8). May we repent of all these forms of idolatry.

A second avenue by which demons and evil spirits can gain access to our lives is through occult practices. According to Prince, modern examples of divination include fortunetelling, palm reading, psychics, Ouija boards, and horoscopes. Sorcery is similar to divination, but involves the use of tools such as "drugs, potions, charms, amulets, magic, spells, incantations and various forms of music."[8] A third branch of the occult includes spiritism. A medium or spiritist's general form of activity is known as a séance.[9]

The final area Prince refers to concerning the occult is witchcraft. He writes, "Witchcraft is the universal, primeval religion of fallen humanity. When the human race turned from God in rebellion, the power that moved in was witchcraft. As the Bible says, *'Rebellion is as the sin of witchcraft'* (1 Samuel 15:23)." Prince notes that primitive witchcraft normally includes a form of priesthood, rituals and liturgies, sacrifices, and covenants that bind the participants to whatever demonic or satanic being is the focal point of their activity.[10]

Prince lists four main purposes of witchcraft: "(1) To propitiate a higher spiritual being. . . . (2) To control the forces of nature. . . . (3) To ward off sickness and infertility. . . . (4) To control other human beings—to terrify enemies in battle or to produce sexual desire in one person toward one another."[11] Witchcraft in the west, according to Prince, operates on four levels: (1) open, public, "respectable"; (2) "underground"—covens; (3) disguised within society and the Church; (4) a work of the flesh.[12]

When I was a kid, not bathing for a week didn't faze me. I just went right along playing basketball and football every day after school, getting dirty and smelly with the other boys who were hygienically challenged like myself. I'm sure I was detestable in the nostrils of many of my teachers and female class-mates. Know that while people in your circles of influence may look on some of these occult practices as fun, helpful, neutral, or laughable, God has strong feelings about them. In Deuteronomy 18:9-12, God tells us the practices listed above are detestable and the people who do such things are detestable to Him. The word "detestable" is used three times in those verses.

In 1 Samuel 15, King Saul was given a mission to completely destroy all the Amalekites and their possessions. Saul obeyed partially, but not fully. He left their king alive, kept the best of their possessions, and set up a monument for himself. When Samuel confronted Saul about his disobedience, Saul claimed to have kept the spoils of the battle as offerings to the Lord, but he couldn't make up a decent lie for keeping the king alive against God's orders. Samuel said to him, *"Has the Lord as much delight in burnt offerings and sacrifices as in obeying the voice of the Lord? Behold, to obey is better than sacrifice, and to heed than the fat of rams. For rebellion is as the sin of divination, and insubordination is as iniquity and idolatry"* (verses 22-23). God soon allowed an evil spirit to begin tormenting Saul.

From this story we can deduce our third point: an attitude of rebellion, or rebellious actions, can lead to demonization. Jesus said, *"When the unclean spirit goes out of a man, it passes through waterless places seeking rest, and does not find it. Then it says, 'I will return to my house from which I came'; and when it comes, it finds it unoccupied, swept, and put in order. Then it goes and takes along with it seven other spirits more wicked than itself, and they go in and live there; and the last state of that man becomes worse than the first. That is the way it will also be with this evil generation"* (Matthew 12:43-45).

After the house was emptied (the evil spirit was cast out), the house wasn't subsequently filled. Jesus says the man's lack of being filled allowed for seven additional evil spirits to invade him. What, then, prevented the man from having his house (life) filled and opened him to demons?

Derek Prince writes, "Any act of deliberate wrongdoing may open the way for a demon. Many such acts are possible—telling a premeditated lie, for instance, or shoplifting, or cheating on exams. Again, it may not be a single act that opens the door. It may well be the deliberate, persistent practice of a sinful act that eventually becomes a habit. Secret sins like repeated masturbation or fornication or pornography almost inevitably open the way for demons. But other more 'respectable' habits can have a similar effect. Frequent overeating opens the way for a demon of gluttony. . . . Habitual exaggeration in conversation opens the way for a lying spirit."[13]

I realize seeing phrases like "demon of gluttony" or "lying spirit" may be unfamiliar to you. Perhaps you've only been exposed to teaching that states there are only generic demons and evil spirits. But the Bible is much more specific. Excluding the ranks of rebellious angels Paul writes about in Ephesians 6:12, some other names of demonic spirits found in Scripture include: *goat demon* (see Leviticus 17:7), *evil spirit* (see 1 Samuel 16:14), *lying spirit* (see 1 Kings 22:23; 1 Timothy 4:1), *spirit of judgment* (see Isaiah 4:4), *spirit of burning* (see Isaiah 4:4), *spirit of distortion* (see Isaiah 19:14), *spirit of harlotry* (see Hosea 4:12), *unclean spirit* (see Mark 1:23), *deaf and mute spirit* (see Mark 9:25), *spirit of divination* [python spirit] (see Acts 16:16) and a *spirit of fear* (see 2 Timothy 1:7). There are several additional types of demons not specifically listed in Scripture but connected with sin issues, sicknesses, or strongholds in our lives.

Sometimes, the sinful act committed by one person leads to demonization in another. Such is the case with spirits of trauma. Francis MacNutt writes that spirits of trauma "enter a person not through the victim's sin, but through someone else's."[14] A person is almost killed by a drunk driver. A man abuses his wife or child. A person performs satanic ritual abuse. A young lady is raped. A parent is forced to bury his child. A single mom gets laid off. A little boy is kidnapped. Traumas come in all kinds of forms.

MacNutt continues, "Spirits of trauma are the most common category of evil spirits that afflict people. . . . When these spirits identify themselves, they give names like *grief, rejection,* or *fear.* These are not sins, of course, but represent our most common emotions. Emotions are one of God's gifts to humanity and help move us to action. Fear is not in itself a problem, but *fear* as a spirit can invade the emotion of excessive fear, which *is* a problem, and make it more of a problem. Demonic fear blocks its victim's free will so that he behaves irrationally and is tempted to commit desperate acts."[15]

A fourth way Christians allow demons to oppress them is through sustained anger combined with an unwillingness to forgive. In Ephesians 4:26-27, Paul writes, "BE ANGRY, AND YET DO NOT SIN; DO NOT LET THE SUN GO DOWN ON YOUR ANGER, AND DO NOT GIVE THE DEVIL AN OPPORTUNITY." The word translated "opportunity" in this verse (*topon*) has a lexical range that includes "place," "region," "seat," and "opportunity."[16] Jesus says in John 14:2

that He is going to God the Father to prepare a *topon*, a dwelling place, for His disciples.

Staying angry with someone and refusing to forgive him or her is like handing a thief the key to our house. Specifically, Paul tells us this thief is the devil, and the house for which the key is made is our body. To be sure, handing over the key to our house is not the same as signing over the deed to that person. Just because someone has a key to our house does not mean he or she owns it. We still own the house.

If you have been born again, God has bought you with a price and your body has become the temple of the Holy Spirit. The devil cannot own or possess something that is owned or possessed by God. However, if you have given away the key to your house to him, he has the ability to cause much damage to your life. Again, as Jesus said, *"The thief comes only to steal and kill and destroy"* (John 10:10). Knowing this, why would you willingly give the key to your house to the thief?

Unfortunately, I have seen two situations in which prolonged anger combined with an unwillingness to forgive allowed evil spirits to torment a Christian. These two individuals had anger toward family members, and their unwillingness to obey the Lord and forgive caused them to be actively tormented by evil spirits. Both of these people would frequently hear audible, evil, and berating voices. One of these people heard voices telling him to do harmful, malevolent things to others.

Both individuals experienced deliverance once they repented of the sins of prolonged anger and unforgiveness. They experienced the Spirit of God cast out the evil spirits from their bodies through the power, authority, name, and blood of Jesus Christ. Both of these Christians felt incredible spiritual and physical relief as a result of the repentance and deliverance that had taken place. One of the two was finally able to start having a full night's sleep after roughly two decades of restless nights.

A lack of repentance of past sins is the fifth reason a person can be demonized even after receiving Christ. Just like new wine needs to be put into fresh wineskins, repentance must accompany a born-again experience; if it doesn't, many messes will ensue. John the Baptist, Jesus, the 12 apostles, and Paul all preached the necessity of repentance. However, though repentance is sometimes preached in today's Church, it is often just given lip service when someone comes forward to become a Christian. A pastor will ask, "Have you repented of your sins?" If the person says yes and affirms general questions about the deity and saving work of Jesus, he or she is allowed to be baptized. This was not the case with the early Christians. Second-century Christian apologist Justin Martyr writes:

> I will also relate the manner in which we dedicated ourselves to God when we had been made new through Christ. . . . As many as are persuaded and believe that what we teach and say is true, and undertake to be able to live accordingly, are instructed to pray and to entreat God with fasting, for the remission of their past sins. The rest of us pray and fast with them. They are brought by us where there is water, and are regenerated in the same manner in which we were regenerated ourselves. They there receive the washing with water in the name of God (the Father and Lord of the universe), of our Savior Jesus Christ, and of the Holy Spirit. For Christ also said, "Unless you are born again, you will not enter into the kingdom of heaven."[17]

Can you imagine how much healthier our churches would be if we took repentance and baptism as seriously as the early Church? Can you imagine how tightly knit our communities of faith would be if we fasted and prayed with a new brother or sister who was also fasting and praying in preparation for baptism? Jesus said that when we are one, just as He and the Father are one, the world will know that God sent Him and loves us just as He loves Jesus (see John 17:22-23). Can you imagine scores upon scores of non-Christians putting their complete trust in Christ and the Church being perfected in unity?

If you've been involved in any of the practices I've discussed, know there is hope for you. The God of hope is ready and willing to incline to you, hear your cry, and rescue you if you fully yield yourself to Him and repent. Find someone—a pastor, Christian counselor, Bible study leader, someone strong in the faith—and practice in faith the words of James 5:16: *"Therefore, confess your sins to one another, and pray for one another so that you may be healed."* Agree with God about the evil nature of these practices, fully turn away from them, and then turn your life over to Jesus.

Don't let the devil beat you down, keep you in shame, and cause you to resist grace. You probably didn't realize the full weight of what you were doing. Many of the leaders who were responsible for killing Jesus, the Author of Life, also acted in ignorance. As Peter said to them, *"Brethren, I know that you acted in ignorance, just as your rulers did also. But the things which God announced beforehand by the mouth of all the prophets, that His Christ would suffer, He has thus fulfilled. Therefore repent and return, so that your sins may be wiped away, in order that times of refreshing may come"* (Acts 3:17-19).

Peter was a man who made many mistakes. Have you ever wondered why, after His resurrection, Jesus asked Peter three times, "Do you love Me?" I've heard sermons about this passage in John 21, and often the preacher will say Jesus was restoring Peter to ministry since Peter had earlier denied knowing Jesus three times. But let me suggest there was more going on in that moment.

In 2 Corinthians 1:20, Paul writes, *"For as many as are the promises of God, in Him they are yes."* Basically, that means God keeps every promise He makes. Earlier in Jesus's ministry, Peter heard Jesus promise, *"Everyone who confesses Me before men, I will also confess him before My Father who is in heaven. But whoever denies Me before men, I will also deny him before My Father who is in heaven"* (Matthew 10:32-33). I believe Peter remembered the latter portion of that promise and thought all hope for him was lost. That is why he was almost to the point of giving up on being a disciple of Jesus and had decided to go back into the fishing business.

However, Jesus keeps *all* of His promises. In Romans 2:4, Paul tells us the kindness of God leads us to repentance. So, in His kindness, Jesus helped Peter do the hard work of repentance on that beach. Three times He asked Peter, "Do you love Me?" Three times Peter said yes and called Jesus his Lord in front of the others. Three times Jesus then told Peter to be a shepherd to His flock, the Church. Yes, Peter was restored to ministry that day, but more crucially, he was restored spiritually.

When Peter addressed the crowd in Acts 3 and called them to repent, promising times of refreshing from the Lord if they would obey the promptings of the Spirit, he was speaking from empathy, experience, and a hope-filled, repentant heart that knew the depth of God's kindness. If God can spiritually restore Peter and many of the people who played a part in having Jesus killed, He can restore you as well.

May the Lord of heaven and earth bring you up out of the pit of destruction, out of the miry clay, and set your feet on the rock to make your footsteps firm. May the Lord rescue you and deliver you as you submit fully to Him. May you turn away from evil and do good. May you seek peace and pursue it. And as you do, may the Lord of peace Himself give you peace at all times and in every way.

Chapter 12

A PERSON OF INFLUENCE

Have you ever heard the statement that Christianity is not a religion but a relationship? After being married for eight years now, I have come to realize there are several things I can do, both good and bad, to affect the levels of intimacy, peace, and happiness with my wife. Stephanie worked many years as a night-shift labor and delivery nurse, and sometimes she would ask me to take care of the dishes when she was leaving. I would always tell her I'd do them, but there were many occasions when she came home in the morning to find dirty dishes still in the sink, and me eating breakfast while reading the news. I told you I can be a jerk.

However, there are other times when I'm at the grocery store and see a beautiful orchid, one of my wife's favorite flowers, and bring it home for her just because I love her. Or there's the "buy your wife a present on your own birthday" birthday gift. I can't take credit for that one. That's a Mike Satterfield special, and it works.

The Scriptures tell us there are several things we can do to affect the influence of the Holy Spirit in our lives and our relationship with Him. First, in Ephesians 4:29-32, Paul says we can grieve the Holy Spirit when we engage in certain behaviors: *"Let no unwholesome word proceed from your mouth, but only such a word as is good for edification according to the need of the moment, so that it will give grace to those who hear. Do not grieve the Holy Spirit of God, by whom you were sealed for the day of redemption. Let all bitterness and wrath and anger and clamor and slander be put away from you, along with all malice. Be kind to one another, tender-hearted, forgiving each other, just as God in Christ also has forgiven you."* The word "grieve" means to cause immense emotional sorrow or sadness. The negative actions Paul lists distress the Holy Spirit in a manner similar to the emotions we feel when grieving the loss of a loved one.

There was a young man in a church where I used to work who had a rocky relationship with his father. I spent a lot of time discipling this young man and heard numerous stories of broken promises and other heart-wrenching things. This young man could not remember ever hearing his Christ-professing father tell him "I love you" or give him a hug after age seven.

The young man was seeking to do well in all areas of life—academically, vocationally, and spiritually. Yet one day, a darkness came over him, and a crisis of faith ensued. We talked over the phone that day, and he explained various problems he was encountering at school and work. He asked how a good God could allow such things. Doubt and anger were filling his mind as he wondered if he had ever actually experienced God at all.

I suddenly felt led to ask him about his father. Knowing their history, I asked if he had told his father he forgave him. The young man said he hadn't. I told him that if he had ever said the Lord's Prayer, he had asked God to forgive him in the manner that he forgives others. I then directed him to Ephesians 4 and told him about how we grieve the Holy Spirit when we don't forgive others, especially other Christians. I told him the remedy for this is to imitate Christ, who loved and forgave His enemies. I prayed for him, and we hung up our phones.

The next day, the young man met with his dad at his house. Eventually, he began to confront the issues that had caused him bitterness for so many years. He expressed his feelings to his dad without yelling or name-calling. Neither of them got defensive. They expressed apologies to each other and offered forgiveness. They hugged, and the father told the young man, "I love you." The darkness that once hovered over the young man now fled, and a deep sense of joy and peace filled his spirit.

Not only can we grieve the Holy Spirit, but Paul says we can also quench the Spirit: "*Rejoice always; pray without ceasing; in everything give thanks; for this is God's will for you in Christ Jesus. Do not quench the Spirit; do not despise prophetic utterances. But examine everything carefully; hold fast to that which is good; abstain from every form of evil*" (1 Thessalonians 5:16-22). The word "quench" means to extinguish or suppress.[1] It's like using a hose when suddenly the water stops running. You trace the hose backward and realize a kink has developed, cutting off the flow of water. In a similar way, we can develop spiritual "kinks" that suppress the flow the Holy Spirit in our lives.

To illustrate this point, I'm going to pay attention to Paul's instructions to "*rejoice always; pray without ceasing; in everything give thanks.*" From spring 2013 to spring 2015, I worked as a chaplain. Radio stations, construction companies, restaurants, and other businesses would ask my company to come to their job sites each week and check up on every member of the company. We would ask how they and their families were doing and if there was anything we could do for them that week. We would also provide various forms of pastoral care-like services such as hospital visits, funerals, counseling, or just meeting someone for coffee or lunch if he or she wanted to talk.

Throughout the first few months of this vocation, I would be flooded with feelings of anxiety as I drove to each job site. A couple of times I sat in the parking lot of the establishments for about 15 minutes, focusing on how I was about to say many stupid things and inevitably look like a fool. Basically, how it was about to be middle school and high school all over again. Then, giving into my fears, I would drive off to find comfort in a Chick-fil-A #1 with no pickles, telling myself many reasons why tomorrow would be a much better day to make a visit.

Our heavenly Father has promised to meet all our needs according to His glorious riches in Christ Jesus. He has promised a steady flow of Living Water for His children. However, He has also promised we have the ability to control, to a great extent, how freely that river flows in our lives. Paul tells us in 1 Thessalonians 5:16-22 that one key to maintaining a steady flow of the Holy Spirit is by engaging God throughout our day with an awareness of His goodness, His greatness, and His Fatherly care.

One morning as I was about to do my chaplain work, I was again inundated with worry and fear concerning the task ahead of me. This time, however, I chose to engage God. I began to sing one of my favorite hymns, "How Great Thou Art." I dwelt on how the great and awesome God of the universe loved me enough to send His Son to die for me and take away my sin and how He is coming back to take me home to be with Him forever.

I sang louder and louder, engaging not just my heart but also my mind and spirit. I sang until I entered God's presence and believed the truth of the words I was singing more than the lies of enemy. I kept singing until it was a prayer. I sang until I was worshiping God. By the grace of God, I worshiped until I was no longer in a place of quenching the Spirit but rather in a place of excitement about obeying God out of a love for Jesus. I kept that posture of prayer during the ride to the establishment, and God did amazing things in the lives of the people I encountered that day.

In Galatians 5:16-25 Paul teaches us the third way we can affect the influence of the Holy Spirit in our lives. He says, "*But I say, walk by the Spirit, and you will not carry out the desire of the flesh. For the flesh sets its desire against the Spirit, and the Spirit against the flesh; for these are in opposition to one another, so that you may not do the things that you please. But if you are led by the Spirit, you are not under the Law. Now the deeds of the flesh are evident, which are: immorality, impurity, sensuality, idolatry, sorcery, enmities, strife, jealousy, outbursts of anger, disputes, dissensions, factions, envying, drunkenness, carousing, and things like these, of which I forewarn you, just as I have forewarned you, that those who practice such things will not inherit the kingdom of God. But the fruit of the Spirit is love, joy, peace, patience, kindness, goodness, faithfulness, gentleness, self-control; against such things there is no law. Now those who belong to Christ Jesus have crucified the flesh with its passions and desires. If we live by the Spirit, let us also walk by the Spirit."*

My sister-in-law, Leanna, is a full-time missionary in Mozambique. She and her missionary friend Ally have been faithfully serving there for nearly a decade. On December 24, 2012, Ally's father was beaten to death as he walked to his church to play the organ for their evening Christmas Eve service. The men who committed the vicious murder had no motive. They did not know Ally's father, he had done nothing wrong, and they had nothing to hold against him. They took his life in a brutal way, without hesitation and without provocation.

As Ally's mom and her family sat in court, it was impossible to perceive any repentance or remorse on the part of the murderers. When the men heard the sadistic nature of their crime described in painful detail, they displayed only anger and frustration at being caught. They didn't seem in the least bit sorry for what they had done.

The story was highly publicized in the national news, and the courthouse was crawling with reporters with cameras ready to catch the family's response. Anyone would have understood if Ally's mom lashed out in anger toward her husband's killers. However, she surprised millions by publicly offering forgiveness to the murderers. She explained she was doing so because that is what Jesus did for her. That is what He did for all of us.

The response was incredible. Scores of people began to get in touch with her, looking for a better understanding of how she could forgive such a crime. Ally's mother had the joy of pointing them all to Christ. Strangers showed up on her doorstep wanting to talk, and people stopped her in the supermarket or when she was in line at the bank. She began to receive hundreds of letters from people all over the country who were moved by what they had witnessed. Many described how they had been convinced to turn back to a Christ they had abandoned years ago, or how they had been inspired to forgive an offense they had been holding onto for decades, or how they wanted to know more about God.

Various television programs invited Ally's mom to talk about her stance on forgiveness, and the church asked her to talk at various peace and reconciliation forums. Everywhere she went she encountered people who were hungry to know more about God from her in a way that she, a natural evangelist, had longed for her entire life. People who had never met her before could look at her life and recognize, in what was for many the first time, a true demonstration of God's love.

I believe Ally's mother was able to reach so many people during such a difficult time because she allowed herself to be led by the Spirit rather than the flesh. She admits that forgiving her husband's murderers would not have been something she would have been able to achieve in her own goodness or her own strength. It was not possible for her to forget what those men had done to make her husband suffer so much, or how they had shown him no mercy, or how they had hurt him over and over again.

Forgiveness was not her instinctive response. However, after many years of following Jesus and wondering at His willingness to forgive her own offences, it was her heart's desire to let the Spirit do His work in her. When Paul says we should be *"led by the Spirit"* (Galatians 5:18), he paints a picture of a person walking beside a horse or donkey, holding the reigns and leading it to a desired destination. He also implies the horse or donkey is willingly submitting itself to the one leading it.

Walking with and being led by the Spirit means allowing the Holy Spirit to set the course of our thoughts and actions. When this is true in our lives, we think and act more like the Lord Jesus, because *"the Lord is the Spirit"* (2 Corinthians 3:17). Second Peter 3:9 tells us the Lord is patient with us, *"not wishing for any to perish but for all to come to repentance."* This is even true for the murderers of a man who was on his way to honor Him at a Christmas Eve service.

Ally's mother's reaction displayed the heart of a person who is being transformed by the Gospel. Many people, including other Christians she knew, responded to the killers with a message that sounded more like, "Go to hell!" Some people living through the situation might have been tempted to exact revenge by seeking to have the two men murdered. Ally's mom, though, lived out what it means to love our neighbors as ourselves.

One summer day when I was in elementary school, my older brother and I went to my cousin's house to swim in their pool. I wasn't the strongest swimmer, which my brother knew, and at some point he convinced me to come out to the deep end. Once I got there, he playfully grabbed me and put my head under water. I began to flail about, kicking and swinging—basically doing anything I could to get back above water. After a couple of seconds, he let me back up. I called him a name and said I was telling Mom.

Have you ever been in that kind of situation where you feel like you're desperately fighting to take your next breath and stay alive? Realize now that however low of a self-esteem you may have, or however much you think you hate yourself, you actually love yourself more than anything else in this world. To prove it, all someone has to do is force your head under water, and, if you're like most people, you'll do almost anything to stay alive.

Jesus tells us it's with that same fervor, passion, and fight that we are supposed to love our neighbors, and even our enemies. We are supposed to love them as ourselves. Right now as you're reading this, something inside you may be revolting against Jesus's teaching. Understand that's what Paul says happens all the time. "*For the flesh sets its desire against the Spirit, and the Spirit against the flesh; for these are in opposition to one another*" (Galatians 5:17).

However, if we stay close to the Spirit and are led by Him, we produce the fruit of the Spirit in abundance. Jesus said, "*Abide in Me, and I in you. As the branch cannot bear fruit of itself unless it abides in the vine, so neither can you unless you abide in Me. I am the vine, you are the branches; he who abides in Me and I in him, he bears much fruit, for apart from Me you can do nothing*" (John 15:4-5). The word "abide" also translates as "remain." Ally's mom has produced much fruit for the kingdom of God because she has remained close to the Spirit through this ordeal and allowed Him to lead her each step of the way.

The fourth way to affect the influence of the Holy Spirit in our lives is by being filled with the Spirit. As Paul writes in Ephesians 5:18, "*Do not get drunk on wine, which leads to debauchery. Instead, be filled with the Spirit.*" The phrase "filled with the Spirit" literally means to be under the influence or control of the Spirit.

I got drunk for the first time at the age of 15. I had been at a house party for 30 minutes and had consumed enough alcohol to get a middle linebacker drunk after four or five hours. Ten minutes later, completely under the influence, I passed out in the cup of a girl I was speaking with. Later, I knocked over a cooler. People tell me I talked to a tree for a while like a long-lost friend. I remember the host angrily telling my ride to get me out of there. As my friend opened the car door, I vomited all over the host, who had continued to chew us out all the way to the street. Then I vomited on my pants and in my friend's air ducts.[2]

In Ephesians 5:18, Paul tell us, *"Do not get drunk with wine, for that is dissipation."*[3] He then uses this picture of being inebriated to make his point that we need to be *"filled with the Spirit."* Paul is not insinuating a Spirit-filled Christian is physically out of control like a drunk person, but he is stating a Christian who is filled with the Spirit has chosen to become completely occupied by God.

Some people teach that Christians are *always* filled with the Spirit, but if that were the case, Paul wouldn't have to command us to be filled. Also, continuing with the analogy of getting drunk, no one is *always* drunk—people have to do things to get drunk. And a person can't just take a sip of alcohol to get drunk. You have to be intentional about it.

Others teach that when people are filled with the Spirit, they must speak in tongues. In the book of Acts we find that sometimes they do, but the primary result of people being filled with the Spirit is boldly speaking the word of the Lord. We see this in the case of Elizabeth (see Luke 1:41-45), Zachariah (see Luke 1:67-79), Peter (see Acts 4:8-12), the believers in the early Church (see Acts 4:23-31), and Paul (see Acts 9:17-22). As Christians, it should be a great joy for us to boldly speak words from God. And God promises that if we seek Him and yield ourselves to Him, we can be under His influence and do mighty things for His kingdom!

Let us then take heed of Peter's words: *"For the time already past is sufficient for you to have carried out the desire of the Gentiles, having pursued a course of sensuality, lusts, drunkenness, carousing, drinking parties and abominable idolatries. . . . The end of all things is near; therefore, be of sound judgment and sober spirit for the purpose of prayer. Above all, keep fervent in your love for one another, because love covers a multitude of sins. Be hospitable to one another without complaint. As each one has received a special gift, employ it in serving one another as good stewards of the manifold grace of God. Whoever speaks, is to do so as one who is speaking the utterances of God; whoever serves is to do so as one who is serving by the strength which God supplies; so that in all things God may be glorified through Jesus Christ, to whom belongs the glory and dominion forever and ever. Amen (1 Peter 4:3, 7-11)."*

Being a good steward of what God has entrusted to us is the fifth way to affect the influence of the Holy Spirit in our lives. Jesus said in Luke 16:10-11, *"He who is faithful in a very little thing is faithful also in much; and he who is unrighteous in a very little thing is unrighteous also in much. Therefore if you have not been faithful in the use of unrighteous wealth, who will entrust the true riches to you?"*

After I accepted the invitation to go to Swaziland, I was informed I had to raise more than $2,000 to make the trip. It was a daunting task, but by God's grace I was able to raise about half of the required amount. Unfortunately, half was not adequate. Several of the other students were in the same financial boat as me, and we had only one week to go before the deadline to turn in our money. Then, out of the blue, an anonymous donor wrote a check to the school covering all of our remaining expenses. Hallelujah! What a clear demonstration that God wanted us all to be on that trip!

When we arrived in Africa, we spent a week doing training in an area close to Johannesburg, South Africa. It was kind of like summer camp in central Texas, and I didn't really feel like I was in Africa. However, when we crossed the border into Swaziland and I began to see poverty like never before, something changed inside of me. I began to feel overwhelmed with shame, anxiety, and a strong sense I needed to go home.

I told a couple of my group members what was going on, and during the next day God sent several brothers and sisters in Christ to show genuine concern and to pray for me. But I would not be dissuaded. I called my dad that night and told him I needed to come home. He gently asked if that would be the best way to honor all the people who contributed financially to get me there. But he also told me he would get me back to Houston if that's what I really felt was the best course of action.

The next day, I had a meeting with the ministry's main counselor. We talked for about 20 minutes, but she could tell she wasn't getting anywhere. I was defensive and had made up my mind. So she raised the stakes. She asked if I had ever read Jesus's parable in Matthew 25:31-46 about the sheep and the goats. I told her I had, but she read it anyway. (Take a moment right now to open your Bible and read those verses simply and seriously, like an intelligent 12-year-old child.)

I asked what the parable had to do with me. After all, I wasn't a goat; I was a Jesus-confessing sheep. She reminded me how the goats all professed Jesus as their Lord as well. They called Him their Lord, but they didn't walk as their professed Lord walked. She told me it wasn't enough to *call* Jesus my Lord—the way we steward what He has placed in our care reveals whether He really *is* our Lord. She said this was a defining moment that would prove my true sheep or goat nature. Then she got up and walked away.

I went back to my room and cried. I wailed and screamed at God in agony on my knees with my face pressed into my mattress. For what seemed like two hours, though it was probably only 45 minutes, I prayed for forgiveness and cleansing for my disrespect and doubt. Then I pleaded with God to carry me and give me strength to fulfill His mission for me. Just then, I sensed Him telling me to turn to Isaiah 42, where I read, "*I am the Lord, I have called You in righteousness, I will also hold You by the hand and watch over You, and I will appoint You as a covenant to the people, as a light to the nations, to open blind eyes, to bring out prisoners from the dungeon and those who dwell in darkness from the prison*" (verses 6-7).

I broke down after reading these lines, and then again and again. I have never wept that much in my life. At the same time, I began to feel God strengthening me and filling me with His Spirit. Though I knew this portion of Isaiah was messianic in nature, I could feel God encouraging me with the truth that the same Holy Spirit who had indwelt and empowered God's only Son also indwells and empowers His adopted children (see Romans 8:11-17).

A little while later, as I was reading Scripture and praying, I sensed God wanted to heal one of the members of my team of some physical ailment. God showed me which member of the team it was. We'll call her Courtney. As I tell the rest of this story, remember this happened toward the beginning of the trip, before any of the other miraculous stuff had taken place.

The next evening, my team was supposed to have a meeting at 9 PM. I knew God wanted me to speak up during the meeting and ask if anyone needed to be healed, but I was a bit nervous, to say the least. Around 10 PM, AS the meeting was wrapping up and our team leader was getting reading to dismiss us, I blurted out, "I know this sounds weird, but does anyone need to get healed of anything?" Sure enough, Courtney raised her hand and said she had been suffering from excruciating pain in her left hip for several years.

We gathered around her, with my friend Jaco taking the lead. As he prayed for her, Courtney, an American Protestant, went limp. No one had pushed her. She just went limp. Then she came to, with an exceeding amount of joy, and declared all her pain was gone! Before the new things came to pass, God declared them. He took me by the hand and then went "*forth like a warrior . . . [to] prevail against His enemies*" (Isaiah 42:13).

Though I was angry with the counselor who pointed me to Jesus's parable of the sheep and the goats, I'm so thankful now she was a good steward of the spiritual gift of exhortation. That confrontation helped me to be a good steward of the wealth that had been invested in me, and God then blessed me with spiritual riches in return. If not for that good and faithful servant of Jesus, I know this book would not have been written.

The final way we can affect the influence of the Holy Spirit in our lives is to simply ask for more of the Holy Spirit's influence in our lives. In Luke 11:9-10, Jesus says, *"Ask, and it will be given to you; seek, and you will find; knock, and it will be opened to you. For everyone who asks, receives; and he who seeks, finds; and to him who knocks, it will be opened."*

The other day I needed to take my lawn mower to the shop. So I raised my garage door, dragged out the mower, and lifted the heavy beast into my vehicle. When I came home, I complained to Stephanie about how I must have pulled a muscle in my lower back while lifting the mower. She looked at me and said, "Why didn't you just ask me to help you?"

God has given us an amazing yet difficult task. We are to be the light of the world. We are to overcome evil with good. We are to love our neighbors as ourselves. We are to abide in the Vine of Jesus Christ and produce good fruit. We are to go into all the world making disciples of Christ, teaching them to obey all He commanded. We are to persevere in Christ to the very end, even through torture and death. We are to walk as Jesus walked. With such a high calling, it's no wonder God calls us to ask for His help.

However, there are two other verses that concern our ability to experience the abundant spiritual life God desires for us and our ability to help others experience more of Him. The first is 1 Corinthians 12:31, where Paul writes, *"But earnestly desire the greater gifts."* The second is 1 Corinthians 14:1, where we are told, *"Pursue love, yet desire earnestly spiritual gifts, but especially that you may prophesy."* These are commands God has given all Christians.

So I ask you, are you earnestly desiring the greater gifts? Are you earnestly desiring *all* the spiritual gifts, especially prophecy? Remember, God has given these gifts for the common good. Often, our spiritual gifts will give credibility to the message of the Gospel to non-Christians (see Mark 2:1-12). Sometimes, as James 4:2 says, we have not because we ask not. Indeed, it may be that our non-Christian friends, family members, co-workers, and neighbors have not experienced God because we ask not. If we are commanded to ask, to not ask is a sin—a sin that is depriving the world of experiencing more of God.

In Luke 11:13, Jesus says, *"If you then, being evil, know how to give good gifts to your children, how much more will your heavenly Father give the Holy Spirit to those who ask Him?"* If you are a Christian, how are you stewarding the precious gift of the Holy Spirit that God has entrusted to your care? As Jesus said, "For to everyone who has, more shall be given, and he will have an abundance; but from the one who does not have, even what he does have shall be taken away" (Matthew 25:29).

May you be a good and faithful servant of the King of kings. May you be a good steward of all He has entrusted in your care. May you never grieve or quench the Holy Spirit. May you walk with the Spirit, be led by the Spirit, and produce much fruit of the Spirit. And may you seek Christ with all your heart and find the door has been opened to you.

PART 3

NEW WINESKINS OF THE OLD TESTAMENT

Chapter 13

MIRACLES ON THE THIRD DAY

Every year we've been married, Stephanie and I have taken a trip together, usually overseas. So when we began the process of adopting two beautiful kids, we realized 2013 might be the final opportunity for us to take one of those major trips for a while. We prayed about it and decided to take a 10-day tour of Israel. I'm a big fan of Christian teacher Ray Vander Laan taking tour groups through important biblical sites, and we definitely wanted a Christian guide for our tour. We also didn't want to spend an arm and a leg. Fortunately, Stephanie found a great deal on a tour that had Jesus's name in the title.

We thought this would be a vacation where we could relax and receive spiritual nourishment from a Christian tour guide while walking in the same places as our Lord. Life, though, is full of surprises. When we got there, we quickly realized our tour guide was not a follower of Jesus. Rather, he stated he was Jewish, which was unexpected, but fine.

I love Jewish people, and many of them have played a positive role in helping shape me into the person I am today. Our tour guide, however, was Jewish by blood but more of an agnostic in his beliefs. Though he was nice and helpful, early on Stephanie and I began to notice he was subtly painting Jesus as a sort of false messiah. I can't fault him for taking this approach. Like me, he had been raised with old wineskins concerning Jesus that had shaped his worldview in a way contrary to a simple reading of Scripture.

The night before we were to go to Capernaum, he issued a challenge to us while we were on the bus. (As far as I'm aware, all but one of the more than 30 of us on the tour professed to be Christians.) He said the next day he would give us a chance to explain why John chose to write that Jesus's first miracle of turning water into wine happened on "the third day." The bus went silent and stayed that way until we arrived at our hotels. I couldn't sleep that night, so I sought God for wisdom concerning the matter of Jesus's first miracle. After 45 minutes I felt He had given me a sound-enough reply, so I turned the light off and went to bed.

The next morning, our guide tried to convince us of his opinion about Jesus's first miracle. His answer was succinct but strange. He said that according to the Jewish tradition of Kabbalah, three is the number of good luck. Now, Kabbalah is widely understood by Christians to be one of the most ancient forms of the occult and Gnosticism.[1] Thus, our guide was not only implying that John was an endorser of Kabbalah, but that Jesus was as well. After he finished, he asked if anyone else had an opinion. No one raised their hand, so I asked if I could address the group. The following is the gist of what I said.

John's Gospel is different from the others because his begins with a creation account. *"In the beginning was the Word, and the Word was with God, and the Word was God. He was in the beginning with God. All things came into being through Him, and apart from Him nothing came into being that has come into being"* (John 1:1-3). I believe John did this to show that Jesus and the Lord God of Genesis, who created all things, are one.

Genesis also begins with a creation account: *"In the beginning God created the heavens and the earth"* (Genesis 1:1). Before we see the days of creation listed, God is there, and the Spirit of God is moving over the surface over the waters. Then on day one, God creates light and separates it from darkness. On day two, God creates an expanse to separate the waters below from the waters above, and calls the expanse heaven. On day three, God creates dry ground and brings forth all sorts of vegetation, with plants and trees reproducing according to their kind. That feat is spectacular because the sun will not be created until day four.

Jesus's public ministry begins in John 1:35, which is two days before the wedding at Cana (day three). Remember how the Spirit of God was hovering over the surface of the waters before the first day of creation? Here is what John said happened the day before the first day of the Creator's ministry on earth:

> *The next day [John the Baptist] saw Jesus coming to him and said, "Behold, the Lamb of God who takes away the sin of the world! This is He on behalf of whom I said, 'After me comes a Man who has a higher rank than I, for He existed before me.' . . . I have seen the Spirit descending as a dove out of heaven, and He remained upon Him. I did not recognize Him, but He who sent me to baptize in water said to me, 'He upon whom you see the Spirit descending and remaining upon Him,*

this is the One who baptizes in the Holy Spirit.' I myself have seen, and have testified that this is the Son of God" (John 1:29-30, 32-34).

In John's account, the Spirit of God descends from heaven, hovers over a body of water, and remains with Jesus, the Word of God and agent of creation. Then, on the first day of Jesus's ministry, the True Light comes on the scene. John the Baptist points Him out, and some of his disciples begin to follow Jesus, believing Him to be the Messiah (see verses 35-42). On the second day, Jesus explains to Nathanael that He is the true bridge that crosses the great expanse between heaven and earth (see verses 43-51). On the third day, a tremendous miracle takes place with a seed-bearing plant. Wine is produced not from grapes fermenting over time, but instantly from Jesus blessing water.

Early Christian writer Theophilus wrote that God created the sun on the fourth day to show it is He who ultimately gives life to all things and sustains all things, not the forces of nature.[2] Similarly, John says Jesus's first miracle was also a sign of something greater (see 2:11). Roughly three years later, Jesus was crucified for our sins. Jesus prophesied, *"The Son of Man will be delivered to the chief priests and scribes, and they will condemn Him to death, and will hand Him over to the Gentiles to mock and scourge and crucify Him, and on the third day He will be raised up* (Matthew 20:18-19)." The greatest miracle of all, the empty tomb, happened on the third day.

Of course, there is no resurrection without the crucifixion. John adds a detail about that gruesome crime: *"So the soldiers came, and broke the legs of the first man and of the other who was crucified with Him; but coming to Jesus, when they saw that He was already dead, they did not break His legs. But one of the soldiers pierced His side with a spear, and immediately blood and water came out"* (John 19:32-34). In Cana, through the power of Christ, water and wine turned a party foul into a wedding feast for the ages. At Golgotha, blood and water flowed out from the Messiah's side, bringing salvation to all who fully entrust themselves to Him.

I said other things that morning, but those were the main points. God gives us what we need at just the right time to help others in need and bring glory to His name.

I do not believe John was saying three is the number of good luck. However, I do believe he was demonstrating a critical lesson Jesus taught the disciples after He rose from the dead. In Luke 24, the risen Christ appears to two of His disciples as they are walking to Emmaus, but He conceals His identity. The disciples are quite disheartened, because they thought Jesus was the Messiah, but He was killed. Also, they say it is the third day, the day He said He would rise from the dead. To their knowledge He hasn't come back to life, though some of the female disciples said they saw Him earlier that day.

Jesus responds, "*O foolish men and slow of heart to believe in all that the prophets have spoken! Was it not necessary for the Christ to suffer these things and to enter into His glory?' Then beginning with Moses and with all the prophets, He explained to them the things concerning Himself in all the Scriptures*" (verses 25-27). Later that day, Jesus appears to the remaining disciples and says, "*These are My words which I spoke to you while I was still with you, that all things which are written about Me in the Law of Moses and the Prophets and the Psalms must be fulfilled*" (verse 44). Jesus opens their minds to understand the Scriptures and says, "*Thus it is written, that the Christ would suffer and rise again from the dead the third day, and that repentance for forgiveness of sins would be proclaimed in His name to all the nations, beginning from Jerusalem*" (verses 46-47).

I believe the most important lesson Jesus is revealing is that all the Old Testament is designed to point to Him—that no matter what section of the first 39 books of the Bible we study, there will always be something to direct us to Christ. To illustrate my point, let's consider the first nine chapters of Genesis:

- Genesis 1: Jesus is the life that comes out of the ground on the third day.
- Genesis 2: He is killed on the tree with which we sinned so that one day we can again eat from the tree of life.
- Genesis 3: He is the seed of the woman who crushes the head of the serpent.
- Genesis 4: He is the better Abel who is murdered out of envy, and thus becomes the perfect offering for the sins of the world.
- Genesis 5: Jesus is the better Seth, the true image-bearer of the Father, and the better Enoch, the one who walked with God without sinning all the days of His life.
- Genesis 6: He is the better Noah, the true preacher of righteousness, who proclaims the way of salvation.

- Genesis 7: He is the true ark to whom the humble will run, and the true door we must enter through to escape the flood of judgment.
- Genesis 8: He is the true dove who declares peace to the world.
- Genesis 9: He is the covenant-establishing God who gives His life to keep His covenant of love with humanity.

A false doctrine again creeping into the Church states the God of the Old Testament is not the same as the God of the New Testament. I say it is creeping in again because it's well documented that during the second century, a man named Marcion was denounced as a heretic for promoting that and other Gnostic teachings.[3] Oftentimes, people who are holding to this ancient heresy will say that while they don't believe in the God of the Old Testament, they do believe in Jesus and the God of the New Testament. It's quite interesting, though, if you read the New Testament, how often Jesus identifies Himself with the God of the Old Testament.

Maybe you've heard that Jesus never claimed to be God. That's simply not true. He absolutely claimed to be God; He just did it in a Jewish way, since He was a Jew. For instance, in Mark 14, Jesus has been arrested and is standing trial before Caiaphas, the high priest. Many false charges have brought by false witnesses, yet Jesus remains silent. Mark records, *"The high priest was questioning Him, and saying to Him, 'Are You the Christ, the Son of the Blessed One?' And Jesus said, 'I am; and you shall see the Son of Man sitting at the right hand of Power, and coming with the clouds of heaven.' Tearing his clothes, the high priest said, 'What further need do we have of witnesses? You have heard the blasphemy; how does it seem to you?' And they all condemned Him to be deserving of death"* (verses 61-64).

How did Jesus slander God's name? In fact, He didn't. What Jesus actually did was quote a loaded messianic text and apply it to Himself. The passage Jesus quoted was from Daniel 7:13-14: *"I kept looking in the night visions, and behold, with the clouds of heaven one like a Son of Man was coming, and He came up to the Ancient of Days and was presented before Him. And to Him was given dominion, glory and a kingdom, that all the peoples, nations and men of every language might serve Him. His dominion is an everlasting dominion which will not pass away; and His kingdom is one which will not be destroyed."*

When Jesus called Himself the "Son of Man," He wasn't merely highlighting His humanity. Rather, He was calling attention to the fact He was the fulfillment of the Daniel 7 prophecy. He was the messianic cloud rider, the Son of Man who becomes the everlasting king of all the earth. All nations will serve Him. So you can see why the priests were so angry. They were thinking, *"We will never serve you!"* Yet that was what Jesus was saying. But where does this passage say the cloud rider is God? One answer, in addition to Jesus's use of *ego eimi* (I AM), is that His words link with another messianic prophecy found in Isaiah.

In Daniel 7, the cloud-riding Son of Man is a king whose kingdom will cover the earth and never end. In Isaiah 9:6-7 we read, *"For a child will be born to us, a son will be given to us; and the government will rest on His shoulders; and His name will be called Wonderful Counselor, Mighty God, Eternal Father, Prince of Peace. There will be no end to the increase of His government or of peace, on the throne of David and over his kingdom, to establish it and to uphold it with justice and righteousness from then on and forevermore."*

This child, this son of man, is going to be called some remarkable things like Mighty God and Eternal Father. And this God-man is going to reign on David's throne forever, meaning He will be the messiah and there will be no end to the increase of His reign. So, all the Jews understand full and well that Jesus has just said He is one with the Lord God of the Old Testament. They consider him a blasphemer, and the punishment for that crime is death.

Let's rewind a bit to find another example of Jesus saying He is God. In John 10:14-16, Jesus says to the Pharisees, *"I am the good shepherd, and I know My own and My own know Me, even as the Father knows Me and I know the Father; and I lay down My life for the sheep. I have other sheep, which are not of this fold; I must bring them also, and they will hear My voice; and they will become one flock with one shepherd."*

Later, as Jesus is walking in the Temple, the Jews gather around Him and ask, *"How long will You keep us in suspense? If You are the Christ, tell us plainly"* **(verse 24)**. Jesus answers, *"I told you, and you do not believe; the works that I do in My Father's name, these testify of Me. But you do not believe because you are not of My sheep. My sheep hear My voice, and I know them, and they follow Me; and I give eternal life to them, and they will never perish; and no one will snatch them out of My hand. My Father, who has given them to Me, is greater than all; and no one is able to snatch them out of the Father's hand. I and the Father are one"* (verses 25-30). At this, the Jews pick up stones to kill Jesus, saying, *"For a good work we do not stone You, but for blasphemy; and because You, being a man, make Yourself out to be God"* (verse 33).

Once again, we need to look at the Old Testament to understand why the Jews believed Jesus was blaspheming by making Himself out to be God. In Ezekiel 34:1-10, God speaks harsh rebukes against the shepherds and leaders of Israel for exploiting the people, the flock of Israel, for their own gain. The Lord pronounces woes on the shepherds and says He is now against them. He then declares that since none of the shepherds and leaders of Israel are doing this critical job right, He will do it Himself. "*For thus says the Lord GOD, 'Behold, I Myself will search for My sheep and seek them out. As a shepherd cares for his herd in the day when he is among his scattered sheep, so I will care for My sheep and will deliver them. . . . I will feed My flock and I will lead them to rest,' declares the Lord GOD. 'I will seek the lost, bring back the scattered, bind up the broken and strengthen the sick'"* (verses 11-12, 15-16).

God then gives them a messianic prophecy: "*I will set over them one shepherd, My servant David, and he will feed them; he will feed them himself and be their shepherd. And I, the Lord, will be their God, and My servant David will be prince among them*" (verses 23-24). Of course, by Ezekiel's time David had been dead for hundreds of years. Therefore, it is widely understood the David reference is to the Messiah who would come (see, for example, Bartimaeus's confession in Mark 10:46-52).

However, the Lord doesn't leave any doubt about the true nature of the Good Shepherd, for He states, "*Then they will know that I, the Lord their God, am with them, and that they, the house of Israel, are My people. . . . As for you, My sheep, the sheep of My pasture, you are men, and I am your God*" (Ezekiel 34:30-31). The Lord God is the Good Shepherd, and God's servant, the Son of David, is also the Good Shepherd. Jesus is the Son of David and the Good Shepherd, who is the Lord God. So now you see why the Jews wanted to kill Him.

Jesus not only quotes Ezekiel to show He is God but also Deuteronomy 32:39, where Yahweh says, "*See now that I, I am He, and there is no god besides Me; it is I who put to death and give life. I have wounded and it is I who heal, and there is no one who can deliver from My hand.*" Jesus has just said He is the one who gives life and no one can snatch someone out of His hand. He then says He and the Father are one. But Yahweh says in Deuteronomy there is no god besides Him. This is yet another reason why the religious leaders wanted to stone Him.

Let's look at one last example of Jesus identifying Himself with the Lord God of the Old Testament. However, this time we will begin with the passage from the Old Testament. In Isaiah 6, the prophet writes:

In the year of King Uzziah's death I saw the LORD *sitting on a throne, lofty and exalted, with the train of His robe filling the temple. Seraphim stood above Him, each having six wings: with two he covered his face, and with two he covered his feet, and with two he flew. And one called out to another and said, "Holy, Holy, Holy, is the* LORD *of hosts, the whole earth is full of His glory."*

And the foundations of the thresholds trembled at the voice of him who called out, while the temple was filling with smoke. Then I said, "Woe is me, for I am ruined! Because I am a man of unclean lips, and I live among a people of unclean lips; for my eyes have seen the King, the LORD *of hosts."*

Then one of the seraphim flew to me with a burning coal in his hand, which he had taken from the altar with tongs. He touched my mouth with it and said, "Behold, this has touched your lips; and your iniquity is taken away and your sin is forgiven."

Then I heard the voice of the LORD, *saying, "Whom shall I send, and who will go for Us?" Then I said, "Here am I. Send me!" He said, "Go, and tell this people: 'Keep on listening, but do not perceive; keep on looking, but do not understand.' Render the hearts of this people insensitive, their ears dull, and their eyes dim, otherwise they might see with their eyes, fear with their ears, understand with their hearts, and return and be healed"* (verses 1-10).

In verse 1, Isaiah said he saw the Lord on the throne, lofty and exalted. The Hebrew word used here for "Lord" is *Adonai*. So, Isaiah testified he saw the Lord, *Adonai*, high and lifted up on the throne. Second, in verse 5 Isaiah says he is in deep trouble because he is a man of unclean lips and his eyes have seen the King, the Lord of hosts. This is the same Lord of hosts the Seraphim said was *"Holy, Holy, Holy"* in verse 3. The phrase "Lord of hosts" in Hebrew is *Yahweh Sabaoth*; or, if you'd prefer, *Jehovah Sabaoth*. Therefore, we are able to easily deduce that Isaiah saw a manifestation of Yahweh in his vision recorded in Isaiah 6.

Now we will move back to the New Testament. In John 12, we find Jesus in the last week of His life. He has already raised Lazarus from the dead and is popular with most of the people. But the leaders of the Jews are plotting to kill both Him and Lazarus. John writes:

> *Though He had performed so many signs before them, yet they were not believing in Him. This was to fulfill the word of Isaiah the prophet which he spoke:* "LORD, WHO HAS BELIEVED OUR REPORT? AND TO WHOM HAS THE ARM OF THE LORD BEEN REVEALED?" *FOR THIS REASON THEY COULD NOT BELIEVE, FOR ISAIAH SAID AGAIN,* "HE HAS BLINDED THEIR EYES AND HE HARDENED THEIR HEART, SO THAT THEY WOULD NOT SEE WITH THEIR EYES AND PERCEIVE WITH THEIR HEART, AND BE CONVERTED AND I HEAL THEM." *These things Isaiah said because he saw His glory, and he spoke of Him. Nevertheless many even of the rulers believed in Him, but because of the Pharisees they were not confessing Him, for fear that they would be put out of the synagogue; for they loved the approval of men rather than the approval of God* (verses 37-43).

John quotes Isaiah 6 and then writes that Isaiah said these things because he saw "*His glory, and he spoke of Him.*" Who is the "Him" whom John says Isaiah saw? The answer is found in verses 37 and 42, where John says even though Jesus was performing many signs the Jews refused to believe in Him, and the ones who did believe wouldn't confess Him because they were afraid of being put out of the synagogue.

No one would get put out of the synagogue for confessing belief in Yahweh. All Jews confessed that truth every time they said the *Shema* (see Deuteronomy 6:4-5). But a person *would* get put out of the synagogue for confessing the truth that Jesus was Yahweh. Many of them were seeing, yet they weren't believing. Isaiah, however, saw His glory and believed. He saw Yahweh. So, once again, John tells us Jesus and Yahweh are one.

After Isaiah saw the pre-incarnate Jesus, his life was never the same. As his old wineskins were burst, he was filled with an excitement and boldness to do anything for the Lord God no matter the cost. Just as Isaiah's life was turned rightside up when he actually saw the Lord God after serving Him for so many years, my world was rocked when I began to discover how the entire Old Testament was designed to point us to Jesus. It changed everything.

Many of my old wineskins were burst, which helped me make sense of so many things in the Old Testament that had troubled me in the past.

As you read the rest of this book, may you have a similar eye-opening, heart-warming, and spiritually-invigorating experience. And may it produce a renewed love for studying the Scriptures and living them out due to an overwhelming sense of gratitude for the great things Jesus has done, is doing, and is going to do for you.

Chapter 14

THE DIVINE MESSENGER

A while ago, two nice Jehovah's Witnesses came to my door, inviting me to attend their annual Lord's Supper service. I used to be hostile to the Witnesses and the Mormons and try to get them away from my front porch as quickly as possible. But now I try to be friendly, calm, and compassionate, asking questions and directing the conversation toward the person and nature of Jesus, while being careful to not interrupt them as they speak. (Just so you're aware, Jehovah's Witnesses believe Jesus is the first of Jehovah's creations and that Jesus was known in the Old Testament as the archangel Michael.)

After I let my two visitors tell me why they were visiting me, I asked if we could read two passages of Scripture. They gladly agreed, and they read aloud from their Bibles. We started with Isaiah 6. Interestingly, in verse 1 where the word *Adonai* is used in the Hebrew, their translation used Jehovah (meaning *Yahweh*). But in verses 3 and 5, their translation used Jehovah correctly where *Yahweh Sabaoth* was used.[1]

I asked who they believed Isaiah saw, and they agreed he saw Jehovah. The trap was set. We turned to John 12:37-43. Once again, in their translation John used the name Jehovah when quoting Isaiah, and then John stated Isaiah wrote those things because he beheld His glory and spoke of Him; that "Him" being Jesus, of course. And many of the Jewish leaders believed in Him but wouldn't confess Him publically for fear of being put out of the synagogue.

One of the witnesses stood there stunned, mouth literally open. The other tried to steer the conversation back to their original purpose for coming. After this visitor finished, I gently showed them John's linking of Jesus and Jehovah in John 10 with Ezekiel 34 and Deuteronomy 32:39. I also invited them to visit our church that Sunday. It was easy to tell God was doing a good work in that conversation and graciously bursting many old wineskins.

I've had conversations with other Jehovah's Witnesses about their belief that Jesus and Michael are the same. On one such occasion, I asked the man I was speaking with to show me one passage in the Bible where it says Jesus is the archangel Michael. At first he couldn't think of one, but then he took me to 1 Thessalonians 4:13-17.

I asked the man where that passage said Jesus and the archangel Michael were the same, and directed me to verse 16: "*The Lord Himself will descend from heaven with a shout, with the voice of the archangel and with the trumpet of God, and the dead in Christ will rise first.*" I again asked what about that verse made him believe the archangel Michael is the same person as Jesus, and he tried to change the subject.

Think about this for a moment. When LeBron James is introduced before basketball games, he often comes onto the court shouting. The voice of the announcer also shouts his name, and the fans blow bullhorns and use other noise-making devices. Does that mean LeBron is the announcer, the fans, or the bullhorns being blown? Of course not. So why should we make that grammatical stretch with the Scriptures?

In Hebrews 1:5-14 the writer makes a clear distinction between angels and Jesus, the only begotten Son of God. The writer makes it abundantly clear that Jesus is on a completely different level than all the angels. Jesus *is* God and all the angels worship Him. However, starting in the book of Genesis, a mysterious character appears on the scene whom the author meticulously demonstrates is linked with Yahweh. His name? The angel of the Lord.[2]

The first time we encounter this being is in Genesis 16, when Hagar, Sarai's maidservant, flees to the wilderness to escape Sarai's mistreatment. Sarai, Abram's wife, had given Hagar to Abram to have children with her, yet when Hagar conceived, Sarai despised and persecuted her, causing Hagar to run away. We pick up the story in Genesis 16:7-14:

> *Now the angel of the LORD FOUND HER BY A SPRING OF WATER IN THE WILDERNESS, BY THE SPRING ON THE WAY TO SHUR. HE SAID, "HAGAR, SARAI'S MAID, WHERE HAVE YOU COME FROM AND WHERE ARE YOU GOING?" AND SHE SAID, "I AM FLEEING FROM THE PRESENCE OF MY MISTRESS SARAI." THEN THE ANGEL OF THE LORD SAID TO HER, "RETURN TO YOUR MISTRESS, AND SUBMIT YOURSELF TO HER AUTHORITY." MOREOVER, THE ANGEL OF THE LORD SAID TO HER, "I WILL GREATLY MULTIPLY YOUR DESCENDANTS SO THAT THEY WILL BE TOO MANY TO COUNT."*

> *The angel of the LORD SAID TO HER FURTHER, "BEHOLD, YOU ARE WITH CHILD, and you will bear a son; and you shall call his name Ishmael, because the LORD HAS GIVEN HEED TO YOUR AFFLICTION. He will be a wild donkey of a man, his hand will be against everyone, and everyone's hand will be against him; and he will live to the east of all his brothers." Then she called the name of the LORD WHO SPOKE TO HER, "YOU ARE a God who sees"; for she said, "Have I even remained alive here after seeing Him?" Therefore the well was called Beer-lahai-roi; behold, it is between Kadesh and Bered.*

Notice it was the angel of the Lord who said he would greatly multiply Hagar's descendants. In response, *"[Hagar] called the name of the LORD WHO SPOKE TO HER, 'YOU ARE a God who sees'; for she said, 'Have I even remained alive here after seeing Him?'"* (verse 13). When you look back over the story, only the angel of the Lord speaks to Hagar—the Lord Himself isn't mentioned in the divine encounter. Yet Hagar called the one who spoke to her "the Lord" (*Yahweh*) and "the God who sees" (*El Roi*).[3] Also notice how Hagar was amazed she remained alive after seeing the one she believed to be God. This is a theme that spans the course of the Bible. Paul sums it up clearly in 1 Timothy 6:15-16 when he writes, *"[God] is the blessed and only Sovereign, the King of kings and Lord of lords, who alone possesses immortality and dwells in unapproachable light, whom no man has seen or can see."*

Though Adam and Eve originally had bodies that were capable of walking with God in the cool of the morning, the corruption humanity experienced when they sinned prevented them from being able to dwell in the presence of God. Think of it like the sun. Though the sun is beneficial to humanity and helps sustain life, if we were to get too close to it, we would die. In fact, if we stare at it for too long, it will blind us. Kind of like Aslan in *The Lion, the Witch, and the Wardrobe*, God is not safe, but He is good.

A bit later we will address how Hagar could be in the presence of God and yet not be destroyed. For now, let's examine another example of the angel of the Lord found in Genesis 22. This is the famous story of Abraham being tested to offer Isaac, the son of the covenant, as a sacrifice. In verses 1-2, God (*Elohim*) tells Abraham to take Isaac and sacrifice him on the mountain that He will show him. God is the one orchestrating this event. Then, in verse 11, just as Abraham is about to plunge his knife into Isaac, the angel of the Lord speaks to Abraham out of heaven and tells him to stop. He says, *"Do not stretch out your hand against the lad, and do nothing to him; for now I know that you fear God, since you have not withheld your son, your only son, from Me."* The text states Abraham did not withhold his one and only son from the angel of the Lord, but God was the one who initiated this event and told Abraham to offer his son as a sacrifice.[4]

Moving on, we are introduced to one of Abraham's grandsons, Jacob. In Genesis 32:24-32, Jacob is about to come face to face with his brother, Esau, who has sworn to kill him for deceitfully obtaining the firstborn birthright from their father, Isaac. Jacob has split his camp into two parts and sent them across a river. There, all by himself, Jacob has a divine encounter that will prove to be a defining moment in his life.

According to the writer of Genesis, a "man" wrestles with Jacob from evening until morning. Seeing Jacob will not relent, the "man" touches Jacob's hip, and it is thrown out of socket. Jacob has been permanently crippled and will walk with a limp for the rest of his life. Then, when dawn is breaking, this "man" says Jacob must let him go. When Jacob says the "man" must bless him first, the "man" does so by giving Jacob a name change.

Jacob then names the land on which this famous wrestling match occurred Peniel, which means "face of God." He gives it this name because, *"I have seen God face to face, yet my life has been preserved"* (verse 30). It seems clear the writer of Genesis is saying that Jacob wrestled with God in a man's form. But does any other Scripture back up that interpretation?

Not surprisingly, Hosea 12:3-5 puts forth that very idea. Speaking of Jacob, the prophet Hosea writes, *"In the womb he took his brother by the heel, and in his maturity he contended with God. Yes, he wrestled with the angel and prevailed; he wept and sought His favor. He found Him at Bethel and there He spoke with us, even the Lord, the God of hosts, the Lord is His name."* Jacob wrestled with God. The angel. The Lord.

Later, when Jacob blesses Joseph's two sons, Ephraim and Manasseh, he states, *"The God before whom my fathers Abraham and Isaac walked, the God who has been my shepherd all my life to this day, the angel who has redeemed me from all evil, bless the lads"* (Genesis 48:15-16). Once again, Jacob equates the *God* before whom his fathers walked and the *God* who shepherded him all his life with the *angel* of the Lord who redeemed him from all evil.

Previously, we cited Exodus 3:1-9, the critical passage of Moses and the burning bush. As you look at that story again, notice it is the angel of the Lord who is in the midst of the burning bush. *"The angel of the LORD appeared to* him in a blazing fire from the midst of a bush; and he looked, and behold, the bush was burning with fire, yet the bush was not consumed" (verse 2). Verse 4 then states that God (*Elohim*) calls to Moses from the midst of the bush, and verse 7 shifts to Yahweh as the speaker. The angel of the Lord. God. Yahweh.

One last example—though there are other passages to pull from—is found in Judges 6. In this story, a young man named Gideon is threshing wheat in a winepress because his people are scared of the Midianites, who have been raiding and pillaging their villages:

> *Then the angel of the LORD came and sat under the oak that was in Ophrah, which belonged to Joash the Abiezrite as his son Gideon was beating out wheat in the wine press in order to save it from the Midianites. The angel of the LORD appeared to him and said to him, "The LORD is with you, O valiant warrior."* . . .
>
> *But the LORD said to him, "Surely I will be with you, and you shall defeat Midian as one man." So Gideon said to Him, "If now I have found favor in Your sight, then show me a sign that it is You who speak with me. Please do not depart from here, until I come back to You, and bring out my offering and lay it before You." And He said, "I will remain until you return."*
>
> *Then Gideon went in and prepared a young goat and unleavened bread from an ephah of flour; he put the meat in a basket and the broth in a pot, and brought them out to him under the oak and presented them. The angel of God said to him, "Take the meat and the unleavened bread and lay them on this rock, and pour out the broth." And he did so. Then the angel of the LORD put out the end of the staff that was in his hand and touched the meat and the unleavened bread; and fire sprang up from the rock and consumed the meat and the unleavened bread. Then the angel of the LORD vanished from his sight. When Gideon saw that he was the angel of the LORD, he said, "Alas, O Lord GOD! For now I have seen the angel of the LORD face to face." The LORD said to him, "Peace to you, do not fear; you shall not die." Then Gideon built an altar there to the LORD and named it The LORD is Peace. To this day it is still in Ophrah of the Abiezrites* (verses 11-12, 16-24).

At first the angel of the Lord is sitting under the oak tree, then the story indicates it is the Lord, and then it again seems to say it is the angel of the Lord (see verses 11, 14, 21). Similarly, at first the angel of the Lord speaks to Gideon, then the Lord, then the angel of the Lord, then the Lord—all from the same spot (see verses 12, 14, 20, 23). In verses 16-18, we read that Gideon was preparing an offering for the Lord, but then in verses 19-21 he presents it before the angel of the Lord, who touches the food with his staff and consumes it with fire. Gideon responds the same way Hagar and Jacob did when they realized they had seen God, except Gideon is amazed he has seen the angel of the Lord face to face and yet lived.

It seems Gideon had come to understand a key theological principle that had been developing over the centuries before him. God knew it was not safe for Him to dwell with humanity, but since He is good and full of love, He longed to personally help humanity. So, at important times in human history, God sent an embodied messenger of His same will and substance, in a way that His glory would not consume people, to interact with them and speak and act on His behalf. This being was not one of the seraphim, cherubim, archangels, or regular angels. This being was not part of the created order. This being was the ultimate angel of the Lord, the begotten messenger of Yahweh.

To help bridge the gap to the New Testament and bring clarification to who this divine uncreated messenger of Yahweh is, let's look at one more passage from Genesis. In Genesis 12, God called Abram and said He would bless him and make him into a great nation. Many years pass, and now, in Genesis 15, God reminds Abram of the promises and adds some clarification. In verse 1 we read, "*After these things the word of the LORD came to Abram in a vision.*" No, that's not an acid trip where someone is seeing sound or hearing colors. The Bible clearly states Abram *sees* the word of the Lord.

Then Abram says, "*O Lord God, what will You give me, since I am child-less?*" (verse 3). The word of the Lord takes Abram outside, tells him to count the stars, and promises that is what his descendants will be like. Abram believes in the Lord, and God reckons it to him as righteousness (see verses 4-6). The word of the Lord seems to act and speak quite similarly to the angel of the Lord.

The word of the Lord came to Abram, and by faith Abram believed and received the Lord God. About 2,000 years later, the Word of God came to humanity again, this time as both fully human and fully God. Not only did we need a redeemer, but we also needed God to show us what He is truly and fully like. We needed God Himself to show us how we were originally designed to live as His image bearers.

> *In the beginning was the Word, and the Word was with God, and the Word was God. He was in the beginning with God. All things came into being through Him, and apart from Him nothing came into being that has come into being. . . . He was in the world, and the world was made through Him, and the world did not know Him. He came to His own, and those who were His own did not receive Him. But as many as received Him, to them He gave the right to become children of God, even to those who believe in His name, who were born, not of blood nor of the will of the flesh nor of the will of man, but of God. And the Word became flesh, and dwelt among us, and we saw His glory, glory as of the only begotten from the Father, full of grace and truth. . . . No one has seen God at any time; the only begotten God who is in the bosom of the Father, He has explained Him* (John 1:1-3, 10-14, 18).

Jesus, the Divine Word of God, perfectly reveals and explains God the Father to a world that is desperate to understand the reason for its existence. May you receive the only begotten Son of God the Father, Jesus Christ, and believe fully in His name. May you take delight in studying the words of and about the Word of God, and may they lead you to love the Lord your God with all that you are, and your neighbors as yourself.

Chapter 15

THE FLOOD, GIANTS, AND RICHARD DAWKINS

Richard Dawkins believes "the God of the Old Testament is arguably the most unpleasant character in all fiction: jealous and proud of it; a petty, unjust, unforgiving control-freak; a vindictive, bloodthirsty ethnic cleanser; a misogynistic, homophobic, racist, infanticidal, genocidal, filicidal, pestilential, megalomaniacal, sadomasochistic, capriciously malevolent bully."[1] These ideas are nothing new; they pervade the foundational beliefs of Gnosticism.[2] Unfortunately, much of that line of thinking is still alive and well in the new atheist culture, agnosticism, and, I've noticed, even in the Church.

Frankly, it can be difficult to reconcile a God who calls Himself slow to anger and full of mercy with actions such as the Great Flood and His order of "the ban" during the occupation of the Promised Land. If that's where you are today, know that I was once there too. However, as God helped me dig into the Scriptures and the historical writings surrounding those events, my confusion vanished and the Bible became more exciting and intriguing than ever before.

To begin our quest, let's look at the account setting up the Flood story in Genesis 6:

> *Now it came about, when men began to multiply on the face of the land, and daughters were born to them, that the sons of God saw that the daughters of men were beautiful; and they took wives for themselves, whomever they chose. . . . The Nephilim were on the earth in those days, and also afterward, when the sons of God came in to the daughters of men, and they bore children to them. Those were the mighty men who were of old, men of renown. . . . Noah was a righteous man, blameless in his time; Noah walked with God. . . . God looked on the earth, and behold, it was corrupt; for all flesh*

> had corrupted their way upon the earth. Then God said to
> Noah, "The end of all flesh has come before Me; for the earth
> is filled with violence because of them; and behold, I am about
> to destroy them with the earth (verses 1-2, 4, 9, 12-13).

When I watched the *Noah* movie starring Russell Crowe, I was glad my ticket had already been purchased. I wholeheartedly agree with the director, Darren Aronofsky, who called his movie the least biblical biblical film ever made.[3] There are numerous examples I could cite, but the main issue I had with the movie, other than Noah being an incredibly violent man, was the role of the rock monsters.

In Aronofsky's movie, the rock monsters were supposed to be benevolent angels who came to earth. God had cursed them and turned them into rock monsters because they had abandoned the heavenly realm and helped humanity become civilized. People then enslaved many of the former-angels-now-rock monsters, so the rock monsters helped Noah build the ark and fight off the wicked people. Because the former-angels-now-rock monsters were willing to sacrifice their lives to help Noah, God allowed them to be redeemed and ascend back into heaven. You know something is fishy when a director paints biblical antagonists as protagonists.

Let's start by examining who these "sons of God" were and why they did what they did. The phrase "sons of God" in Hebrew is *bene ha elohim*.[4] It is seen again in Job 1:6: "*Now there was a day when the sons of God came to present themselves before the Lord, and Satan also came among them.*" It next appears in Job 2:1: "*Again there was a day when the sons of God came to present themselves before the Lord, and Satan also came among them.*" Finally, we see *bene ha elohim* once more in Job 38:4-7: "*Where were you when I laid the foundation of the earth? Tell Me, if you have understanding, who set its measurements? Since you know. Or who stretched the line on it? On what were its bases sunk? Or who laid its cornerstone, when the morning stars sang together and all the sons of God shouted for joy?*"

No human beings were around when God laid the cornerstone of the earth, but the angels were.[5] This means that in Genesis 6, "the sons of God" were angels who looked down on humanity and lusted after the women. They began to intermarry with them and produce offspring called the Nephilim. The Septuagint (LXX), the first Greek translation of the Hebrew text made by the Jews in the third century BC, states plainly the Nephilim were giants in the land. (Interestingly, you'll find that Jesus and the apostles almost always quoted from the Septuagint when referencing Old Testament passages instead of the Hebrew text.)

I was taught in my Christian upbringing that the "sons of God" and "daughters of men" mentioned in Genesis 6 were the sons of Seth (Adam and Eve's third son) and the daughters of Cain. However, no one in ancient Judaism taught that theory. In fact, the first teacher to promote the sons of Seth theory was Saint Augustine in the fifth century CE.[6] Every major Jewish writer and early Church teacher before that time promoted the straightforward biblical stance of the angels being the sons of God.[7] It's a little unsettling when seminaries and pastors teach that orthodox Christianity began after Constantine came to power or when Luther and Calvin began to forcefully impose their doctrines on the masses.

Here are a few early Jewish and Christian quotes you can read for your own edification:

> And the angels, the children of the heaven, saw and lusted after them, and said to one another: "Come, let us choose us wives from among the children of men and beget us children." . . . And all the others together with them took unto themselves wives, and each chose for himself one, and they began to go in unto them and to defile themselves with them. . . . And they became pregnant, and they bare great giants. . . . And when men could no longer sustain them, the giants turned against them and devoured mankind. And they began to sin against birds, and beasts, and reptiles, and fish, and to devour one another's flesh, and drink the blood. Then the earth laid accusation against the lawless ones (1 Enoch).[8]

> On what principle was it that giants were born of angels and women? . . . [Moses] relates that these giants were sprung from a combined procreation of two natures, namely, from angels and mortal women; for the substance of angels is spiritual; but it occurs every now and then . . . that they have imitated the appearance of men, and transformed themselves so as to assume the human shape; as they did on this occasion, when forming connections with women for the production of giants (Philo).[9]

For many angels of God accompanied with women, and begat sons that proved unjust, and despisers of all that was good, on account of the confidence they had in their own strength; for the tradition is, that these men did what resembled the acts of those whom the Grecians call giants (Josephus, 93 CE).[10]

The angels transgressed this appointment and were captivated by love of women. And they begat children, who are those who are called demons (Justin Martyr, 160 CE).[11]

In the days of Noah, He justly brought on the Deluge for the purpose of extinguishing that most infamous race of men then existent, who could not bring forth fruit to God. For the angels who sinned had commingled with them (Irenaeus, 180 CE).[12]

Such was the beauty of women that it turned the angels aside. As a result, being contaminated, they could not return to heaven. Being rebels from God, they uttered words against Him. Then the Highest uttered His judgment against them. And from their seed, giants are said to have been born. . . . When they died, men erected images to them (Commodianus, 240 CE).[13]

Of course, none of the early Jewish and Christian writings matter if the New Testament doesn't affirm a straightforward reading of the Old Testament. In fact, both 2 Peter and Jude corroborate the Old Testament account and inform us of the consequence of the angels' sin:

> For if God did not spare angels when they sinned, but cast them into hell [Tartarus, not Gehenna] and committed them to pits of darkness, reserved for judgment; and did not spare the ancient world, but preserved Noah, a preacher of righteousness, with seven others, when He brought a flood upon the world of the ungodly; and if He condemned the cities of Sodom and Gomorrah to destruction by reducing them to ashes, having made them an example to those who would live ungodly lives thereafter; and if He rescued righteous Lot . . . then the Lord knows how to rescue the godly from temptation, and to keep the unrighteous under punishment for the day of

*judgment, and especially those who indulge the flesh in its cor-
rupt desires and despise authority* (2 Peter 2:4-7, 9-10).

*Angels who did not keep their own domain, but abandoned
their proper abode, He has kept in eternal bonds under darkness for the judgment of the great day, just as Sodom and
Gomorrah and the cities around them, since they in the same
way as these indulged in gross immorality and went after
strange flesh, are exhibited as an example in undergoing the
punishment of eternal fire* (Jude 6-7).

According to these verses in 2 Peter and Jude, the sin of the fallen angels
was similar to the sin of Sodom and Gomorrah. In Ezekiel 16:49-50, God
declares, *"Behold, this was the guilt of your sister Sodom: she and her daughters had arrogance, abundant food and careless ease, but she did not help the
poor and needy. Thus they were haughty and committed abominations before
Me. Therefore I removed them when I saw it."* However, the final factor that
decided Sodom and Gomorrah's fate was the men of Sodom trying to have
intercourse with two good angels who had come to Lot's house in the form
of men (see Genesis 19).

Hollywood loves to call good evil and evil good. The movies *Noah* and
City of Angels would have us cheer for biblical antagonists like these fallen
angels, as if they were hopeless romantics punished by God for caring too
much. The Bible, though, reveals the malevolent conspirators in action and
exposes them for what they are. However, it's even more insidious than that.
To understand what these fallen angels had in mind when they decided to
commit their atrocities, we need to go back to the messianic prophecy made
in the Garden of Eden.

The Lord had said to the serpent, *"I will put enmity between you and
the woman, and between your seed and her seed; He shall bruise you on the
head, and you shall bruise Him on the heel"* (Genesis 3:15). God said *the offspring of Eve* would crush the head of the serpent. In his book *Corrupting
the Image,* author and biblical language scholar Douglas Hamp demonstrates
how this prophecy was the first of several stating the Messiah would be
genetically connected to Adam and Eve, who were made in the image of God:

God created man in His own image and likeness; when man
sinned that image was marred, but not lost. However, as a
result man cannot be with God in person since man's genetic

code (and spiritual composition) has been compromised (or corrupted). . . . The principle verse of this book is found in the declaration of Genesis 3:15: her seed brought forth the Savior; Satan's seed will bring the destroyer. . . . Ever since the fall in the garden and in a manner similar to the virgin birth of Jesus, Satan has been trying to find a way for "his seed" to become a reality. He almost succeeded in the days of Noah when the sons of God (fallen angels) came down and took women as wives and engendered a race called the Nephilim, which were genetic hybrids (Genesis 6).[14]

In the Garden, God told Satan the offspring of the woman would lead to his demise. But what if Satan could corrupt the seed of the woman? What if he could alter every human being's DNA so there were no longer any image-bearing humans left? Genesis 6:12 tells us that in the days of Noah *all flesh had corrupted their way upon the earth,* and only Noah and his family were not found to be corrupt in God's sight. After hundreds of years, the original eugenics campaign led by the fallen angels and Nephilim resulted in the DNA of the rest of humanity being tainted beyond the scope of redemption. Thus, God brought forth the Great Flood, and Satan's first plan to prevent the Messiah's purpose was thwarted.

Unfortunately, though the Great Flood brought an end to all the Nephilim living at the time of the Noah, that was not the end of the Nephilim in the Bible. In Numbers 13, we read that when the Israelites were ready to enter into the Promised Land, Moses sent 12 spies to scout the quality, people, and fortifications of the land and give a report of what they had seen. The spies returned 40 days later and told Moses and the people:

> We went in to the land where you sent us; and it certainly does flow with milk and honey, and this is its fruit. Nevertheless, the people who live in the land are strong, and the cities are forti-fied and very large; and moreover, we saw the descendants of Anak there. . . . The land through which we have gone, in spying it out, is a land that devours its inhabitants; and all the people whom we saw in it are men of great size. There also we saw the Nephilim (the sons of Anak are part of the Nephilim); and we became like grasshoppers in our own sight, and so we were in their sight (verses 27-28, 32-33).

Before we move on, keep in mind that the spies said *all* the people in the land were of great size, and Caleb and Joshua did not discount their testimony. So, how did the giant Nephilim hybrids return and cover the Promised Land? The most common theory is that a second incursion of angels cohabitating with women took place. Genesis 6:4 says, "*The Nephilim were on the earth in those days, and also afterward, when the sons of God came in to the daughters of men, and they bore children* to them" (emphasis mine). However, author Rob Skiba suggests that one of Noah's sons' wives could have been a carrier of the Nephilim's genetic information, as Nephilim offspring can be traced through the lineage of Ham.[15]

One way to research this issue, in addition to studying Genesis 10–11, is to find all the names the Bible uses to refer to the Nephilim. (See chart on page 138) Fortunately, Douglas Hamp has already done this for us in his book *Corrupting the Image*.[16]

At the beginning of this chapter, I mentioned something called "the ban," which means devoted to destruction. It is mentioned several times in Scripture, but a good example is found in Deuteronomy 20:16-18, when Moses told the Israelites, "*Only in the cities of these peoples that the LORD YOUR GOD IS GIVING YOU AS AN INHERITANCE, YOU SHALL NOT LEAVE ALIVE ANYTHING THAT BREATHES. BUT YOU SHALL UTTERLY DESTROY THEM, THE HITTITE AND THE AMORITE, THE CANAANITE AND THE PERIZZITE, THE HIVITE AND THE JEBUSITE, AS THE LORD YOUR GOD HAS COMMANDED YOU, SO THAT THEY MAY NOT TEACH YOU TO DO ACCORDING TO ALL THEIR DETESTABLE THINGS WHICH THEY HAVE DONE FOR THEIR GODS, SO THAT YOU WOULD SIN AGAINST THE LORD YOUR GOD.*"

Notice the ban was only to be enforced on these people groups residing in the Promised Land. These were the Nephilim of Numbers 13—the part-angelic, part-human creatures of great size residing in the Promised Land. Thus, the only "people" God ever called the Israelites to wipe off the face of the earth were the same "people" He had wiped off the earth with the Great Flood. They weren't people at all. They were the Nephilim part two; Satan's second attempt at eugenics and the corruption of humanity.[17]

I've had conversations with Christians who've used passages like the Israelites' occupation of the Promised Land to justify wars or killing for whatever reason the person feels is acceptable. Sadly, many of these people were indoctrinated with teaching that simply isn't orthodoxy. It is interesting how Jesus said in Mark 10:15, "*Truly I say to you, whoever does not receive the kingdom of God like a child will not enter it at all.*" Failing to read the Scriptures like an intelligent 12-year-old child, and instead holding on to the old wineskins

NAMES	SCRIPTURES
Nephilim = Anakim	The descendants of Anak came from the giants [Nephilim]. (Numbers 13:33)
Anakim = Rephaim = Emim	The Emim formerly lived there, a people great and many, and tall as the Anakim. Like the Anakim, they are also counted as Rephaim, but the Moabites call them Emim. (Deuteronomy 2:10-11 ᴇꜱᴠ)
Rephaim = Zamzummim = Anakim	It is also counted as a land of Rephaim. Rephaim formerly lived there—but the Ammonites call them Zamzummim—a people great and many, and as tall as the Anakim. (Deuteronomy 2:20-21 ᴇꜱᴠ)
Og, King of Bashan = Rephaim	Og the king of Bashan was left of the remnant of the Rephaim. (Deuteronomy 3:11 ᴇꜱᴠ)
Bashan = Rephaim	All that portion of Bashan is called the land of the Rephaim. (Deuteronomy 3:13 ᴇꜱᴠ)
Sihon of the Amorites = Rephaim = Amorites	For Heshbon was the city of Sihon the king of the Amorites. (Numbers 21:26 ᴇꜱᴠ)
Og, King of Bashan = Rephaim = Amorites	His land and the land of Og, the king of Bashan, the two kings of the Amorites who lived to the east beyond the Jordan. (Deuteronomy 4:47 ᴇꜱᴠ) What you did to the two kings of the Amorites […] Sihon and Og. (Joshua 2:10)
Goliath and his brothers = Anakim = Rephaim	At Gath, where there was a man of great stature, […] and he was also descended from the giants [Rephaim, LXX reads: from the giants, γιγαντων]. (2 Samuel 21:20 ᴇꜱᴠ) Lahmi the brother of Goliath the Gittite [Gath]. […] at Gath, […] he also was descended from the giants [Rephaim, LXX reads: giants, γιγαντες]. […] These were descended from the giants in Gath. (1 Chronicles 20:5-6, 8 ᴇꜱᴠ)

of Augustinian and Calvinistic teachings, have caused many to feel justified in destroying people made in the image of God and others to flat out reject Him altogether.

Remember the quote from Richard Dawkins at the beginning of the chapter that the God of the Old Testament is a vindictive, racist, infanticidal, genocidal, bloodthirsty, capriciously malevolent bully? That might make sense if you don't take the biblical stance concerning the fallen angels and the Nephilim. However, if you take the words of Scripture seriously, the God of the Old Testament is just as merciful, caring, and loving as He is in the New Testament. He desires that no humans perish but that all come to repentance, and He will go to great lengths to defeat our true enemies who seek our eternal destruction.

That leads us to our final stop in this chapter. How does all this point us to Jesus? Not only did Jesus and the apostles frequently quote from the Septuagint, but the early Christian writers did as well. It was basically their go-to Old Testament. Interestingly, throughout the first three centuries of Christendom, one of the key figures these writers referenced from the Old Testament as being a typological representation of Christ was a man we know as Joshua son of Nun. However, in the early translations of the Septuagint, he is called Jesus son of Nave.

When we understand this, we are easily able to connect the dots between many of the stories in the Old Testament about Joshua and the stories in the New Testament about the life of Jesus. Here are two examples of the early Christian writers making these connections from a passage about Moses, Joshua, and the Amalekites in Exodus 17:

> When the people . . . waged war with Amalek, and the son of Nave (Nun) by name Jesus (Joshua), led the fight, Moses himself prayed to God, stretching out both hands, and Hur with Aaron supported them during the whole day, so that they might not hang down when he got wearied. For if he gave up any part of this sign, which was an imitation of the cross, the people were beaten, as is recorded in the writings of Moses; but if he remained in this form, Amalek was proportionally defeated, and he who prevailed prevailed by the cross. For it was not because Moses so prayed that the people were stronger, but because, while one who bore the name of Jesus (Joshua) was in the forefront of the battle, he himself made the sign of the cross (Justin Martyr, 165 CE).[18]

Also in the Acts of the Apostles . . . "Be it known unto you all, and to all the people of Israel, that in the name of Jesus Christ of Nazareth, whom ye have crucified, whom God hath raised up from the dead, by Him he stands whole in your presence, but by none other. This is the stone which was despised by you builders, which has become the head of the corner. For there is no other name given to men under heaven in which we must be saved." . . .This is the stone in Exodus upon which Moses sat on the top of a hill when Jesus the son of Nave fought against Amalek; and by the sacrament of the stone, and the steadfastness of his sitting, Amalek was overcome by Jesus, that is, the devil was overcome by Christ (Cyprian, 250 CE).[19]

Not only is Jesus the seed of the woman who crushes the head of the serpent, but He is also our ultimate leader who vanquishes our enemies and brings us into the true Promised Land. So in the midst of a depraved culture, may you be righteous and blameless like Noah and walk with God. May you follow Jesus, the Lamb of God, wherever He goes, even when the odds seem stacked against you. And may you see God slay giant after giant in your life as He triumphantly leads you into His Promised Land.

Chapter 16

FEASTING WITH JESUS

I remember the first time I read the Bible all the way through in one year. It was such an amazing experience, but the worst part was Leviticus. What drudgery. It took me twice as long as it should have to get through the book because I fell asleep after only a few paragraphs of reading. So the next year, I was a naughty boy and went straight from Exodus to Numbers. Needless to say, I just didn't get it. After all, Jesus seemed to think Leviticus was incredibly important, as He said it contained the second greatest commandment in the entire Bible (see Leviticus 19:18 and Mark 12:28-31).

A couple of years ago, as I was doing sermon preparation for a Pentecost message, a portion of Leviticus I had previously sped-read stopped me in my tracks and exploded old wineskins. This passage, Leviticus 23, has since deepened my faith and love for Jesus and furthered my enjoyment of studying the Old Testament as it pertains to the first and second comings of Christ. In this chapter, we will look at the first four of seven Feasts of the Lord given in Leviticus 23, and I will highlight a few ways those feasts point us to Jesus.

The first thing we must understand is that these are the Feasts of the *Lord*. As God told Moses, "*The LORD's appointed times which you shall proclaim as holy convocations—My appointed times are these*" (verse 2). The Bible does not say these are the feasts of Israel or the feasts of the Jews; these are the *Feasts of the Lord*. Therefore, if we belong to the Lord, these Feasts should matter to us. Second, the command to celebrate the feasts is a lasting ordinance for all generations to come. The Lord's people are not to stop celebrating them.

Finally, though the term "feasts" is frequently used to describe the celebrations, the *New American Standard Bible* accurately translates these as "*appointed times of the LORD, HOLY CONVOCATIONS WHICH YOU SHALL PROCLAIM AT THE TIMES APPOINTED FOR THEM*" (verse 4). These are fixed, appointed convocations for the Lord's people to meet and proclaim the gracious past, present, and even future acts the Lord will accomplish on their behalf and for His name. Dr. Michael Brown states, "These [feasts] are not just ancient things that had past meaning and no relevance to today. These find their fulfillment in Jesus Yeshua."[1] Even though these festivals celebrated significant moments in Israel's history, they were, and are, prophetic dress rehearsals for major messianic events.

Passover was the first of the seven Feasts of the Lord. *"In the first month, on the fourteenth day of the month at twilight is the LORD's PASSOVER"* (Leviticus 23:5). A fuller explanation of the first Passover is found in Exodus 12, where God told Moses:

> *This month shall be the beginning of months for you; it is to be the first month of the year to you. . . . On the tenth of this month [the people] are each one to take a lamb for themselves, according to their fathers' households, a lamb for each household. Now if the household is too small for a lamb, then he and his neighbor nearest to his house are to take one according to the number of persons in them; according to what each man should eat, you are to divide the lamb. Your lamb shall be an unblemished male a year old; you may take it from the sheep or from the goats. You shall keep it until the fourteenth day of the same month, then the whole assembly of the congregation of Israel is to kill it at twilight. Moreover, they shall take some of the blood and put it on the two doorposts and on the lintel of the houses in which they eat it. They shall eat the flesh that same night, roasted with fire, and they shall eat it with unleavened bread and bitter herbs. . . . The blood shall be a sign for you on the houses where you live; and when I see the blood I will pass over you, and no plague will befall you to destroy you when I strike the land of Egypt* (verses 1-8, 13).

It stands to reason that because Jesus is the Lord, and these are the Feasts of the Lord, all these feasts will ultimately be about Him. Sure enough, during the last year of His ministry, on the fourteenth day of the first month of the Hebrew calendar (the month of Nisan or Aviv), Jesus, the Lamb of God (see John 1:29), had the Passover meal with His disciples in the upper room and explained to them the fulfillment of the feast.

At four important points of a Passover meal, called a Seder, four cups of wine would be passed around the table from which each family member would drink. These cups were based on the four expressions of God's redemption of the Israelites from the Egyptians, as found in Exodus 6:6-8: *"Say, therefore, to the sons of Israel, 'I am the LORD, and (I will bring you out) from under the burdens of the Egyptians, and (I will deliver you from their bondage). (I will also redeem you) with an outstretched arm and with great judgments. Then (I will take you for My people), and I will be your God; and you shall know that I am the Lord your God, who brought you out from under the burdens of the Egyptians.'"*[2]

The first cup was known as the cup of blessing. The second was called the cup of deliverance, after which the family would eat the unleavened bread, bitter herbs, and Passover lamb. The third was the cup of redemption. The fourth was the cup of praise, and then the family would sing part of the *Hallel* (Psalms 113–118) to conclude the Passover meal.[3]

In the Gospels, only the first and third cups are mentioned (see Luke 22:14-18; Matthew 26:27). However, before Jesus took the third cup and He and the disciples ate the most important part of the meal, *"Jesus took some bread, and after a blessing, He broke it and gave it to the disciples, and said, 'Take, eat; this is My body.' And when He had taken a cup and given thanks, He gave it to them, saying, 'Drink from it, all of you; for this is My blood of the covenant, which is poured out for many for forgiveness of sins'"* (Matthew 26:26-28).[4]

The next morning—still considered the fourteenth of Nisan since the Jews viewed days as progressing from sundown to sundown (see Genesis 1:3-5)—Jesus was crucified. Mark tells us, *"When the sixth hour came, darkness fell over the whole land until the ninth hour. . . . And Jesus uttered a loud cry, and breathed His last. And the veil of the temple was torn in two from top to bottom"* (15:33, 38). Why does Mark gives us these details?

The Lord sent 10 plagues against the Egyptians to convince Pharaoh to let the Israelites go. For the last plague, the Lord went throughout Egypt and killed every firstborn son who was not inside a house with the blood of a lamb smeared over the doorposts. Right before the Passover lamb was slain, the plague of darkness covered the land for three days. On the day of Passover in Jesus's last year, darkness covered the land for three hours as He hung on the cross. At 3 PM, just as a lamb was being slain in the temple for the sins of the people, the true and better Passover lamb was slain.

Jesus is the fulfillment of Passover. In fact, the apostle Paul says exactly that in 1 Corinthians 5:7: *"For Christ our Passover also has been sacrificed."* By grace through faith in Jesus Christ, we are brought out of the kingdom of darkness and transferred into God's kingdom (see 1:13-14). Jesus delivers us from bondage to our old sin nature and makes us adopted sons and daughters of God (see Romans 8:11-17). We are not redeemed from our futile way of life with perishable things like gold or silver but with Christ's precious blood as of a lamb unblemished and spotless (see 1 Peter 1:18-19). Because of Jesus's redemptive work on the cross that Passover, He is able to bring us to Himself as the bride of Christ, pure and radiant (see Revelation 19:7-9).

Leviticus 23:6-7 introduces us to the Feast of Unleavened Bread. The Lord said, *"Then on the fifteenth day of the same month there is the Feast of Unleavened Bread to the LORD; FOR SEVEN DAYS YOU SHALL EAT UNLEAVENED BREAD. On the first day you shall have a holy convocation; you shall not do any laborious work."* In Exodus 12:14-15, God gives these instructions to the Israelites as to how to keep this feast: *"Now this day will be a memorial to you, and you shall celebrate it as a feast to the LORD; THROUGHOUT YOUR GENERATIONS YOU ARE TO CELEBRATE IT AS A PERMANENT ORDINANCE. Seven days you shall eat unleavened bread, but on the first day you shall remove leaven from your houses; for whoever eats anything leavened from the first day until the seventh day, that person shall be cut off from Israel."*

From these passages, we see the Feast of Unleavened Bread began the day after Passover, at sundown, which was considered a Sabbath. The day before the Sabbath, what we would consider Thursday at sundown to Friday at sundown, was the "preparation day." The Hebrews were to remove all leaven from their houses during this feast, for leaven was symbolic for sin.[5] Finally, we see this is an annual feast to Yahweh that is to be celebrated forever.

Jesus was crucified on a Passover that was a preparation day, and the first day of that year's Unleavened Bread took place on a regular Sabbath. *"[Joseph from Arimathea] went to Pilate and asked for the body of Jesus. And he took it down and wrapped it in a linen cloth, and laid Him in a tomb cut into the rock, where no one had ever lain. It was the preparation day, and the Sabbath was about to begin. Now the women who had come with Him out of Galilee followed, and saw the tomb and how His body was laid. Then they returned and prepared spices and perfumes. And on the Sabbath they rested according to the commandment"* (Luke 23:52-56).

Jesus was crucified on Passover, and on Unleavened Bread the sinless Son of God was laid His resting place, the borrowed tomb. Many people think Jesus surely sinned at some point during His life, yet Scripture says He was without sin. The author of Hebrews writes, *"Therefore, since we have a great high priest who has passed through the heavens, Jesus the Son of God, let us hold fast our confession. For we do not have a high priest who cannot sympathize with our weaknesses, but One who has been tempted in all things as we are, yet* without sin" (Hebrews 4:14-15). The apostle Paul agrees: *"He made Him who knew no sin to be* sin on our behalf, so that we might become the righteousness of God in Him" (2 Corinthians 5:21).

Peter demonstrates how Jesus fulfilled Isaiah 53, which is loaded with messianic prophecies, when he writes, *"For you have been called for this purpose, since Christ also suffered for you, leaving you an example for you to follow in His steps,* WHO COMMITTED NO SIN, NOR WAS ANY DECEIT FOUND IN HIS MOUTH; AND WHILE BEING REVILED, HE DID NOT REVILE IN RETURN; WHILE SUFFERING, HE UTTERED NO THREATS, BUT KEPT ENTRUSTING HIMSELF TO HIM WHO JUDGES RIGHTEOUSLY; *and He Himself bore our sins in His body on the cross, so that we might die to sin and live to righteousness; for by His wounds you were healed"* (1 Peter 2:21-24).

Finally, just in case you've been told that since Jesus fulfilled the Feasts of the Lord we don't need to continue celebrating them, the apostle Paul writes, *"Clean out the old leaven so that you may be a new lump, just as you are in fact* unleavened. For Christ our Passover also has been sacrificed. Therefore let us celebrate the feast, not with old leaven, nor with the leaven of malice and wickedness, but with the unleavened bread of sincerity and truth" (1 Corinthians 5:7-8). Christ doesn't want us to keep killing animals as offerings to God, but He calls us to continue celebrating the Lord's feasts in ways that bring honor to Him.[6]

Many of the Christians who resided in Asia Minor during the first and second century celebrated Passover on the fourteenth day of Nisan. John was an elder in Ephesus, and as stated earlier, he discipled Polycarp, who became the bishop of Smyrna. Polycarp discipled Irenaeus while Irenaeus lived in Smyrna, and Irenaeus eventually became the bishop of Lyons in Gaul.[7] Here is what Irenaeus wrote in 180 CE concerning the Passover tradition handed down from Jesus, to John, to Polycarp, and finally to him:

> Whatsoever things he had heard from them respecting the Lord, both with regard to His miracles and His teaching, Polycarp having thus received [information] from the eyewitnesses of the Word of life, would recount them all in harmony with the Scriptures.... And when the blessed Polycarp was sojourning in Rome in the time of Anicetus ... neither could Anicetus persuade Polycarp to forego the observance [in his own way], inasmuch as these things had been always

> [so] observed by John the disciple of our Lord, and by other apostles with whom he had been conversant; nor, on the other hand, could Polycarp succeed in persuading Anicetus to keep [the observance in his way], for he maintained that he was bound to adhere to the usage of the presbyters who preceded him. And in this state of affairs they held fellowship with each other; and Anicetus conceded to Polycarp in the Church the celebration of the Eucharist, by way of showing him respect; so that they parted in peace one from the other, maintaining peace with the whole Church.[8]

The earliest Christians continued to observe Passover, but they did so recognizing Jesus was the fulfillment of the Feasts of the Lord. Early Christian teacher Origen wrote in 228 CE, "The Passover of the Jews consists of a sheep that is sacrificed, each taking a sheep according to his father's house. And the Passover is accompanied by the slaughter of thousands of rams and goats, in proportion to the number of the households of the people. But our Passover is sacrificed for us, namely, Christ."[9]

Not only did Jesus fulfill Passover and Unleavened Bread on their respective feast days, but He also fulfilled the third spring feast, Firstfruits, on the Feast of Firstfruits. In Leviticus 23:9-11, God said to Moses, "*Speak to the sons of Israel and say to them, 'When you enter the land which I am going to give to you and reap its harvest, then you shall bring in the sheaf of the first fruits of your harvest to the priest. He shall wave the sheaf before the LORD FOR YOU TO BE ACCEPTED; ON THE DAY AFTER THE SABBATH THE PRIEST SHALL WAVE IT.'"*

As previously mentioned, that Passover Jesus celebrated with His disciples was on a preparation day, and Unleavened Bread took place on the regular Sabbath (Friday sundown to Saturday sundown). God said that Firstfruits was to be commemorated on the day after the Sabbath of Unleavened Bread. In the year that Jesus died, this feast would have taken place on the sixteenth of Nissan, and on the first day of the week.

Luke 24:1 says the resurrection took place at early dawn on the first day of the week, Sunday. Matthew 28:1 records the resurrection occurred after the Sabbath, as it began to dawn on the first day of the week. Mark 16:1-2 tells us this event happened when the Sabbath was over, early on the first day of the week. Finally, John 20:1 records the first witness of the resurrection came early to Jesus's tomb on the first day of the week while it was still dark.

Jesus rose from the dead on Firstfruits, the third feast day of the Lord. That detail gave me a better understanding as to why Jesus said in Luke 18:31-33, *"All things which are written through the prophets about the Son of Man will be accomplished. For He will be handed over to the Gentiles, and will be mocked and mistreated and spit upon, and after they have scourged Him, they will kill Him; and the third day He will rise again."* Matthew corroborates Luke's account when records that Jesus told His disciples, *"The Son of Man is going to be delivered into the hands of men; and they will kill Him, and He will be raised on the third day"* (17:22-23).

It's easy to get flustered concerning the prospect of Jesus not being in the tomb for a full 72 hours. Admittedly, it frustrated and confounded me for many years. Even if Jesus had been immediately brought to the tomb after He breathed His last on Friday around 3 PM, and then raised right around sunrise on Sunday, He would have only been buried for 39 hours at most. However, if we understand Jesus came to fulfill His feast days, it makes all the sense in the world that He said He would rise on the third day.

Paul picks up on this connection between Jesus, the resurrection, and Firstfruits when he writes, *"If Christ has not been raised, your faith is worthless; you are still in your sins. . . . But now Christ has been raised from the dead, the first fruits of those who are asleep. For since by a man came death, by a man also came the resurrection of the dead. For as in Adam all die, so also in Christ all will be made alive. But each in his own order: Christ the first fruits, after that those who are Christ's at His coming, then comes the end, when He hands over the kingdom to God the Father, when He has abolished all rule and all authority and power"* (1 Corinthians 15:20-24).

Twice in this passage Paul calls Jesus the Firstfruits. I've heard this section of Scripture taught innumerable times, and on each occasion the point was always that if Christ had not been raised from the dead our faith would be worthless; however, since Christ was raised, we can have supreme confidence in life and in death. Those points are true, but they miss one of the main points Paul is making: Christ is the Firstfruits of God.

William Francis writes, "On [the Feast of Firstfruits], the early crops of the spring planting, the *first fruits*, were presented in the Temple. The Feast of Firstfruits was not merely a harvest festival, however. It was an acknowledgement of Israel's total dependence on God. In gratitude and recognition of God's providential care, the people presented part of the fruit that ripened first."[10] The people would give God the first and the best of the spring harvest.

What did God give? *"For God so loved the world, that He gave His only begotten Son, that whoever believes in Him shall not perish, but have eternal life. For God did not send the Son into the world to judge the world, but that the world might be saved through Him"* (John 3:16-17). God gave His first and His best: Jesus, the Firstfruits.

The people made this offering in total dependence on God and in faith that because He was the giver of every good and perfect gift, He would continue to supply all their needs, even though they had already given their best to Him. Paul writes that Jesus did the same: *"Christ Jesus . . . although He existed in the form of God, did not regard equality with God a thing to be grasped, but emptied Himself, taking the form of a bond-servant, and being made in the likeness of men. Being found in appearance as a man, He humbled Himself by becoming obedient to the point of death, even death on a cross"* (Philippians 2:6-8).

Jesus lived in total dependence on God and entrusted Himself to the One who judges justly. He lived the life we should have lived and died the death we should have died. But because of Jesus's humble faithfulness to His Father, death couldn't keep its hold on Him. Paul continues, *"For this reason also, God highly exalted Him, and bestowed on Him the name which is above every name, so that at the name of Jesus EVERY KNEE WILL BOW, OF THOSE WHO ARE IN HEAVEN AND ON EARTH AND UNDER THE EARTH, and that every tongue will confess that Jesus Christ is Lord, to the glory of God the Father"* (verses 9-11).

The fourth Feast of the Lord is called Shavuot, or Pentecost. In Leviticus 23:15-16, God said to Moses, *"You shall also count for yourselves from the day after the sabbath, from the day when you brought in the sheaf of the wave offering; there shall be seven complete sabbaths. You shall count fifty days to the day after the seventh sabbath; then you shall present a new grain offering to the LORD."* The feast would begin 50 days after Firstfruits; seven Sabbaths and one day. In Greek the name of the feast is *Pentecost*, meaning "fiftieth day."[11]

All the feast days held great importance in Israel's history. On Passover, the lamb was slain to protect the people from being destroyed. The next day, on Unleavened Bread, the Israelites left Egypt. On the third day, Firstfruits, they passed through the sea on dry ground and saw the Egyptian army destroyed behind them. In Jesus's day, it was Hebrew tradition that God had given Moses the Law to Moses on Pentecost.[12]

The Feast of Pentecost was a celebratory feast, and one of three (along with Passover and Sukkot) that every Hebrew male was required to attend. Since Pentecost falls in late May or early June each year, traveling conditions were ideal for vast numbers of people to come to Jerusalem. Jews from all over the known world came into the city on that feast day, for "it was *the international day in Jerusalem*."[13] In Acts 2:1-4, we read that 50 days after Unleavened Bread in the year Jesus died and rose again:

> *[The followers of Jesus] were all together in one place. And suddenly there came from heaven a noise like a violent rushing wind, and it filled the whole house where they were sitting. And there appeared to them tongues as of fire distributing themselves, and they rested on each one of them. And they were all filled with the Holy Spirit and began to speak with other tongues, as the Spirit was giving them utterance.*

Luke tells us that when the Jews in Jerusalem heard the sound, they were amazed because the disciples were speaking in their own language. Yet some said, *"They are full of sweet wine"* (verse 13). Peter explained the disciples were not drunk; what was happening was that the prophecy in Joel 2:28-32 was being fulfilled right before their eyes. He also explained that by them crucifying Jesus, and God raising Him from the dead and pouring out His Spirit, Psalm 16:8-11 and Psalm 110:1 had now also been fulfilled. Peter's hearers were cut to the heart by these words and asked what they should do in response. Peter replied, *"Repent, and each of you be baptized in the name of Jesus Christ for the forgiveness of your sins; and you will receive the gift of the Holy Spirit"* (Acts 2:38).

Luke writes that those who received Peter's message were baptized, and 3,000 people were added to the Church that day! What an amazing ingathering that Pentecost! But why is the number 3,000 significant? To answer that question, we must look at what happened the day Moses came down from Mt. Sinai with the Ten Commandments:

> *When the people saw that Moses delayed to come down from the mountain, the people assembled about Aaron and said to him, "Come, make us a god who will go before us."... Then all the people tore off the gold rings which were in their ears and brought them to Aaron. He took this from their hand, and fashioned it with a graving tool and made it into a molten calf; and they said, "This is your god, O Israel, who brought you up from the land of Egypt." Now when Aaron saw this,*

he built an altar before it; and Aaron made a proclamation
and said, "Tomorrow shall be a feast to the LORD." SO THE
NEXT DAY THEY ROSE EARLY AND OFFERED BURNT OFFER-
INGS, AND BROUGHT PEACE OFFERINGS; AND THE PEOPLE
SAT DOWN TO EAT AND TO DRINK, AND ROSE UP TO PLAY"
(Exodus 32:1, 3-6).

Unlike the Israelites in Moses's day, the disciples waited patiently and
faithfully for the Holy Spirit to be poured out on them. Fire came upon the
gold of the Israelites, and out came an abominable idol. Fire from God came
down upon the disciples, and it sparked the revival of all revivals. When the
Law of Moses came down, *"about three thousand men of the people fell that*
day" (verse 28). When the Law of the Spirit came down, *"that day there were*
added about three thousand souls" (Acts 2:41).

On the first Pentecost, God brought a blessing after the Levites destroyed
everyone who had acted wickedly. But on the best Pentecost, God poured out
a far better blessing. *"They were continually devoting themselves to the apos-*
tles' teaching and to fellowship, to the breaking of bread and to prayer. Everyone
kept feeling a sense of awe; and many wonders and signs were taking place
through the apostles. And all those who had believed were together and had all
things in common; and they began selling their property and possessions and
were sharing them with all, as anyone might have need. Day by day continuing
with one mind in the temple, and breaking bread from house to house, they
were taking their meals together with gladness and sincerity of heart praising
God and having favor with all the people. And the Lord was adding to their
number day by day those who were being saved" (Acts 2:42-47).

This is a description of what should be normative in our lives when we
put selfish ambition aside, put on the attitude of Christ, and seek to glorify
God. When God's Spirit invades us, it should not only birth in us a new devotion to the Scriptures, other members of the body of Christ, and communion
with God, but we should also long to gather more and more people into His
family, regardless of the sacrifices required.

My mother's parents, Horace and Alto, were committed Christians who
lived in the West Texas town of Rankin during the early 1960s. One day,
the small Baptist church where most of the African American community
attended burned down, leaving them without a church home. Alto, feeling
this was what Jesus wanted them to do, invited an African American child
to go with her and Horace to the all-white First Baptist Church of Rankin,

where they attended. This happened before laws were passed to end segregation, and needless to say my grandparents' decision caused quite a stir in the church and in the town. Yet they continued to bring this girl. Soon, African American children from two families were coming with them each week, and eventually several Hispanic children came with them as well.

Sunday after Sunday, my grandparents brought these children to church despite subtle and not-so-subtle resistance from church members and friends. One day, the oldest girl told my grandmother she wanted to give her life to Jesus and be baptized. Once again, this was a problem for the majority of white members who felt they had already made significant strides in allowing these children to attend their white church. After all, getting baptized at First Baptist Rankin meant membership. My grandfather, a deacon, dug in his heels and stood up for this new daughter of the King of kings. The pastor said he would meet with the others and thought things would be all right. When the deacon body met, they voted to allow the child to be baptized into the church. And so she was.

In spite of intimidations and persecutions, First Baptist Rankin was integrated, and my grandparents became living examples of how the power of the Holy Spirit given at Pentecost enables us to walk as Jesus walked. It is a tall order *"to do justice, to love kindness, and to walk humbly with your God"* (Micah 6:8). It can often feel like an impossibility to deny ourselves, pick up our crosses, and follow Jesus (see Matthew 16:24). It is a tremendous task to go into all the world making disciples of Jesus, teaching them to obey everything He commanded (see 28:19-20). However, those whom God calls He equips.

Jesus was killed on Passover as the Passover lamb of God who takes away the sins of the world. He was in the tomb on Unleavened Bread as the sinless Son of God who became sin on our behalf. He was raised from the dead on Firstfruits so that we who have been born again by the word of truth could become a kind of firstfruits among His creation, giving the first and best of ourselves to Him in total dependence on Him (see James 1:18). And Jesus gave us the Holy Spirit on Pentecost so that through His Spirit dwelling in us, we could become conformed to His image and character and do the works He did.

Now may the God of peace, who through the blood of the eternal covenant brought back from the dead our Lord Jesus, that great Shepherd of the sheep, equip you with everything good for doing His will. And may He work in you what is pleasing to Him, through Jesus Christ, to whom be glory for ever and ever. Amen.

Chapter 17

TIME TO RISE AND SHINE

In an earlier chapter, I wrote that I was a bit of a stinky child. For some strange reason I despised bath time, and it didn't help that I was active outdoors. I remember lying to my mom and dad several times about taking my nightly shower, and they would catch me since I still stunk to high heaven the next morning. One night, my mom surprised me after I supposedly had taken my shower by calling me over to the couch and smelling my head. Of course, I failed the test. However, the next night I was prepared. Instead of taking a shower, I washed my hair in the bathroom sink. I passed the smell test that night, but I guess the joke was on me since I was still the stinky kid at school.

Showering at summer camp was more terrifying. All that separated me from 15 or so other young, hyperactive, prank-loving kids was a thin curtain hung between two small, dirty stalls. I wasn't having any of it. Several years at that five-day camp I went the entire time without showering. Bless my little heart. ("Bless your heart" is a southern phrase often meaning, "You stupid idiot.") Worse than the showers, though, was the noise of "Reveille" played on a bugle every morning around sunrise. If you were sleeping on a top bunk, you might hit your head on the ceiling when you shot upward in a panicked state. I was used to my mother's gentle voice being my alarm clock, so that bugle made me feel the apocalypse was upon us.

The fifth Feast of the Lord, the Feast of Trumpets, is known as Yom Teruah, which means "day of blowing," or Zikhron Teruah, meaning "memorial of blowing." God states the reason for these names in Leviticus 23:24-25: "*On the first day of the seventh month you are to have a day of sabbath rest, a sacred assembly commemorated with trumpet blasts. Do no regular work, but present a food offering to the Lord.*" Yom Teruah is the first of the three fall Feasts of the Lord.[1]

However, Yom Teruah is more commonly referred to as Rosh Hashanna, which means "head of the year." As Meria Merola explains, "Why do the

Jewish people refer to this day as *'Rosh Ha'Shanah?'* To put it simply, there are two different 'New Year's.' The first 'New Year' is mentioned in Exodus 12:2 and 13:4 as *'the month Abib,'* and it commemorates the time when [Yahweh] took [Israel] out of Egypt. It is the first of the year for the seven feasts annually. This calendar runs its course for seven months, and it measures the seven months of feasts as well as the *'four harvests'* in [Israel] (barley, first wheat, second wheat, grapes). The other 'New Year' measures *'linear time'* itself, and this it is when the *'seven year sabbatical cycles'* are measured, called the *'shmitta,'* as well as the *'fifty year'* Jubilee cycles."[2]

Rosh Hashanna, the first day of the seventh month, was the day the Jews believed God completed His creation by creating Adam and Eve. On that first day of humanity's existence, God blew His Spirit into them, and they awakened to become living souls. Then, on a later Yom Teruah at Mount Moriah, the angel of the Lord stopped Abraham from sacrificing his beloved son Isaac to the Lord God.[3] When Abraham looked up, he saw a ram caught in a thicket by its horns. Abraham sacrificed the ram to the Lord God and called Yahweh his provider.

The Israelites began to use a ram's horn to make shofars, what was basically an ancient type of trumpet. Most likely due to that moment on Mount Moriah, the blowing of a trumpet or shofar became a symbol of redemption for God's people. The first time we see a trumpet blast in Scripture is found in Exodus 19. In this crucial moment in history, the Israelites are about to receive the Ten Commandments from God at Mount Sinai, and a great trumpet blast plays a critical role in the story.

> *So it came about on the third day, when it was morning, that there were thunder and lightning flashes and a thick cloud upon the mountain and a very loud trumpet sound, so that all the people who were in the camp trembled. And Moses brought the people out of the camp to meet God, and they stood at the foot of the mountain. Now Mount Sinai was all in smoke because the Lord descended upon it in fire; and its smoke ascended like the smoke of a furnace, and the whole mountain quaked violently. When the sound of the trumpet grew louder and louder, Moses spoke and God answered him with thunder. The Lord came down on Mount Sinai, to the top of the mountain; and the Lord called Moses to the top of the mountain, and Moses went up (verses 16-20).*

The Lord God descended in the midst of thick clouds and to the sound of an increasingly loud trumpet blast. When the people heard the blast, they were allowed to come up to the mountain. Several hundred years later, the prophet Isaiah wrote of another gathering up at the sound of a trumpet blast: *"In that day the Lord will start His threshing from the flowing stream of the Euphrates to the brook of Egypt, and you will be gathered up one by one, O sons of Israel. It will come about also in that day that a great trumpet will be blown, and those who were perishing in the land of Assyria and who were scattered in the land of Egypt will come and worship the Lord in the holy mountain at Jerusalem"* (27:12-13). Could it be that the Feast of Trumpets will ultimately be fulfilled with a future event comprising a trumpet blast and gathering with God's people and the risen Lord Jesus Christ?

Remember, all the Feasts of the Lord are memorial festivals that God commands His people to celebrate forever. The Lord God fulfilled each of the four spring feasts on their exact days in their exact orders during His first coming. Doesn't it then make sense He would do the same with the fall feasts on His second coming?

Let's look at what Jesus has to say about His second coming and see if it corresponds with what we've learned so far about Yom Teruah. Jesus told His disciples, *"Immediately after the tribulation of those days the sun will be darkened, and the moon will not give its light, and the stars will fall from the sky, and the powers of the heavens will be shaken. And then the sign of the Son of Man will appear in the sky, and then all the tribes of the earth will mourn, and they will see the Son of Man coming on the clouds of the sky with power and great glory. And He will send forth His angels with a great trumpet and they will gather together His elect from the four winds, from one end of the sky to the other"* (Matthew 24:29-31).

Like on Mount Sinai, the Lord will descend with the clouds at the sound of a great trumpet to gather His people to Himself. As we've discussed, Paul also writes about Christ's return with similar details. In 1 Thessalonians 4:15-17 he states, *"We who are alive and remain until the coming of the Lord, will not precede those who have fallen asleep. For the Lord Himself will descend from heaven with a shout, with the voice of the archangel and with the trumpet of God, and the dead in Christ will rise first. Then we who are alive and remain will be caught up together with them in the clouds to meet the Lord in the air, and so we shall always be with the Lord."* The Lord descends with a trumpet blast, and those currently in Christ, whether dead or alive, are caught up with Him.

Paul also writes, *"We will not all sleep, but we will all be changed, in a moment, in the twinkling of an eye, at the last trumpet; for the trumpet will sound, and the dead will be raised imperishable, and we will be changed"* (1 Corinthians 15:51-52). Notice the important detail Paul adds to this event: Christ's return will not just happen at a great trumpet blast, but it will be at the *last* trumpet. Therefore, we should investigate when the Bible says this last trumpet of God will sound.

Beginning in Revelation 8, John describes the final seven trumpet blasts of God, which bring tribulation on the earth. Just imagine how the first trumpet alone will affect all mankind. When this trumpet is blown, hail and fire mixed with blood are thrown down to the earth. A third of the earth is burned up, a third of the trees are burned up, and all the green grass is burned up. When the second trumpet is blown, something like a great mountain burning with fire is thrown into the sea. A third of the creatures in the sea die, and a third of the ships are destroyed.

At the third trumpet a great star named Wormwood falls from heaven to the rivers and spring waters, causing many people to die from the bitter water. Jesus tells us in Revelation 1:20 that stars represent angels, so this Wormwood fellow is most likely an evil angel, whom Paul would refer to as one of the rulers of darkness in heavenly places (see Ephesians 6:12). It is possible this great star is Satan, the ultimate evil angel (see Isaiah 14:12; Revelation 12:7-12).

When the fourth trumpet is blown, a third of the sun, moon, and stars are struck so that a third of the day and night are without light. Then, before the fifth trumpet is blown, John sees an eagle flying in mid-heaven, crying out, *"Woe, woe, woe to those who dwell on the earth, because of the remaining blasts of the trumpet of the three angels who are about to sound!"* (Revelation 8:13). Those "woes" aren't like Keanu Reeves's "whoa" in *Bill and Ted's Excellent Adventure*. Just so you know, woes in the Bible mean *really*, really bad news for those on whom they are pronounced. If you want to see an example of woes spoken by Jesus, read Matthew 23. Jesus isn't the buddy-Christ that Hollywood would love for you to believe He is.

When the fifth trumpet is sounded, a star from heaven that had fallen to earth unlocks the bottomless pit, releasing an army of demonic hybrid locusts:

> *They were told not to hurt the grass of the earth, nor any green thing, nor any tree, but only the men who do not have the seal*

of God on their foreheads. And they were not permitted to kill anyone, but to torment for five months; and their torment was like the torment of a scorpion when it stings a man. And in those days men will seek death and will not find it; they will long to die, and death flees from them. The appearance of the locusts was like horses prepared for battle; and on their heads appeared to be crowns like gold, and their faces were like the faces of men. They had hair like the hair of women, and their teeth were like the teeth of lions. They had breast-plates like breastplates of iron; and the sound of their wings was like the sound of chariots, of many horses rushing to bat-tle. They have tails like scorpions, and stings; and in their tails is their power to hurt men for five months. They have as king over them, the angel of the abyss; his name in Hebrew is Abad-don, and in the Greek he has the name Apollyon (Revelation 9:4-11).

There are two things to notice about this fifth trumpet. First, it is those with the seal of God on their foreheads—those who belong to Jesus—who are not harmed by the demonic hybrid locusts. Interestingly, in Exodus 13 the Lord God told the Hebrews that whenever they continued to celebrate the festival of Unleavened Bread, and whenever they redeemed a firstborn male with a lamb, those actions served as a sign on their hand and forehead of God's deliverance. It is through faith in the sinless body and redeeming blood of our Messiah, Jesus, that we are delivered and become marked as God's people.

Second, the Bible says a star from heaven opened the bottomless pit to let out the demonic locusts. As previously mentioned, stars are usually inter-preted as angels in this book. In Revelation 9, we see this star was in heaven but had already fallen to earth. Could this fallen, rebellious angel be Satan, possibly known as Wormwood? Similarly to the Hindu god Shiva, this evil angel's name was Abaddon and Apollyon, which means "destruction" and "destroyer," respectively. Whether Satan or someone else, he is an evil angel of destruction. He brings his destructive acts on everyone without the seal of God on their foreheads to the extent that people try to kill themselves, yet somehow are forced to endure the torture.[4]

When the sixth trumpet is blown, four angels who have been bound up at the great river Euphrates are released to kill one-third of humanity. They lead an army of horsemen numbering 200 million and, like the locusts, these horseman are most likely demonically enhanced. "*The heads of the horses are like the heads of lions; and out of their mouths proceed fire and smoke and brimstone. A third of mankind was killed by these three plagues, by the fire and the smoke and the brimstone which proceeded out of their mouths. For the power of the horses is in their mouths and in their tails; for their tails are like serpents and have heads, and with them they do harm*" (Revelation 9:17-19).

It shouldn't surprise us that such strange evil creatures will be roaming the earth during this time. Jesus said in Matthew 24:27, "*For the coming of the Son of Man will be just like the days of Noah.*" Genesis 6 tells us that in the days of Noah, "*The Nephilim were on the earth in those days, and also afterward, when the sons of God came in to the daughters of men, and they bore children to them. Those were the mighty men who were of old, men of renown. . . . God looked on the earth, and behold, it was corrupt; for all flesh had corrupted their way upon the earth*" (verses 4, 12).[5] According to the Bible and the Dead Sea Scrolls, the days of Noah were about as weird as it gets, making the fiction of C. S. Lewis look more like fact.

Going back to Revelation 9, one would think humanity would turn back to God after such tribulation had come on the earth. Unfortunately, though, like Pharaoh, humanity only chooses to harden their hearts in continued rebellion at the signs and plagues. "*The rest of mankind, who were not killed by these plagues, did not repent of the works of their hands, so as not to worship demons, and the idols of gold and of silver and of brass and of stone and of wood, which can neither see nor hear nor walk; and they did not repent of their murders nor of their sorceries nor of their immorality nor of their thefts*" (Revelation 9:20-21).

At last, we come to the seventh and final trumpet. In Revelation 10:7, a strong angel gives John a critical piece of information about this trumpet: "*In the days of the voice of the seventh angel, when he is about to sound, then the mystery of God is finished, as He preached to His servants the prophets.*" According to this passage, in the days of the seventh trumpet the mystery surrounding who God is and what He is like will be brought to completion. This sounds like the glorious second coming of Christ.

Just before the seventh trumpet is sounded, we read in Revelation 11:1-14 that two witnesses of God come to earth to prophesy to humanity for roughly three and a half years. If anyone seeks to harm them, fire comes out of their mouths and kills their assailants. They have the power to bring drought during the days of their prophesying and to strike the earth with all the plagues of Egypt. At the end of that time the Antichrist, the one who comes up out of the Abyss (see Revelation 9:1, 11; 13:1-10), kills the two witnesses in the streets of Jerusalem.

As the bodies of the two witnesses lie dead, people give gifts to each other, celebrating the witnesses' deaths like it's Christmas morning. However, after three and a half days, God breathes life back into them, and they stand back up on their feet in front of everyone. Just then, a voice from heaven says, "Come up here," and they rise up to God in the clouds. That is likely one of the last events preceding the seventh trumpet: two of God's faithful followers being called up into the clouds to be with Him forever, while the disobedient look on.

When the seventh trumpet is blown, the voices in heaven say, "*The kingdom of the world has become the kingdom of our Lord and of His Christ; and He will reign forever and ever*" (11:15). The King comes to rule the earth, and the prayer Jesus taught us to pray reaches its completion as His kingdom and His will fully come on earth as they are in heaven. The seventh trumpet also ushers in the outpouring of God's wrath on the earth through the seven bowls. In addition, "*the temple of God which is in heaven*" is opened, and the ark of God, which symbolizes His presence, becomes visible (verse 19).

Just before the seven bowls of God's wrath are poured out on the earth, John says, "*I looked, and behold, a white cloud, and sitting on the cloud was one like a son of man, having a golden crown on His head and a sharp sickle in His hand. And another angel came out of the temple, crying out with a loud voice to Him who sat on the cloud, 'Put in your sickle and reap, for the hour to reap has come, because the harvest of the earth is ripe.' Then He who sat on the cloud swung His sickle over the earth, and the earth was reaped*" (14:14-16). Those who are left after the earth is reaped are thrown into the great winepress of the wrath of God.

There has been a popular teaching since the mid-1800s that Jesus will take His followers out of the world before the event known as the "Great Tribulation" happens. However, that teaching was not orthodoxy in early Christendom. Also, I believe a straightforward reading of Scripture shows us Christ's return and His followers meeting Him in the air occurs close to the end of the Great Tribulation.

Jesus also told His disciples, "*Now learn the parable from the fig tree: when its branch has already become tender and puts forth its leaves, you know that summer is near; so, you too, when you see all these things, recognize that He is near, right at the door. Truly I say to you, this generation will not pass away until all these things take place"* (Matthew 24:32-34). Jesus says His generation of believers won't pass away until all the things He listed come to pass.

Earlier in this same conversation, Jesus said He would return in the clouds to gather His people to Himself after the tribulation of those days. *"When you see the* ABOMINATION OF DESOLATION *which was spoken of through Daniel the prophet, standing in the holy place (let the reader understand), then those who are in Judea must flee to the mountains. . . . For then there will be a great tribulation, such as has not occurred since the beginning of the world until now, nor ever will. Unless those days had been cut short, no life would have been saved; but for the sake of the elect those days will be cut short. Then if anyone says to you, 'Behold, here is the Christ,' or 'There He is,' do not believe him. For false Christs and false prophets will arise and will show great signs and wonders, so as to mislead, if possible, even the elect"* (Matthew 24:15-16, 21-24).

Paul notes in 2 Thessalonians 2:1-4 that Jesus's return and our being gathered to Him will not occur until after the Antichrist is revealed. *"Let no one in any way deceive you, for [the coming of Jesus and our gathering to Him] will not come unless the apostasy comes first, and the man of lawlessness is revealed, the son of destruction, who opposes and exalts himself above every so-called god or object of worship, so that he takes his seat in the temple of God, displaying himself as being God"* (verses 3-4). The early Christian writers likewise affirmed the Church would remain on earth while the Antichrist was bringing tribulation on humanity:

> He shall come from heaven with glory, when the man of apostasy, who speaks strange things against the Most High, will venture to do unlawful deeds on earth against us Christians (Justin Martyr, 160 CE).[6]

> Once this Antichrist has devastated everything in this world, he will reign for three years and six months, and sit in the temple at Jerusalem. And then the Lord will come from heaven in the clouds (Irenaeus, 180 CE).[7]

> [The Antichrist] will order censers to be set up by everyone, everywhere, so that no one among the saints may be able to buy or sell without first sacrificing. For this is what is meant by the mark received upon the right hand. And the phrase, "on their forehead," indicates that all are crowned. That is,

they put on a crown of fire. This is a crown of death, not of life (Hippolytus, 200 CE).[8]

Even the Antichrist, when he begins to come, will not be allowed to enter into the church just because he threatens. We will not yield to his arms and violence, even though he declares he will destroy us if we resist. . . . The Antichrist is coming. Yet, above him, comes Christ also (Cyprian, 250 CE).[9]

Earlier, we read how Isaiah prophesied the Lord would gather up His people at the sound of a trumpet blast (see 27:12-13). In verse 1, Isaiah describes a different scene occurring at roughly the same time: "*In that day the Lord will punish Leviathan the fleeing serpent, with His fierce and great and mighty sword, even Leviathan the twisted serpent; and He will kill the dragon who lives in the sea.*" In Revelation, John says the Antichrist is the beast that comes out of the sea with the power, throne, and authority of the dragon, Satan (see 11:7; 13:1).[10]

Isaiah and Paul both affirm the words of John and Jesus concerning the coming of Christ being connected to the Antichrist who is already on the scene. Isaiah and Paul's words are also in line with Jesus's concerning His arrival being connected to the great trumpet blast of God. All this testimony from Scripture makes a strong case that there will not only be many visible events preceding the second coming of Christ, but also Jesus's return will happen on the fifth Feast of the Lord, Yom Teruah.

I can picture many folks reading this and thinking, *Wait a minute. Didn't Jesus say in Matthew 24 that no one knows the day or hour of His return?* Yes, He did, and I believe every word He said. It is important, though, for us to remember that Jesus was a Jewish rabbi who was speaking to other Jews in a Jewish context. Once again, Maria Merola demonstrates how understanding the Scriptures in their original context can help us determine the author's intent: "Many of us have read the famous quote of our Messiah in the gospels when he declared that his second coming would come at a time that '*no man knows.*' But how many of us knew that he was actually making a reference to the *Feast of Trumpets?* The *Feast of Trumpets* was known by those in ancient Jerusalem as '*The Day That No Man Knows.*' And why is it called this? Because it is the only feast that is determined by the sighting of the new moon, and so '*no man*' can calculate the exact day or hour of when this feast day will begin."[11]

Ancient Hebrews determined their months by the lunar calendar. New moons occur on the first day of a lunar month, when the moon has been at its darkest and now the first sliver is visible in the night sky. Merola continues, "In ancient Jerusalem, *'two witnesses'* would stand on the walls of Jerusalem and *'watch'* for the first sighting of the new moon. When the Father in heaven decided to allow the new moon to appear in the sky, then the *'two witnesses'* would sound the showfar (trumpet) and all the people in the city would immediately drop what they were doing, and they would run to the Temple for the celebration of *'The Day of Blowing'* called *Yom Teruw'ah* in Hebrew. The Temple doors were only open for a short period of time, and if they failed to make it to the Temple before the doors were shut, those who were slack in running to the Temple were left out of the feast because the *'doors were shut.'"*[12]

With this context in mind, we see in Matthew 24 that Jesus gives us clue after clue as to when His return will take place: "*But immediately after the tribulation of those DAYS THE SUN WILL BE DARKENED, AND THE MOON WILL NOT GIVE ITS LIGHT, AND THE STARS WILL FALL from the sky, and the powers of the heavens will be shaken. And then the sign of the Son of Man will appear in the sky, and then all the tribes of the earth will mourn, and they will see the SON OF MAN COMING ON THE CLOUDS OF THE SKY with power and great glory. And He will send forth His angels with A GREAT TRUMPET AND THEY WILL GATHER TOGETHER His elect from the four winds, from one end of the sky to the other*" (verses 29-31).

Jesus's coming will be "*just like the days of Noah*" (verse 37), and in those days the people witnessed several signs before the wrathful judgment of God came upon them. They heard Noah's righteous preaching and saw him building an ark for around 100 years before the prophesied deluge came. Seven days before the Great Flood, everyone saw Noah, his family, and the animals enter the ark. Everyone surely saw the sky grow dark and the heavy clouds gather above them—and then came the downfall.

Noah and his family were not spared from living in an increasingly violent and wicked world filled with demonically enhanced enemies of God. They remained in that world right up until the judgment. They were watching and obedient to God, and because of this they were given a heads-up before the deluge came. They then went into the ark and were taken up and away before the God's wrath was poured out on the earth. Everyone who remained disobedient despite God's warnings were left to suffer His wrath.

The same will be true of Jesus's second coming. Furthermore, it shouldn't be surprising that this second coming will happen on the Feast of Trumpets. Think about it: there are two advents of Christ, and two sets of feasts—spring and fall. During the first advent, Jesus died on Passover, was in the tomb on Unleavened Bread, resurrected on Firstfruits, and poured out His Holy Spirit on Pentecost. He fulfilled each of the spring feasts on their exact days in their exact order. Doesn't it make sense then that the first event in Christ's second advent—His second coming and the Church's gathering to Him—would occur on the first of the fall feasts? These are the Lord Jesus's feasts, after all.

I am going to steer clear of how Christians should celebrate the fall feasts in their assemblies. The Old Testament gives some details that would apply in a New Testament context, but there are often many sacrifices involved, and we know the Lord Jesus is the sacrifice to end all sacrifices (see Hebrews 10:10-14). Something to keep in mind is that the Bible says these are the *Lord's Feasts*, so we should be celebrating them in remembrance of the Lord Jesus, as is done with the Lord's Supper. Many Christians celebrate the Lord's Supper various ways, and I think that's fine as long as it is done with holiness and in remembrance of the Lord Jesus. I believe the same liberty should apply in the practice of the Feasts of the Lord.

Finally, I know many Christians have placed their hopes in escaping this world before the Great Tribulation. However, in light of the straightforward reading of the Scriptures we have discussed and the testimony of the early Church, I think it would be best for us to prepare to persevere through it. I admit I could be wrong about this, but I would rather we be prepared to endure tribulation with Jesus and then be surprised by an early exit than to bet on an early exit and wind up being overwhelmed in a worldly sorrow surrounded by apostates.

So may you be a faithful and wise servant of the King of kings, whom Jesus finds doing His will when He returns on the day of the awakening blast. May you be a son or daughter of the day who is alert and sober, having put on a breastplate of faith and love and the hope of salvation as a helmet. May you overcome with Jesus and keep His commandments until the end. And may you be faithful until death, that you may receive the crown of life.

Chapter 18

CANCELING DEBTS AND CONQUERING DARKNESS

When I was 24, I took out the first loan of my life to buy an engagement ring for a woman I would be disengaged to within a couple of months. That was obviously not a wise investment. It took several years to pay back the loan, and by the time that burden was taken off my shoulders, I had a car payment. Then, at age 29, my wife and I took on a house payment. Fortunately, about two years after moving into our house we were able to pay off my car and refinance our house payment from a 20- to a 15-year mortgage.

I hate having debt, even if all we have is our house payment. According to a report in 2013 by GoBankingRates, which tracks interest and banking rates nationwide, the average credit card debt among indebted households in the United States is $15,263. The average mortgage debt is $147,591, the average outstanding student loan balance is $31,646, and the average auto loan debt is $30,738. Meanwhile, a mere 59 percent of Americans possess at least $500 in savings.[1] Wouldn't it be amazing if there were a day when all of those debts would be canceled and our slates wiped clean?

Interestingly, in Leviticus 25:8-13 the Lord told the Hebrews that every fiftieth year, on the tenth day of the seventh month, all enslaved debtors would be released and all family property would be returned to the original owners. This was called the year of Jubilee, and the Lord determined it would happen on the sixth Feast of the Lord: the Day of Atonement, or Yom Kippur. This was an incredibly solemn, holy convocation and became known as "the Fast" (see Acts 27:9). In Leviticus 23:27-32, we see just how serious God takes this feast:

> On exactly the tenth day of this seventh month is the day of atonement; it shall be a holy convocation for you, and you shall humble your souls and present an offering by fire to the Lord. You shall not do any work on this same day, for it is a

> *day of atonement, to make atonement on your behalf before*
> *the Lord your God. If there is any person who will not humble*
> *himself on this same day, he shall be cut off from his people. As*
> *for any person who does any work on this same day, that per-*
> *son I will destroy from among his people. You shall do no work*
> *at all. It is to be a perpetual statute throughout your genera-*
> *tions in all your dwelling places. It is to be a sabbath of com-*
> *plete rest to you, and you shall humble your souls; on the ninth*
> *of the month at evening, from evening until evening you shall*
> *keep your Sabbath.*

The Lord means business about this feast day. He says that any of His people who refuse to humble themselves will be cut off from the people of God. There are many things about Yom Kippur that can help us understand who Jesus is, what He has done, and what He will do soon. So let's start digging.

In Leviticus 16, the Lord gives instructions to Moses on how the high priest was to perform his duties on the Day of Atonement. Interestingly, judging by its actual length, chapter 16 falls in the center of Leviticus, which itself is the middle book of the Pentateuch, the first five books of the Bible. God's decision to place these instructions in this spot emphasizes the importance of the activities that occurred on this feast day.

The first thing we glean from Leviticus 16 is the reason why Yom Kippur was instituted. The main purposes of this feast were: (1) to atone for and cleanse the sins of the priests and the people of Israel, (2) to cleanse the sanctuary from the pollution those sins caused, and (3) to release the scapegoat to Azazel so the liability for those sins would be removed from the community. The Day of Atonement thus gives us a sober look at the way sin affects us, our communities, and our relationship with the Lord God.

J.E. Hartley writes, "In seeking to understand these achievements, it is important to be aware of the multiple consequences that result from a sin. In committing a sin, a person harms the one sinned against and simultaneously commits an offense against God. In addition, every act of sinning releases a pollution. In ancient Israel the penetrating force of that pollution into the tabernacle depended on the standing of the one who had sinned and on the character of the sin. . . . Pollution released by blatant sins entered the holy of holies. In addition, committing a sin unleashed a negative power that strengthened the force of evil in the community."[2]

The instructions carried out on the Day of Atonement ensured the pollution caused by the people's sins during the past year would be cleansed and they would remain in relationship with God for another year. The main player on this day was the high priest, who entered the holy place of the temple with a bull for a sin offering and a goat for a burnt offering. The high priest did not wear his customary attire but rather a simple white linen garment as a sign of his humility and weakness before the Lord. Instead of merely washing his hands and feet, as was customary when he served at the altar, he completely immersed himself in water before beginning his ministry of atonement.

The high priest would then offer the young bull as a sin offering to atone for himself and his family. Next he would take two unblemished male goats to the doorway of the tent of meeting to present before the Lord. The high priest would cast lots for the two goats. One goat would be for the Lord and one would be for Azazel, with this second goat sometimes referred to as the "scapegoat." The goat whose lot fell for the Lord was offered as a sin offering.

The high priest sacrificed both the bull and the goat on the main altar. He then took the blood of each animal into the holy of holies, the innermost room of the temple where God manifested His presence. The high priest sprinkled the blood of each animal onto the mercy seat, or atonement slate, which covered the ark of the covenant. God would appear in a glory cloud on top of the atonement slate of the ark.

The atonement slate was an object made of gold that was placed on top of the ark and served as the base for the cherubim. Hartley writes, "Its primary purpose was to function as the place where Israel could find full expiation from her sins in order to keep in force her covenant relationship with the holy God."[3] The high priest would be reminded of the costly nature of a covenantal relationship with Almighty God as he sprinkled the blood of the sin offering on the ark and atonement slate. As the Lord says in Leviticus 17:11, "*It is the blood by reason of the life that makes atonement.*" Without the shedding of blood, there is no atonement.

The goat whose lot fell to Azazel was presented alive before the Lord to make atonement upon it. After the high priest symbolically placed all the sins of the people on its head, he sent it out into the wilderness to Azazel. So, what's going on with the Azazel stuff? Most of the English translations don't even use the word, preferring to say "scapegoat" instead, but "Azazel" is right there in the Hebrew. Even the King James Version doesn't stay true to the original text, though the *New Revised Standard Version* does a great job with the translation.

To determine who or what is Azazel, we must look to the book of 1 Enoch, a Dead Sea Scroll text we've already cited. This book is mentioned in both 2 Peter and Jude, and the early Christians quoted from it as well. Previously, I discussed how Genesis 6 shows many rebellious angels leaving their habitation to procreate with human women. According to 1 Enoch, Azazel was one of those fallen angels. "Azazel taught men to make swords, and knives, and shields, and breastplates . . . and the beautifying of the eyelids, and all kinds of costly stones, and all colouring tinctures" (1 Enoch 8:1).[4]

Azazel was a powerful fallen angel who taught mankind how to wage war against itself and trained women in the art of seduction. He was a master at manipulating humans to break the sixth and seventh commandments and thus defile the image of God in humanity. However, in 2 Peter 2:4 we read that these original fallen angels who chose to procreate with women are bound. Peter writes, "*God did not spare angels when they sinned, but cast them into hell and committed them to pits of darkness, reserved for judgment.*"

Unfortunately, most versions of the Bible translate the word "hell" incorrectly in this passage. The Greek word is *tartaros*, which, according to the early Christians and secular Greek literature, was the lowest region of Hades, the place of the dead. The word properly translated as "hell," *gehenna* (also known as the lake of fire), is not found in 2 Peter 2:4. Not one of the early Christians translated all three words *hades, gehenna,* and *tartaros* as hell. Those disciples understood them to be what they actually were: three separate places.[5]

A bit later, I will address why God commanded the Hebrews to send the live goat out to Azazel given the fact he was cast into the miry pit of *tartaros* before the Great Flood. For now, let's examine how the Day of Atonement points us to Jesus, beginning with Hebrews 10:1-7. In this passage, the writer doesn't mince words in stating this great feast day was severely lacking without the fullness of Christ:

> *The Law . . . can never, by the same sacrifices which they offer continually year by year, make perfect those who draw near. Otherwise, would they not have ceased to be offered, because the worshipers, having once been cleansed, would no longer have had consciousness of sins? But in those sacrifices there is a reminder of sins year by year. For it is impossible for the blood of bulls and goats to take away sins. Therefore, when He comes into the world, He says, "*SACRIFICE AND OFFERING*

You have not desired, but a body You have prepared for Me; in whole burnt offerings and sacrifices for sin You have taken no pleasure. Then I said, 'Behold, I have come (In the scroll of the book it is written of Me) to do Your will, O God.'"

As mentioned previously, before the high priest served in his atoning ministry on Yom Kippur, he humbled himself and completely immersed himself in water. Similarly, before Jesus, our *"great high priest"* (4:14), began His public ministry, He humbled Himself and chose to be baptized by His cousin, John, even though He was without sin. I was always taught the only reason Jesus chose to be baptized was to validate John as being the forerunner to the Messiah. However, when Jesus told John it was necessary for Him to be baptized in order to fulfill all righteousness (see Matthew 3:15), part of that righteous action was to identify Himself as the true high priest of Yom Kippur.

As the writer of Hebrews states, *"This hope we have as an anchor of the soul, a hope both sure and steadfast and one which enters within the veil, where Jesus has entered as a forerunner for us, having become a high priest forever according to the order of Melchizedek. For this Melchizedek . . . was first of all, by the translation of his name, king of righteousness, and then also king of Salem, which is king of peace"* (6:19–7:2). Like Aaron, the high priest during the first Yom Kippur, Jesus enters within the veil for us as our true high priest. However, unlike Aaron, Jesus remains our high priest of righteousness forever.

In John 2, Jesus said something about Himself and a part of the temple that the people didn't understand at the time. After He cleansed the temple of the moneychangers on Passover, fulfilling Jeremiah 7:1-11 and Psalm 69:9, the Jews asked, *"What sign do You show us as your authority for doing these things?"* Jesus replied, *"Destroy this temple, and in three days I will raise it up."* John writes, *"But He was speaking of the temple of His body. So when He was raised from the dead, His disciples remembered that He said this; and they believed the Scripture and the word which Jesus had spoken"* (verses 18-19, 21-22).

What is fascinating is the Greek word John uses to indicate what part of the temple Jesus equates with His body. The normal Greek word used to describe the entire temple structure is *hieron*, which is where John says this scene took place. However, when John quotes Jesus speaking about the temple of his body, he uses the word *naos*.[6] This refers to the sanctuary of the temple, but more specifically the holy place and holy of holies, where only the high priest was able to enter once a year on the Day of Atonement.

The word *naos* shows up again in 1 Corinthians 3:16-17, where Paul writes, *"Do you not know that you are a temple of God and that the Spirit of God dwells in you? If any man destroys the temple of God, God will destroy him, for the temple of God is holy, and that is what you are."* In Texan lingo, Paul is basically saying, "Don't y'all Jesus followers know that y'all are collectively the holy of holies where the Spirit of God dwells?" Paul goes on to say that if anyone destroys a member of God's temple, God will destroy that person. If Tom Horn is right in his book *Blood on the Altar* that a massive war is coming between Christians, we need to take a long, serious, and sober look at Paul's words before doing anything we will eternally regret.

Paul uses *naos* again in 1 Corinthians 6:19-20 when he tells the believers, *"Do you not know that your body is a temple of the Holy Spirit who is in you, whom you have from God, and that you are not your own? For you have been bought with a price: therefore glorify God in your body."* Paul says we are able to become the *naos* of the Holy Spirit because we were bought with a price. Peter explains how this price was paid: *"You were not redeemed with perishable things like silver or gold from your futile way of life inherited from your forefathers, but with precious blood, as of a lamb unblemished and spotless, the blood of Christ"* (1 Peter 1:18-19).

Paul continues this theme in 2 Corinthians 5:20-21 when he writes, *"Therefore, we are ambassadors for Christ, as though God were making an appeal through us; we beg you on behalf of Christ, be reconciled to God. He made Him who knew no sin to be sin on our behalf, so that we might become the righteousness of God in Him."* Jesus Christ is the true sin offering goat of Yom Kippur. He is the unblemished goat that was slain so atonement could be made for the people's sins. His blood was taken into the true holy of holies and sprinkled on the true atonement slate. As the writer of Hebrews articulates:

> For Christ did not enter a holy place made with hands, a mere copy of the true one, but into heaven itself, now to appear in the presence of God for us; nor was it that He would offer Himself often, as the high priest enters the holy place year by year with blood that is not his own. Otherwise, He would have needed to suffer often since the foundation of the world; but

> *now once at the consummation of the ages He has been mani-*
> *fested to put away sin by the sacrifice of Himself* (9:24-26).

Not only is Jesus Christ the true high priest, the true *naos*, and the true sin offering goat, but He is also the true atonement slate. The writer of Hebrews states that in the holy of holies there was *"a golden altar of incense and the ark of the covenant covered on all sides with gold, in which was a golden jar holding the manna, and Aaron's rod which budded, and the tables of the covenant; and above it were the cherubim of glory overshadowing the mercy seat"* (9:4-5). The Greek word translated as "mercy seat" is *hilasterion,* a derivative of *hilaskomai*.[7]

There are two Scriptures that shed light on how the mercy seat is fulfilled in Jesus. As you read these, remember the atonement slate (*hilasterion*) is the place where God intersects humanity to bring them back in relationship with Him. The first Scripture is Romans 3:23-25, where Paul writes, *"For all have sinned and fall short of the glory of God, being justified as a gift by His grace through the redemption which is in Christ Jesus; whom God displayed publicly as a propitiation in His blood through faith."* The word "propitiation" in Greek is *hilasterion.* So, Paul is saying when Jesus was crucified, God displayed Him as a *public* atonement slate for *all to see.* Why would God do this with His true Mercy Seat, when previously only the high priest was able to see the mercy seat in the holy of holies once each year?

The second Scripture answers that question. In 1 John 2:1-2, the apostle writes, *"If anyone sins, we have an Advocate with the Father, Jesus Christ the righteous; and He Himself is the propitiation for our sins; and not for ours only, but also for those of the whole world."* Once again, the word translated "propitiation" in the Greek is *hilasmos,* a derivative of *hilaskomai.* It makes sense God would put His true Atonement Slate on public display outside the city gate, because Jesus came to be the atoning sacrifice for the whole world, not just a select few.

It's not too difficult to see the connection between Jesus and the sin offering goat, but what about the scapegoat for Azazel? Why did God command the Hebrews to send the goat out to Azazel if he was in the pit of *tartaros*? The book of 1 Enoch indicates that Azazel was one of the worst of the fallen angels who cohabitated with women. From Leviticus 16, we see the sin of all the people was laid on the head of the goat destined for him. Thus, it is quite possible Azazel is representative of the original fallen one, the prince of darkness, who brought rebellion and sin into the universe. If this is the case, every year on the Day of Atonement, God was sending a prophetic reminder to Satan of what was coming his way. Like a Bugs Bunny cartoon when Elmer Fudd lobs a grenade at Bugs, only to see that waskaly wabbit toss it right back, Satan's attempt to destroy the world and the Messiah will only bring about his ultimate destruction.

In 1 Peter 3:18-20, we see how Jesus was a type of both the sin offering goat and the scapegoat for Azazel: "*Christ also died for sins once for all, the just for the unjust, so that He might bring us to God, having been put to death in the flesh, but made alive in the spirit; in which also He went and made proclamation to the spirits now in prison, who once were disobedient, when the patience of God kept waiting in the days of Noah.*" The sinless Lamb of God was first crucified as a sin offering and then became the scapegoat to proclaim to the rebellious spirits in dark prisons how the law of sin had been triumphed through His death.

Remember that God told the people, "*If there is any person who will not humble himself on this same day, he shall be cut off from his people*" (Leviticus 23:29). According to Doug Hamp, even before Jesus walked the earth, the Jews interpreted this period of humbling to begin immediately after the Feast of Trumpets. "According to Jewish custom, three books are opened on the Feast of Trumpets: the Book of Life for the righteous, the Book of Life for the unrighteous, and the Book of Life for those in-between. If a man is deemed righteous, his name is written in the Book of Life for the righteous at the feast of Trumpets. If a man is unrighteous, his name is written in the Book of Life for the unrighteous, and he will not survive the year."[8]

Hamp notes that if a person is deemed in-between, "judgment is delayed for ten days from the Feast of Trumpets to the Feast of the Day of Atonement. It is during that period of time that a man is given the opportunity to repent before the book is closed and his destiny sealed. Thus, most likely at the Feast of Trumpets, the Church will be raptured and the Lord's wrath will begin. . . . It will occupy a relatively brief period of time."[9]

There are 10 days from the Feast of Trumpets to the Feast of the Day of Atonement, called the "days of awe," when all God's people are to humble themselves with prayer, fasting, and repentance. It was in the fall of 2013 that I began to realize the Feasts of the Lord are for Christians, and between the Feast of Trumpets and Yom Kippur I was doing some self-reflection and prayer. Late one night during those 10 days, the Holy Spirit began to convict me of root-issue sins that had been wreaking havoc in my spiritual life.

The Lord showed me that I had been using the Gospel to avoid Jesus and the Gospel. It was almost as if I was studying the Bible in order to win some kind of Christian Trivial Pursuit game instead of using the Bible as a tool in the pursuit of Christ. I began to feel the incredible weight of my hypocrisy and pride as God revealed His purity over me. I was overwhelmed. I felt Jesus saying to me, "What would happen if you died in such a hypocritical state? Do you remember all I've said about hypocrisy? But, Phil, I'm not here to kill you. I'm here to help you. Why are you running from your Helper?"

Godly sorrow flooded my soul, and I began to weep and apologize. Then, in something like a massive computer download, God revealed a detailed outline for this book. It was around 11:30 PM, and for the next 45 minutes God showed me how to apply the central verse for this book, Matthew 9:17, to each of the three sections. I've never experienced anything like it before, and I truly believe a large part of the Lord God pouring out His blessings in that way was tied to me beginning to act in faith concerning the observance of His feast days.

Getting back to how Yom Kippur points us to Jesus, I believe that the rapture of the Church will occur on the Feast of Trumpets, which then ushers in the time of God pouring out His bowls of wrath on the earth. In my opinion, this is what Jeremiah refers to as the "time of Jacob's Trouble" (see 30:4-7, 11). When the Lord gathers His Church at Yom Teruah, this will be a period of such great distress that there will not be a time like it. God says that during this time, while He is destroying the other nations, He will be chastening and disciplining the Hebrews. However, at the end of that time, the Lord will save them. So, what will the time of Jacob's Trouble look like?

We established in the last chapter that the Antichrist is already on the scene, causing all people to take his mark or pay the ultimate price. Revelation 16 describes the seven bowls of God's wrath, which are poured out on the earth after the rapture of the Church. With the first bowl, loathsome, malignant sores are given to all people everywhere possessing the mark of the beast. The second bowl causes all the ocean waters on earth to be turned to blood, causing every living thing in the oceans to die.

At the third bowl, all of the fresh waters are also turned to blood. The fourth bowl brings a scorching heat and fire so fierce that people blaspheme God who had power over these plagues, and refuse to repent and give Him glory. With the fifth bowl, the kingdom of the beast is thrust into darkness, and people gnaw at their tongues due to their pains and sores; yet, they still won't repent.

When the sixth bowl is poured out, the river Euphrates is dried up to prepare the way for the kings from the east. Continuing his description of the sixth bowl, John writes in Revelation 16:13-16, *"I saw coming out of the mouth of the dragon and out of the mouth of the beast and out of the mouth of the false prophet, three unclean spirits like frogs; for they are spirits of demons, performing signs, which go out to the kings of the whole world, to gather them together for the war of the great day of God, the Almighty. ('Behold, I am coming like a thief. Blessed is the one who stays awake and keeps his clothes, so that he will not walk about naked and men will not see his shame.') And they gathered them together to the place which in Hebrew is called Har-Magedon."*

Doug Hamp belives the battle of Armageddon will most likely take place in the Valley of Jehoshaphat, located between the temple mount and the Mount of Olives, not at Megiddo.[10] Jehoshaphat means "Yahweh judges," so the Valley of Jehoshaphat is where Yahweh will pour out His judgment. The Scriptures testify this great battle of the Lord will be fought just outside of the city of Jerusalem, with the armies of the Antichrist surrounding a remnant of Hebrews within Jerusalem. In Joel 3, God says to His people:

> *Behold, in those days and at that time, when I restore the fortunes of Judah and Jerusalem, I will gather all the nations and bring them down to the valley of Jehoshaphat. Then I will enter into judgment with them there on behalf of My people and My inheritance, Israel, whom they have scattered among the nations; and they have divided up My land. . . . Let the nations be aroused and come up to the valley of Jehoshaphat, for there I will sit to judge all the surrounding nations. . . . Put in the sickle, for the harvest is ripe. Come, tread, for the wine press is full; the vats overflow, for their wickedness is great. Multitudes, multitudes in the valley of decision! For the day of the LORD IS NEAR IN THE VALLEY OF DECISION. The sun and moon grow dark and the stars lose their brightness. The LORD ROARS FROM ZION and utters His voice from Jerusalem, and the heavens and the earth tremble. But the LORD IS A REFUGE FOR HIS PEOPLE and a stronghold to the sons of Israel* (verses 1-2, 12-16).

In the last chapter, we discussed how John said the great multitudes of rebellious people would be tread like grapes in God's winepress: *"So the angel swung his sickle to the earth and gathered the clusters from the vine of the earth, and threw them into the great wine press of the wrath of God. And the wine press was trodden outside the city"* (Revelation 14:19-20). The great treading of the grapes of wrath takes place just outside the city, just outside Jerusalem. This is fitting, since Jesus's own blood was shed just outside the city as well.

In Zechariah 12, God states, *"I am going to make Jerusalem a cup that causes reeling to all the peoples around; and when the siege is against Jerusalem, it will also be against Judah. It will come about in that day that I will make Jerusalem a heavy stone for all the peoples; all who lift it will be severely injured. And all the nations of the earth will be gathered against it. . . . I will pour out on the house of David and on the inhabitants of Jerusalem, the Spirit of grace and of supplication, so that they will look on Me whom they have pierced; and they will mourn for Him, as one mourns for an only son, and they will weep bitterly over Him like the bitter weeping over a firstborn. In that day there will be great mourning in Jerusalem, like the mourning of Hadadrimmon in the plain of Megiddo"* (verses 2-3, 10-11). Zechariah also writes:

The LORD . . . WILL GATHER ALL THE NATIONS AGAINST JERUSALEM TO BATTLE, AND THE CITY WILL BE CAPTURED, THE HOUSES PLUNDERED, THE WOMEN RAVISHED AND HALF OF THE CITY EXILED, BUT THE REST OF THE PEOPLE WILL NOT BE CUT OFF FROM THE CITY. THEN THE LORD WILL GO FORTH AND FIGHT AGAINST THOSE NATIONS, AS WHEN HE FIGHTS ON A DAY OF BATTLE. IN THAT DAY HIS FEET WILL STAND ON THE MOUNT OF OLIVES, WHICH IS IN FRONT OF JERUSALEM ON THE EAST; AND THE MOUNT OF OLIVES WILL BE SPLIT IN ITS MIDDLE FROM EAST TO WEST BY A VERY LARGE VALLEY, SO THAT HALF OF THE MOUNTAIN WILL MOVE TOWARD THE NORTH AND THE OTHER HALF TOWARD THE SOUTH. YOU WILL FLEE BY THE VALLEY OF MY MOUNTAINS, FOR THE VALLEY OF THE MOUNTAINS WILL REACH TO AZEL; YES, YOU WILL FLEE JUST AS YOU FLED BEFORE THE EARTHQUAKE IN THE DAYS OF UZZIAH KING OF JUDAH. THEN THE LORD, MY GOD, WILL COME, AND ALL THE HOLY ONES WITH HIM! IN THAT DAY THERE WILL BE NO LIGHT; THE LUMINARIES WILL DWINDLE. FOR IT WILL BE A UNIQUE DAY WHICH IS KNOWN TO THE LORD, NEITHER DAY NOR NIGHT, BUT IT WILL COME ABOUT THAT AT EVENING TIME THERE WILL BE LIGHT (14:1-7).

In Revelation 19, John tells us that though the Antichrist and the armies of the world have gathered to make war against God, He will have no problem defeating them. "*The beast was seized, and with him the false prophet who performed the signs in his presence, by which he deceived those who had received the mark of the beast and those who worshiped his image; these two were thrown alive into the lake of fire which burns with brimstone. And the rest were killed with the sword which came from the mouth of Him who sat on the horse, and all the birds were filled with their flesh*" (verses 20-21).

In Jeremiah 30, God promised He would save the Hebrews after the chastening they receive during the time of Jacob's Trouble. In Zechariah 13:8-9, the prophet also speaks of God's gracious and atoning future actions for the Jewish people. Paul ties these passages together in Romans 11:25-28 when he alludes to this final ingathering of the Hebrews: "*For I do not want you, brethren, to be uninformed . . . that a partial hardening has happened to Israel until the fullness of the Gentiles has come in; and so all Israel will be saved; just as it is written, 'THE DELIVERER WILL COME FROM ZION, HE WILL REMOVE UNGODLINESS FROM JACOB.' 'THIS IS MY COVENANT WITH THEM, WHEN I TAKE AWAY THEIR SINS.'*"

It makes sense that if Jesus returns on the Feast of Trumpets to gather His Church to Himself, He would deliver the remaining faithful Hebrews at the end of the time of Jacob's Trouble on the Day of Atonement. What incredible rejoicing will break out among the Hebrews on that day when spiritual debts are canceled, darkness is conquered, and they cry out, "Blessed is He who comes in the name of the Lord! Blessed is Jesus the Messiah! Blessed is the Lord of Yom Kippur!" It will truly be a day of Jubilee!

So may you delight in the Lord of Yom Kippur, Jesus Christ our high priest. And may you be God's chosen, royal, holy priest in the world so everyone you minister to will glorify Him in the day of His visitation!

Chapter 19

EVERYBODY LOVES A WEDDING

Probably the worst day in Houston professional football history was the day former Oilers owner Bud Adams announced he had decided to move the team to Nashville, Tennessee. Conversely, I remember the sheer jubilation felt all over town when Bob McNair brought professional football back to Houston. They say football is king in Texas, and for a lot of people that may be true. As I write these words, the Houston Texans are in training camp, and I find myself checking their website almost daily for updates on the team's progress.

Something is seriously wrong with me. If I'm honest, I spend more time each day excited about the start of the football season than I do about the fact God wants to dwell with me. I wonder what would happen if I focused my mind on the truth that one day I will be with God face to face to the degree I dwell on a mediocre football team like the Texans. What have the Texans ever done for me anyway? They certainly didn't go through unimaginable torture for six hours on a cross to ransom me out of the domain of darkness. Jesus did, and He is what the Feast of Tabernacles is all about.

The Feast of Tabernacles is the last and greatest of the seven Feasts of the Lord. Like the Day of Atonement was called "the Fast," the Feast of Tabernacles was called "the Feast" (see John 7:37). In Leviticus 23:34-36, 44, God describes it this way:

> *On the fifteenth of this seventh month is the Feast of Booths for seven days to the LORD. ON THE FIRST DAY IS A HOLY CONVOCATION; YOU SHALL DO NO LABORIOUS WORK OF ANY KIND. FOR SEVEN DAYS YOU SHALL PRESENT AN OFFERING BY FIRE TO THE LORD. ON THE EIGHTH DAY YOU SHALL HAVE A HOLY CONVOCATION AND PRESENT AN OFFERING BY FIRE TO THE LORD. . . . NOW ON THE FIRST DAY YOU SHALL TAKE FOR YOURSELVES THE FOLIAGE OF BEAUTIFUL TREES, PALM BRANCHES AND BOUGHS OF LEAFY TREES AND*

WILLOWS OF THE BROOK, AND YOU SHALL REJOICE BEFORE
THE LORD YOUR GOD FOR SEVEN DAYS. YOU SHALL THUS
CELEBRATE IT AS A FEAST TO THE LORD FOR SEVEN DAYS IN
THE YEAR. IT SHALL BE A PERPETUAL STATUTE THROUGHOUT
YOUR GENERATIONS; YOU SHALL CELEBRATE IT IN THE SEV-
ENTH MONTH. YOU SHALL LIVE IN BOOTHS FOR SEVEN DAYS;
ALL THE NATIVE-BORN IN ISRAEL SHALL LIVE IN BOOTHS, SO
that your generations may know that I had the sons of Israel
live in booths when I brought them out from the land of Egypt.

The Feast of Tabernacles was also known as the Feast of Booths, or Suk-kot (see verse 34). The reason for the name is addressed in verses 42-43, where the Lord says He had the Israelites live in temporary shelters when they wandered in the wilderness for 40 years. These *sukkahs* were modest structures without fully covered roofs so the people could see the night sky and remember the Lord was their security, shelter, and peace.

The Feast of Tabernacles, like Passover and Pentecost, was one in which every male Hebrew had to come to Jerusalem. Another difference between Sukkot and the other feasts was that the Lord commanded His people to rejoice for the whole week! For the Hebrews, Sukkot looked forward to the day when the Messiah would gather together all of Abraham's true descen-dants in a revived Hebrew nation.[1] This promise was cause for rejoicing—and don't ever say God didn't like a party. God commanded His people to go camping with their families and celebrate for a week!

Ray Vander Laan writes, "For seven days, the people ate, lived, and slept in these booths. Since this was one of the three feasts in which everyone was commanded to come to Jerusalem (Passover and Shavuot are the others), thousands of people crowded the streets of the city, and there were *sukkot* everywhere. The children loved it, and so did the adults. It was a time to praise God for the past gifts of freedom, land, and bountiful harvests. . . . Truly the feast of Sukkot was one of great celebration. A rabbi once said, 'Whoever has not seen Sukkot has not witnessed real joy.'"[2]

The Feast of Tabernacles took place at the end of September or in early October, during the last part of the dry season in Israel. The Hebrews depended on the rains to come, so at some point, most likely during the second temple period, Sukkot began to take on a ceremony most likely based on Isaiah 12:2-3: "'*Behold, God is my salvation, I will trust and not be afraid;*

for the LORD GOD *is my strength and song, and He has become my salvation.'*
Therefore you will joyously draw water from the springs of salvation."

Vander Laan does a masterful job explaining the water libation ceremony:

> This part of the ceremony involved a procession of priests, accompanied by flutes, marching from the Temple to the Pool of Siloam, which was fed by the Spring of Gihon. One of the priests filled a golden pitcher (more than a quart) with water, and the procession returned to the Temple. . . . The priest carrying the pitcher entered the priests' court through the Water Gate and, to the blast of the shofar, approached the altar. He made one circle around the altar as the crowd sang the *Hallel.*
>
> Then the priest climbed the ramp and stood near the top of the altar. Here there were two silver funnels leading into the stone altar for the daily drink offerings. As the crowd grew silent, the priest solemnly poured the water into one of the funnels. Again the people, accompanied by the Levitical choir, began to chant the *Hallel.* The sound was deafening because of the thousands of pilgrims jammed into the Temple courts. In this way, they asked God for life-giving rain. The living water they used apparently acknowledged it was God who brought rain and life. The chant of the Hosanna— "O Lord, save us!"—now meant "Save us by sending rain as well."
>
> It seems hardly possible, but the celebration became even more intense as the week drew to a close. When the seventh day of the feast arrived, the courts of the Temple were packed with worshipers. Chants of praise were heard throughout the city, and thousands of *lulavim* waved in the air. . . .
>
> As hundreds of priests chanted the Hosanna ("Deliver us! Save us!") and thousands of people jammed into the Temple courts, the procession circled the altar seven times (remembering the walls of Jericho, which fell after seven circuits because of God's great power). Then there were three

blasts on the trumpets, and the crowd grew still as the priest poured the living water into the tunnel.

Now the chanting became even more intense: "Save us, hosanna! Help us, hosanna!" and the next verse: "Blessed is he who comes in the name of the LORD" (Psalm 118:26). The waving of the *lulavim* reached a frenzy as branches were beaten against the ground until the leaves fell off. . . . They had celebrated joyously His presence, thanking Him for His gift of land and the bountiful harvest.[3]

Let's examine how this last and greatest Feast of the Lord is fulfilled in Christ. We will begin with the easiest connection. In John 7, Jesus is in Jerusalem celebrating the Feast of Tabernacles, as He is supposed to do. On the last day of this greatest feast, most likely while the crowd is celebrating the living water God has brought them, Jesus stands and yells, "*If anyone is thirsty, let him come to Me and drink. He who believes in Me, as the Scripture said, 'From his innermost being will flow rivers of living water*" (verse 38). Jesus says He is the true water libation ceremony.

Remember the prophet's words in Isaiah 12:2-3? The word "salvation" in those verses is translated *yeshua* in Hebrew, which is Jesus's name.[4] So, when we look at this passage, we see an incredible picture of the Gospel in the water libation ceremony, especially when we consider John's words that the Holy Spirit is given to those who believe in Christ (see John 7:39). Basically, Isaiah's prophecy reads, "'Behold, God is my Jesus, I will trust and not be afraid; for Yahweh is my strength and my song, and He has become my Jesus.' Therefore you will joyously draw water (the Holy Spirit) from the springs of Jesus."

John connects Jesus to the Feast of Tabernacles more than just through the water libation ceremony. In fact, He begins His Gospel connecting those dots. In John 1:14 we read, "*And the Word became flesh, and dwelt among us, and we saw His glory, glory as of the only begotten from the Father, full of grace and truth.*" As previously mentioned, when John writes of the "Word," he is referring to Jesus. However, what I want to focus on is the word "dwelt" in this verse, which is *eskenosen* in Greek. This word means to tabernacle with someone and specifically refers to God tabernacling with mankind.[5] The event John is referencing here is Jesus's birth.

Although Christians generally celebrate Jesus' birth on December 25, the writers of Scripture left us proof that Jesus was born in the fall, most likely right around the Feast of Tabernacles. In Luke 1:5, we read that John the Baptist's father, Zacharias, was a priest "*of the division [or course] of Abijah.*" When David was king, he divided the priesthood into different courses, and the family of Abijah was in the eighth course (see 1 Chronicles 24:10).

Each of these courses served two weeks of the year. However, during Passover, Pentecost, and Sukkot, when everyone was required to come to Jerusalem, all the priests would serve together. The first feast, Passover, marked the beginning of the year for the Hebrews. Passover usually fell in our month of April (the Hebrew month of Aviv), and the first course of priests would serve on the first week of that month. The second course would follow the second week. The Feast of Unleavened Bread fell on the third week, and all the priests served together that week. So, the third course of priests ministered on the fourth week of the year.

Zacharias's division would have ministered during the eighth week, but the next week was the Feast of Pentecost, when all the priests ministered together. This is why Luke writes "*the whole multitude of the people were in prayer outside at the hour of the incense offering*" (1:10). The multitude was there because it was the Feast of Pentecost.

Next, Luke informs us that Elizabeth conceived soon after Zacharias finished his course, near the middle to end of June, and that she kept herself in seclusion for five months (see verse 24). If you count five months from the middle to end of June, you reach the middle to end of November. Luke reports it was in Elizabeth's sixth month, which would have been sometime in the middle to end of December, that Mary conceived (see verses 26-42). If Mary conceived at this point in December, a 40-week pregnancy would mean Jesus was born in the latter part of September or early October.[6]

The Feast of Tabernacles always occurs during the last few weeks of September to the first few weeks of October. It's never earlier, and never later. Our God is a God of order, so it makes perfect sense He would choose to have His Son tabernacle with us on the Feast of Tabernacles.[7] I would therefore encourage you to pray earnestly about when and how you celebrate the Messiah's birth, since the Scriptures prove to us when Jesus was born.

John also connects Jesus with the Feast of Tabernacles in the book of Revelation. In Revelation 21:3, John tells us that when the new Jerusalem, the bride of Christ, comes down at the Millennium, "*The tabernacle of God is among men, and He will dwell among them.*" The Greek words used for "tabernacle" and "dwell" are *skene* and *skenosei*, respectively. John then writes, "*I saw no temple in it, for the Lord God the Almighty and the Lamb are its temple"* (verse 22). Here, the Greek word for "temple" is *naos*, which means the holy of holies in the tabernacle. In the millennial reign of the Messiah, Jesus tabernacles with His people, and He is the tabernacle of His people. His people need neither the light of the sun, moon, nor a lamp, because He is the shekinah glory of God (see verse 23).

If John stopped here, things would be quite comfortable. However, after stating Jesus is the lamp of the city, he writes, *"The nations will walk by its light, and the kings of the earth will bring their glory into it. In the daytime (for there will be no night there) its gates will never be closed; and they will bring the glory and the honor of the nations into it; and nothing unclean, and no one who practices abomination and lying, shall ever come into it, but only those whose names are written in the Lamb's book of life"* (verses 24-27).

For a long time I had a difficult time reconciling these verses. What does it mean that the kings of the earth will bring their glory into the city? When we left off in the last chapter, we saw the earth laid waste on the future Day of the Atonement, the kings and their armies destroyed at the battle of Armageddon, and the Antichrist and the false prophet thrown into the lake of fire. However, the Scriptures do not say *everyone* on earth came to the battle of Armageddon to fight against God. So, what happened to all the people who didn't choose to fight in the battle? The Bible has an answer, and it involves Sukkot, the Feast of Booths.

In Zechariah 14, the prophet states that after the great battle of God, *"It will come about that any who are left of all the nations that went against Jerusalem will go up from year to year to worship the King, the Lord of hosts, and to celebrate the Feast of Booths. And it will be that whichever of the families of the earth does not go up to Jerusalem to worship the King, the Lord of hosts, there will be no rain on them. If the family of Egypt does not go up or enter, then no rain will fall on them; it will be the plague with which the Lord smites the nations who do not go up to celebrate the Feast of Booths. This will be the punishment of Egypt, and the punishment of all the nations who do not go up to celebrate the Feast of Booths"* (verses 16-19).

I believe this pasage shows the millennial reign of Christ will begin after the great battle of God Almighty. The earth, which had been demolished during the Great Tribulation, will, in a way, be cleansed and purified through fire and transformed into a new earth. *"There will no longer be a curse"* (verse 11), and Satan will be bound and thrown into the abyss until the end of Christ's millennial reign (see Revelation 20:1-3). During this time, those who are not citizens of the new Jerusalem will be required to celebrate the Feast of Booths every year.[8]

Remember, the Feast of Booths is the Feast of Tabernacles. So, one question we need to answer is why Sukkot will still be celebrated if Jesus is now ruling His kingdom. Part of the answer, I believe, concerns Satan's fate following the great battle. Remember that Sukkot was originally about dwelling forever with God, and it was a great time of celebration. During the 1,000-year reign of Christ, when Satan is bound in the Abyss, he is not allowed to tempt or deceive anyone living on earth. Everything seems perfect, but then things take a drastic turn.

In Revelation 20:7-9, we read, "*When the thousand years are completed, Satan will be released from his prison, and will come out to deceive the nations, which are in the four corners of the earth, Gog and Magog, to gather them together for the war; the number of them is like the sand of the seashore. And they came up on the broad plain of the earth and surrounded the camp of the saints and the beloved city.*" Countless hoards of people who have been experiencing heaven on earth now turn against God and surround the New Jerusalem, with Satan himself leading the way. So, how does this relate to Sukkot? Remember that God commanded the people living outside the new Jerusalem to keep His feast every year. An amazing miracle happened on the Feast of Tabernacles when Solomon dedicated the newly-built Temple to Yahweh.

Ray Vander Laan writes, "For seven days, the nation of Israel celebrated and rejoiced because God had chosen to live among them. The ark, the resting place of God's glorious presence, was moved into the Temple, God's earthly home, in a spectacular display of His glory (2 Chronicles 5:13-14). After the people said an impassioned prayer for God's presence (2 Chronicles 6), God sent fire from heaven to consume the sacrifices, a stunning display of His power and love (2 Chronicles 7:1-3). On the day the Temple was dedicated, Solomon and the people offered more than 140,000 sacrifices, a measure of their joy. Afterward, everyone went home filled with happiness (2 Chronicles 7:10)."[9]

In Solomon's day, as the people were praying on this great Sukkot, God sent fire from heaven as a sign of His presence among them. After the Millennium, when Satan surrounds the camp of God's people, the same thing happens. "*They came up on the broad plain of the earth and surrounded the camp of the saints and the beloved city, and fire came down from heaven and devoured them. And the devil who deceived them was thrown into the lake of fire and brimstone, where the beast and the false prophet are also*" (Revelation 20:9-10). During this final Sukkot, fire comes down from heaven, answering the prayers of God's people.

John writes in Revelation that there will be a resurrection of God's people just before the millennial reign of Christ begins (see 20:4-6). Many scholars believe the great sheep and goats judgment of Matthew 25, which I referenced in chapter 12, will take place at this time. In 2 Corinthians 5:10, Paul also attests to the judgment Christians will undergo: *"For we must all appear before the judgment seat of Christ, so that each one may be recompensed for his deeds in the body, according to what he has done, whether good or bad."*

The rest of the dead receive their judgment after Satan is thrown into the lake of fire. John writes, *"I saw the dead, the great and the small, standing before the throne, and books were opened; and another book was opened, which is the book of life; and the dead were judged from the things which were written in the books, according to their deeds. And the sea gave up the dead which were in it, and death and Hades gave up the dead which were in them; and they were judged, every one of them according to their deeds. Then death and Hades were thrown into the lake of fire. This is the second death, the lake of fire. And if anyone's name was not found written in the book of life, he was thrown into the lake of fire"* (Revelation 20:12-15).

Satan has been defeated, but that isn't the last enemy of God and His people. Now, during this final judgment, even Hades and death are thrown into the lake of fire (see verse 14). Now, there is nothing left to oppose God and His people. The apostle Paul joins John as they testify to this truth: *"For He must reign until He has put all His enemies under His feet. The last enemy that will be abolished is death"* (1 Corinthians 15:25-26).

Finally, God and His people can be at complete and perfect rest with each other. Perhaps that's why Sukkot is an eight-day feast that begins and ends on a Sabbath. Though the Sabbath isn't commonly known as one of the seven feasts, God tells Moses in Leviticus 23:2-3 that it is a Feast of the Lord: *"My appointed times are these: 'For six days work may be done, but on the seventh day there is a sabbath of complete rest, a holy convocation. You shall not do any work; it is a sabbath to the Lord in all your dwellings.'"* In fact, Sabbath seems to be a significant feast, since God commands it to be celebrated each week and not just once a year. God took this Sabbath day seriously: *"On the seventh day you shall have a holy day, a sabbath of complete rest to the Lord; whoever does any work on it shall be put to death"* (Exodus 35:2).

So, what was God's purpose in instituting the Sabbath? From Exodus 20:11, we know that *"in six days the Lord made the heavens and the earth, the sea and all that is in them, and rested on the seventh day; therefore the Lord blessed the sabbath day and made it holy."* However, I believe the key to understanding the primary reason why God established the Sabbath is found in the words *"of the Lord"* in verse 10; or, as stated in Levicus and Exodus, *"to the Lord."* Of all the things the Sabbath is about, at its core it is not about a lack of work. There is something deeper going on as it relates to God's people intentionally engaging with Him.

In Exodus 31:13, God tells His people, *"You shall surely observe My sabbaths; for this is a sign between Me and you throughout your generations, that you may know that I am the Lord who sanctifies you."* Yahweh, the Lord, sets His people apart and purifies them for Himself. In Deuteronomy 5:15, God states that on the Sabbath, *"You shall remember that you were a slave in the land of Egypt, and the Lord your God brought you out of there by a mighty hand and by an outstretched arm; therefore the Lord your God commanded you to observe the sabbath day."*

As the Hebrews were resting from their labors, they were supposed to be engaging God and remembering how they were slaves in Egypt until He delivered them with a mighty hand and an outstretched arm. They were to remember He had brought them out of bondage to bring them to Himself and then to bring them with Him into the Promised Land (see Exodus 6:6-8). That's what the weekly Sabbath day rest was all about. As Ray Vander Laan notes, "In the Jewish mind, what God did on Mt. Sinai was a wedding. Was it a wedding? Well, there's an interesting promise in Exodus. He says . . . 'I will take you out from under the yoke of the Egyptians. I will set you free from being slaves to them. I will redeem you.' And then He says, 'I will take you to be my people.' Take you. That's the phrase that's used for marriage."[10]

I believe the major event that will kick off the millennial reign of Christ will be the great wedding supper of the Lamb, held on Sukkot. In Revelation 19:7-9, John writes, *"'Let us rejoice and be glad and give the glory to Him, for the marriage of the Lamb has come and His bride has made herself ready.' It was given to her to clothe herself in fine linen, bright and clean; for the fine linen is the righteous acts of the saints. Then he said to me, 'Write, "Blessed are those who are invited to the marriage supper of the Lamb."'"*[11]

The "bride" represents the saints of God. They are the people from before Jesus's incarnation who were true followers of Yahweh and the people since Jesus's incarnation who demonstrated they were true followers of Yahweh by following Jesus by grace through faith. As Paul wrote in Romans 11, the Gentiles did not *replace* believing Israel as God's treasured possession; rather, they have been *grafted* into believing Israel. After all, the entirety of Jesus's original disciples were Hebrews.

Have you ever noticed how many references there are in the Bible to our relationship with God being like that of an engagement or marriage? There are plenty. We've already discussed Ephesians 5, so let's look at four more passages:

> Thus says the LORD, "I remember concerning you the devotion of your youth, the love of your betrothals. . . . Have I been a wilderness to Israel, or a land of thick darkness? Why do My people say, 'We are free to roam; we will no longer come to You'? Can a virgin forget her ornaments, or a bride her attire? Yet My people have forgotten Me days without number" (Jeremiah 2:2, 31-32).

> Your husband is your Maker, whose name is the Lord of hosts; and your Redeemer is the Holy One of Israel, who is called the God of all the earth.[11] For the Lord has called you, like a wife forsaken and grieved in spirit, even like a wife of one's youth when she is rejected. . . . For a brief moment I forsook you, but with great compassion I will gather you (Isaiah 54:5-7).

> The kingdom of heaven may be compared to a king who gave a wedding feast for his son. And he sent out his slaves to call those who had been invited to the wedding feast, and they were unwilling to come. . . . He said to his slaves, "The wedding is ready, but those who were invited were not worthy. Go therefore to the main highways, and as many as you find there, invite to the wedding feast." Those slaves went out into the streets and gathered together all they found, both evil and good; and the wedding hall was filled with dinner guests (Matthew 22:2-3, 8-10).

> While the bridegroom is with them, the attendants of the bridegroom cannot fast, can they? So long as they have the bridegroom with them, they cannot fast. But the days will come when the bridegroom is taken away from them, and then they will fast in that day (Mark 2:19-20).

I recognize the concept that we become part of the bride of Christ can be more difficult for men to accept than women. Perhaps that's why Jesus followed up His parable about the bridegroom by saying, *"No one sews a patch of unshrunk cloth on an old garment; otherwise the patch pulls away from it, the new from the old, and a worse tear results. No one puts new wine into old wineskins; otherwise the wine will burst the skins, and the wine is lost and the skins as well; but one puts new wine into fresh wineskins"* (Mark 2:21-22).

If we are going to understand what it means to be in a relationship with Jesus, we have to give ourselves to Him like a bride without reservation. For better or worse. For richer or poorer. In sickness and in health. Forsaking all others. New wine must be poured into new wineskins. If we do that, we'll get to take part in the celebration of all celebrations—the wedding feast that will last 1,000 years and then into eternity.

With that said, I want you to consider what you would need in the new Jerusalem for it to be heaven on earth for you. What if you are able to take part in the new heavens and new earth, reigning with Christ, but then find that your favorite pet isn't there? I'm a dog lover, and the favorite dog I've ever owned was a schnauzer named Hazzard. He was incredibly smart, loyal, trainable, brave, sweet, funny, and lovable.

But Hazz was a handful. He tore up furniture, books, and was a constant source of frustration. One night, to deplete him of energy, I took him on a midnight jog around the block in my parents' neighborhood. As he and I were about to turn a corner and pass two minivans in a driveway, Hazz suddenly spun around and lunged at something coming at us in the darkness.

It was a Chow, a dog at least three times Hazzard's size. Hazz had seen it stalking us through the shadows and instinctively gone for its neck, which shocked the dog and sent it lurking back behind the minivans. From that moment on, I was sold. All of his past destructive actions didn't matter anymore, because that little dog had just laid down his life for me.

Fourteen years later, I cried so much the morning Stephanie and I had to put him to sleep. I prayed he would be part of the restoration of creation that Paul writes about in Romans 8:19-21. After all, Isaiah 65:25 speaks of wolves and lambs grazing together in the new earth God creates. Surely dogs will be there too, right? But what if your favorite pet isn't in the new Jerusalem? Would that ruin it for you?

What if you make it to the new Jerusalem and you experience everything you've ever dreamed of and more? Not only is Fluffy there, but y'all can talk back and forth like the animals in Narnia! Everything is just right. The people you want to see are there, and the people you don't want to see aren't. Everything is perfect. Everything, that is, except for one thing. Jesus isn't there. Would you be okay with that?

If we're honest, that one might be a hard pill to swallow. Just like some of us have gotten more wrapped up in the idea of getting married than actually learning to love the person we're getting married to, some of us have cherished the idea of going to heaven much more than learning to love the Lord of heaven and earth. But we are not supposed to view God as our divine benefactor. We are supposed to view Him as our divine bridegroom.

The ultimate reward of a wedding isn't the wedding presents. It isn't being the center of attention and having people clap for us and take our picture. It isn't the ability to change our social networking status to "married" so we can feel equal or superior to some of our peers. The ultimate reward of a wedding is receiving our spouse. To approach that day in any other way is to completely miss the point. In the same way, the ultimate reward of a Christian is neither heaven, the new Jerusalem, nor a glorified body. The ultimate reward is receiving Christ, our Bridegroom, in His fullness forever.

Like a foolish jerk pouring new wine into old wineskins, I missed the point of Christianity for years and hurt many people in the process. I made God a means to an end, rather than an end in Himself. Then, embittered by my unmet expectations, I found myself feeling justified in living like someone without a moral compass—yet grew angry when everyone else wasn't living like Christians. While I was frequently using Christian practices to soothe the pain and fill the emptiness I felt in my life, I did not seek God for who He is and obey Him out of love.

Larry Crabb nailed it when he wrote, "We have become committed to relieving the pain behind our problems rather than using our pain to wrestle more passionately with the character and purposes of God. Feeling better has become more important than finding God."[12] The more I sought to use God and others to alleviate my pain, the more empty and isolated I felt. In the mold of the Samaritan woman of John 4, I talked like a mature follower of God but sought my significance in things God created. I could talk like I had everything under control, but an unbiased look at my decision-making process showed I was a mess. I had a worship problem and didn't know it. In Jeremiah 2:13, the Lord stated my condition perfectly: *"For My people have committed two evils: They have forsaken Me, the fountain of living waters, to hew for themselves cisterns, broken cisterns that can hold no water."*

Do you feel that cosmic thirst? Have you experienced the blessing of an Ecclesiastes 1–2 moment? A moment when you're overcome with a feeling of dissatisfaction and you realize that nothing in this world, including football, will ever satisfy you? Writer and theologian C.S. Lewis once said, "If I find in myself a desire which nothing in this world can satisfy, the most probable explanation is that I was made for another world."[13]

But you weren't just made for another world. You were made for Jesus, and your soul has been trying to communicate that truth to you from your first breath. The psalmist writes in Psalm 42:1-2, "*As the deer pants for the water brooks, so my soul pants for You, O God. My soul thirsts for God, for the living God; when shall I come and appear before God?*" Perhaps that is the ultimate message of Sukkot.

Do you need to drink today from the living waters of Yeshua? If so, Jesus has an invitation for you: "*Let the one who is thirsty come; let the one who wishes take the water of life without cost. . . . He who testifies to these things says, 'Yes, I am coming quickly.' Amen. Come, Lord Jesus. The grace of the Lord Jesus be with all. Amen*" (Revelation 22:17, 20-21).

END NOTES

Introduction

1. Patricia S. and Gregory A. Kuhlman, "Stages of Marriage," Marriage Success Training, accessed February 24, 2015, http://www.stayhitched.com/stages.htm.

Chapter 1: Take Another Little Piece of My Heart, Lord Jesus

1. I dig into the connection of Jesus being one with the Lord God of the Old Testament in chapter 13.

2. *The Ante-Nicene Fathers*, vol. 1, 114 [CD-ROM] (Henderson, TX: Scroll Publishing).

3. R. Banks, "Fasting," cited in Joel Green, Scot McKnight, and I. Howard Marshall, eds., *Dictionary of Jesus and the Gospels* (Downers Grove, IL: InterVarsity Press, 1992), p. 233.

Chapter 2: Sepia Jesus

1. On a side note, I have tremendous respect for both Tim Keller and John Piper, and I certainly don't think either one of them would have any problem with me saying that they aren't greater than Jesus.

2. Martin Luther, "Preface to the New Testament 1545 1522," cited on Bible Explore, accessed February 24, 2015, http://www.godrules.net/library/luther/NEW1luther_f8.htm.

3. Martin Luther, cited in Raymond Taouk, "Luther, Exposing the Myth," accessed February 24, 2015, http://www.catholicapologetics.info/apologetics/protestantism/matluther.htm.

4. Blaise Pascal, *Pensées,* sec. xiv, "Appendix: Polemical Fragments," cited at Bartleby.com, accessed February 24, 2015, http://www.bartleby.com/48/1/14.html.

Chapter 3: John Wayne and Jesus

1. *The Didache,* cited in David Bercot, ed., *A Dictionary of Early Christian Beliefs* (Peabody, MA: Hendrickson Publishers, 1998), p. 609.

2. Aristides, Ibid., p. 474.

3. Justin Martyr, cited in Eberhard Arnold, *The Early Christians in Their Own Words,* fourth edition (Farmington, PA: Plough Publishing House, 1997), p. 106.

4. Athenagoras, cited in *The Ante-Nicene Fathers,* vol. 2, 209 [CD-ROM] (Henderson, TX: Scroll Publishing).

5. Irenaeus, cited in Bercot, *A Dictionary of Early Christian Beliefs,* p. 610.

6. Clement of Alexandria, Ibid., p. 677.

7. Commodianus, Ibid., p. 475.

8. Cyprian, Ibid., p. 680.

9. Lactantius, Ibid., pp. 475-476.

10 David Bercot, "What the Early Christians Believed About War," Scroll Publishing, accessed May 25, 2015, https://www.youtube.com/watch?v=lZo6U-ijfgc.

11. Arnold, *The Early Christians in Their Own Words,* pp. 114-115.

12. Abraham Kuyper, cited in "Abraham Kuyper Quotes," Cambridge Study Center, accessed February 24, 2015, http://www.cambridgestudycenter.com/quotes/authors/abraham-kuyper/.

Chapter 4: Hyperbolic Jesus

1. Charles R. Swindoll, *Insights on John* (Grand Rapids, MI: Zondervan, 2010), p. 213.

2. William L. Lane, *The New International Commentary on the New Testament: The Gospel of Mark* (Grand Rapids, MI: William B. Eerdmans Publishing Company), 1974, p. 1.

3. Ibid., p. 184.

4. M.M. Thompson, "John, Gospel of," *Dictionary of Jesus and the Gospels* (Downers Grove, IL: InterVarsity Press, 1992), p. 370.

5. Swindoll, *Insights on John,* p. 307.

6. Ibid., p. 309.

7. Ibid., p. 309.

Chapter 5: Judas and Jesus

1. This is a modified version of an illustration given by David Bercot in "What the Early Christians Believed About Predestination and Free Will," Scroll Publishing, accessed May 25, 2015, https://www.youtube.com/watch?v=cXbXadet10k.

2. Ignatius, cited in Maxwell Staniforth, *Early Christian Writings* (New York: Dorset Press, 1986), p. 103.

3. Irenaeus, cited in David Bercot, ed., *A Dictionary of Early Christian Beliefs* (Peabody, MA: Hendrickson Publishers, 1998), p. 629.

4. Clement of Alexandria, Ibid., p. 629.

5. Origen, Ibid., p. 631.

6. Cyprian, Ibid., p. 631.

7. Ignatius, Ibid., p. 295.

8. Justin Martyr, Ibid., p. 285.

9. Irenaeus, Ibid., p. 286.

10. Hippolytus, Ibid., p. 288.

11. Origen, Ibid., p. 290.

12. Methodius, Ibid., p. 292.

13. Perhaps the best example of a non-Christian being able to perform good works by God's grace is found in the story of Cornelius in Acts 10, particularly in verses 1-4 where unregenerate Cornelius is told by an angel from God that his prayers and gifts to the poor have ascended as a memorial before God. These good deeds were clearly pleasing to God, yet Cornelius's righteous acts could not save him.

14. Randy L. Maddox, *Responsible Grace: John Wesley's Practical Theology* (Nashville, TN: Kingswood Books, 1994), p. 74. Maddox describes the Eastern view of the effects of the Fall: "The true significance of the Fall was our loss of the Spirit's immediate Presence, resulting in the introduction of mortality into human life. This mortality weakened our human faculties and effaced our moral Likeness of God. Thus, the Fall did render us prone to sin, but not incapable of co-operating with God's offer of healing. As a result, we only become guilty when we reject the offered grace of God, like Adam and Eve did."

15. Bible Hub, δουλεύοντες, accessed March 2, 2015, http://biblehub.com/greek/douleuontes_1398.htm.

16. Bible Hub, *douleuó*, accessed March 2, 2015, http://biblehub.com/greek/1398.htm.

17. David Bercot, "What the Early Christians Believed About Imputed Righteousness," Scroll Publishing, accessed May 25, 2015, https://www.youtube.com/watch?v=58p0iLmUrDE. To see what I believe is Paul's own testimony of this processes taking place in his life as a child, read Romans 7:7-12.

18. C.S. Lewis, *The Lion, the Witch and the Wardrobe* (New York: Collier Books, 1970).

19. Bercot, *A Dictionary of Early Christian Beliefs*, p. 295.

20. Origen, cited in *The Ante-Nicene Fathers*, vol. 2, 756-757 [CD ROM] (Henderson, TX: Scroll Publishing).

21. *The Epistle of Barnabas*, cited in Staniforth, *Early Christian Writings*, p. 220.

Chapter 6: If/Then Jesus

1. Blaise Pascal, *Pensées*, sec. xiv, "Appendix: Polemical Fragments," cited at Bartleby.com, accessed March 2, 2015, http://www.bartleby.com/48/1/14.html.

2. David Bercot, *Will the Real Heretics Please Stand Up* (Tyler, TX: Scroll Publishing, 1999), pp. 66-67.

3. David Bercot, "What the Early Christians Believed About Eternal Security," Scroll Publishing, accessed March 2, 2015, https://www.youtube.com/watch?v=4sduMxpZwe4. I must note that I have been significantly blessed by the teachings of many godly Christians who hold Calvinistic or reformed beliefs, and I reference several of them throughout this book. Also, I do not believe that holding to Calvinistic or reformed theology disqualifies someone from salvation. That would be absurd.

4. David Bercot, "What the Early Christians Believed About Predestination and Free Will," Scroll Publishing, accessed May 25, 2015, https://www.youtube.com/watch?v=cXbXadet10k.

5. For a good explanation of the Gnostics, see Michael L. Brown, *Hyper-Grace* (Lake Mary, FL: Charisma House, 2014), pp. 220-238.

6. Clement of Rome, cited in Maxwell Staniforth, *Early Christian Writings: The Apostolic Fathers* (New York: Dorset Press, 1986), p. 28.

7. Ignatius, cited in David Bercot, David, ed., *A Dictionary of Early Christian Beliefs* (Peabody, MA: Hendrickson Publishers, 1998), p. 580.

8. Polycarp, Ibid., pp. 575-576.

9. *Second Clement*, Ibid., p. 586.

10. Justin Martyr, Ibid., p. 580.

11. Irenaeus, Ibid., p. 581.

12. Clement of Alexandria, Ibid., p. 587.

13. Hippolytus, Ibid., p. 588.

14. Origen, Ibid., p. 588.

15. Cyprian, Ibid., pp. 583-584.

16. Lactantius, Ibid., p. 590.

17. Dr. Michael Brown does a fantastic job succinctly explaining conditional security in the appendix of his book *Hyper-Grace* (see pages 249-251).

18. Bible Hub, πιστεύων, accessed March 2, 2015, http://biblehub.com/greek/pisteuo_n_4100.htm.

19. Bible Hub, *aphistémi*, accessed March 2, 2015, http://biblehub.com/greek/868.htm; *apostasia*, accessed March 2, 2015, http://biblehub.com/greek/646.htm.

20. Bercot, "What the Early Christians Believed About Eternal Security."

Chapter 7: Daddy Issues and Jesus

1. Global Rich List, accessed March 2, 2015, http://www.globalrichlist.com.

2. If you go to globalrichlist.com and enter your annual income, you can find out where you stand financially compared to the rest of the world.

3. David Bercot, "What the Early Christians Believed About the Trinity," Scroll Publishing, accessed May 25, 2015, https://www.youtube.com/watch?v=UpPmXUEK3F8.

4. Bible Hub, "John 1:1," accessed March 2, 2015, http://biblehub.com/interlinear/john/1-1.htm; "John 1:14," accessed March 2, 2015, http://biblehub.com/interlinear/john/1-14.htm.

Chapter 8: WDJD? (What Did Jesus Do?)

1. Bible Hub, *allos*, accessed March 3, 2015, http://biblehub.com/greek/243.htm.

2. Ray Vander Laan, "Dust of the Rabbi," part 1, *That the World May Know,* accessed December 12, 2015, http://v2.followtherabbi.com/uploads/assets/audio/dustoftherabbi1_754.mp3.

Chapter 9: Seeing Things for the First Time

1. "Worldview" can be defined as: "(1) The overall perspective from which one sees and interprets the world; (2) A collection of beliefs about life and the universe held by an individual or a group," *The Free Dictionary,* accessed March 3, 2015, http://www.thefreedictionary.com/worldview.

2. Ray Vander Laan, "Rabbi and Talmidim," *That the World May Know,* accessed May 25, 2015, https://www.thattheworldmayknow.com/rabbi-and-talmidim.

3. Bible Hub, *daimonizomai*, accessed March 3, 2015, http://biblehub.com/greek/1139.htm.

4. Derek Prince, *They Shall Expel Demons* (Grand Rapids, MI: Chosen Books, 1998), pp. 16-17.

Chapter 10: Trailers for the Main Attraction

1. David Bercot, ed., *A Dictionary of Early Christian Beliefs* (Peabody, MA: Hendrickson Publishers, 1998), pp. 299-300.

2. Heidi Baker, "Multiplication of Food," accessed March 3, 2015, https://www.youtube.com/watch?v=ZuH4i1nrgjQ.

Chapter 11: Giving Keys to Thieves

1. Derek Prince, *They Shall Expel Demons* (Grand Rapids, MI: Chosen Books, 1998), p. 103.

2. Ibid., p. 104.

3. Subhas R. Tiwari, "Yoga Renamed Is Still Hindu," Hinduism Today, accessed December 2, 2015, http://www.hinduismtoday.com/modules/smartsection/item.php?itemid=1456.

4. Dave Hunt, *Yoga and the Body of Christ* (Bend, OR: Berean Call, 2006), p. 18.

5. We previously discussed the problem any Christian should have with someone or something else other than Jesus claiming the title of "Lord."

6. Hunt, *Yoga and the Body of Christ,* p. 35.

7. Bible Hub, κοινωνοὺς, accessed March 3, 2015, http://biblehub.com/greek/koino_nous_2844.htm.

8. Prince, *They Shall Expel Demons,* pp. 115-119.

9. Ibid., p. 120.

10. Ibid., p. 129.

11. Ibid., p. 130.

12. Ibid., pp. 130-139.

13. Ibid., pp. 108-109.

14. Francis MacNutt, *Deliverance from Evil Spirits: A Practical Manual* (Grand Rapids, MI: Chosen Books, 2009), p. 187.

15. Ibid, p. 185.

16. Bible Hub, *topos*, accessed March 3, 2015, http://biblehub.com/greek/5117.htm.

17. David Bercot, ed., *A Dictionary of Early Christian Beliefs* (Peabody, MA: Hendrickson Publishers, 1998), p. 56.

Chapter 12: A Person of Influence

1. Bible Hub, *sbennumi*, accessed March 3, 2015, http://biblehub.com/greek/4570.htm.

2. Looking back on that night, I believe it's a miracle I wasn't taken to the hospital for alcohol poisoning.

3. To be clear, I am not implying the Scriptures forbid the consumption of alcohol in appropriate ways.

Chapter 13: Miracles on the Third Day

1. Marcia Montenegro, "Kabbalah: Getting Back to the Garden," CRI, accessed March 3, 2015, http://www.equip.org/articles/

kabbalah-getting-back-to-the-garden-/; Gonz Shimura, "Age of Deceit 2* (Full) Alchemy and the Rise of the Beast Image," accessed March 3, 2015, https://www.youtube.com/watch?v=gfRzUI8hkwo.

2. David Bercot, ed., *A Dictionary of Early Christian Beliefs* (Peabody, MA: Hendrickson Publishers, 1998), p. 179.

3. Ibid., pp. 419-422.

Chapter 14: The Divine Messenger

1. Bible Hub, "Isaiah 6," accessed March 3, 2015, http://biblehub.com/interlinear/isaiah/6.htm; JW.org, "Isaiah 6," accessed March 3, 2015, http://www.jw.org/en/publications/bible/nwt/books/isaiah/6/.

2. Dr. Michael Heiser gives a masterful lecture on this subject. See "Michael Heiser—Two Powers of the Godhead—May 4, 2013," accessed March 3, 2015, https://www.youtube.com/watch?v=CUkhWBKCuXc.

3. Bible Hub, "Genesis 16," accessed March 3, 2015, http://biblehub.com/interlinear/genesis/16.htm.

4. Bible Hub, "Genesis 22," accessed March 3, 2015, http://biblehub.com/interlinear/genesis/22.htm.

Chapter 15: The Flood, Giants, and Richard Dawkins

1. Richard Dawkins, "Ben Stein vs. Richard Dawkins Interview," accessed March 3, 2015, https://www.youtube.com/watch?v=GlZtEjtlirc.

2. David Bercot, *Who Were the Nicolaitans and the Gnostics?*, Scroll Publishing, CD-ROM.

3. Cheryl K. Chumley, "Atheist 'Noah' Director Brags Film Is Least Biblical Bible Movie Ever," The Washington Times, accessed March 3, 2015, http://www.washingtontimes.com/news/2014/mar/24/atheist-noah-director-brags-film-least-biblical-bi/.

4. Bible Hub, "Genesis 6:2," accessed March 13, 2015, http://biblehub.com/interlinear/genesis/6-2.htm.

5. See Dr. Michael Heiser, "Angels Cohabiting with Women—Genesis Six Hybridization," accessed March 3, 2015, https://www.youtube.com/watch?v=RHgjGUbFwhE.

6. A second- and third-century historian named Julius Africanus, who professed to be a Christian, theorized the sons of God could be the

sons of Seth and the daughters of men could be the daughters of Cain. However, he also stated the position of the Church was the literal interpretation of Genesis.

7. Douglas Hamp, *Corrupting the Image* (Crane, MO: Defender Publishing, 2011), pp. 128-129; Stephen Quayle, *Genesis 6: Giants: The Master Builders of the Prehistoric and Ancient Civilizations* (Boseman, MT: End Time Thunder Publishers, 2002).

8. "Book of Enoch," Wesley Center Online, accessed March 3, 2015, http://wesley.nnu.edu/sermons-essays-books/noncanonical-literature/noncanonical-literature-ot-pseudepigrapha/book-of-enoch/.

9. Philo cited in Hamp, *Corrupting the Image,* pp. 125-126.

10. Josephus, Ibid., p. 127.

11. Justyn Martyr, cited in David Bercot, ed.. *A Dictionary of Early Christian Beliefs* (Peabody, MA: Hendrickson Publishers, 1998), p. 18.

12. Irenaeus, Ibid., p. 18.

13. Commodianus, Ibid., p. 19.

14. Hamp, *Corrupting the Image,* pp. 17-18.

15. Ron Skiba, *Babylon Rising: And the First Shall Be the Last* (Carrollton, TX: King's Gate Media, 2013), pp. 33-36.

16. Hamp, *Corrupting the Image,* pp. 144-145.

17. For another resource (in addition to Stephen Quale's *Genesis 6: Giants*) containing written and photographic evidence of giants across the world throughout history, see L.A. Marzulli, *On the Trail of the Nephilim,* vol. 1 (Malibu, CA: Spiral of Life Publishing, 2013).

18. Justin Martyr, cited in *The Ante-Nicene Fathers,* vol. 1, 396 [CD-ROM] (Henderson, TX: Scroll Publishing).

19. Cyprian, Ibid., vol. 5, 918-919.

Chapter 16: Feasting with Jesus

1. Dr. Michael Brown, "Jewish Roots of Christianity 1," accessed May 4, 2015, https://www.youtube.com/watch?v=HjUf9FLODiY.

2. John J. Parsons, "An Overview of the Passover Seder," Hebrew for Christians, accessed March 3, 2015, http://www.hebrew4christians.com/Holidays/Spring_Holidays/Pesach/Seder/Introduction/introduction.html.

3. William W. Francis, *Celebrate the Feasts of the Lord* (Alexandria, VA: Crest Books, 1997), pp. 19, 22-24.

4. Ibid., pp. 24-25.

5. Ibid., pp. 34-35.

6. Parsons, "Chag HaMatzot—Unleavened Bread," Hebrew for Christians, accessed March 3, 2015, http://www.hebrew4christians.com/Holidays/Spring_Holidays/Unleavened_Bread/unleavened_bread.html.

7. David Bercot, ed., *A Dictionary of Early Christian Beliefs* (Peabody, MA: Hendrickson Publishers, 1998), pp. 362, 381-382, 526-527.

8. *The Ante-Nicene Fathers,* vol. 1, 955, 957 [CD-ROM] (Henderson, TX: Scroll Publishing).

9. Bercot, *A Dictionary of Early Christian Beliefs,* p. 501.

10. Francis, *Celebrate the Feasts of the Lord,* pp. 44-45.

11. Ibid, p. 55.

12. Ray Vander Laan, "Shavout," That the World May Know, accessed December 12, 2015, http://v2.followtherabbi.com/uploads/assets/audio/shavout.mp3.

13. Francis, *Celebrate the Feasts of the Lord,* p. 57.

Chapter 17: Time to Rise and Shine

1. William W. Francis, *Celebrate the Feasts of the Lord* (Alexandria, VA: Crest Books, 1997), p. 67.

2. Maria Merola, "Yom Teruw'ah: The Day That No Man Knows!," Double Portion Inheritance, accessed March 4, 2015, http://double-portioninheritance.blogspot.com/2011/05/yom-teruah-day-that-no-man-knows_3315.html.

3. Francis, *Celebrate the Feasts of the Lord,* p. 70.

4. For more information and insight into the matter of Abaddon and Apollyon, see Tom Horn, *Apollyon Rising 2012* (Crane, MO: Defender, 2012), and Rob Skiba, *Babylon Rising* (Charleston, SC: Create Space, 2013).

5. For more information on what modern scientists in the Transhumanism movement are already bringing on the earth, see *Inhuman: The Next & Final Phase of Man Is Here,* Tom Horn, dir., Skywatch TV, October 1, 2015; Tom Horn, "Tom Horn—Trans-Humanism," https://

www.youtube.com/watch?v=S3-AZiQLAkU; or Tom Horn, "Tom Horn Transhumanism—Forbidden Gates," https://www.youtube.com/watch?v=siMpa0vlozc.

6. Justin Martyr, cited in David Bercot, *A Dictionary of Early Christian Beliefs* (Peabody, MA: Hendrickson Publishers, 1998,) p. 23.

7. Irenaeus, Ibid., p. 23.

8. Hippolytus, Ibid., p. 424.

9. Cyprian, Ibid., pp. 24-25.

10. Ibid, pp. 23-24. Hippolytus writes of the Antichrist, "The deceiver seeks to liken himself in all things to the Son of God. . . . Christ is a king, so the Antichrist is also a king. The Savior appeared as a lamb. So he, too, in like manner, will appear as a lamb, though within he is a wolf. The Savior came into the world in the circumcision, and the Antichrist will come in the same manner. The Lord sent apostles among all the nations, and he in like manner will send false apostles. The Savior gathered together the sheep that were scattered abroad. And he, in like manner, will bring together a people who are scattered abroad. . . . The Savior raised up and showed His holy flesh like a temple, and he will raise a temple of stone in Jerusalem. . . . He says, 'Dan is a lion's whelp,' [Deut.33.22]. And in naming the tribe of Dan, he clearly declared the tribe from which the Antichrist is destined to spring. Just as Christ comes from the tribe of Judah, so the Antichrist is to come from the tribe of Dan."

11 Merola, Yom Teruw'ah: The Day That No Man Knows!"

12. Ibid.

Chapter 18: Canceling Debts and Conquering Darkness

1. Burke Speaker, "Report: Average American Is $225,238 in Debt," Investor Place, accessed March 5, 2015, http://investorplace.com/2013/09/report-average-american-in-debt-hundreds-of-thousands/#.U_9SFigwxG5.

2. J.E. Hartley, "Atonement, Day of," *Dictionary of The Old Testament Pentateuch* (Downers Grove, IL: InterVarsity Press, 2003), pp. 55-56.

3. Ibid., p. 57.

4. Wesley Center Online, "Book of Enoch," accessed March 3, 2015, http://wesley.nnu.edu/sermons-essays-books/noncanonical-literature/noncanonical-literature-ot-pseudepigrapha/book-of-enoch/.

5. David Bercot, "What the Early Christians Believed About Life After Death," Scroll Publishing, accessed March 5, 2015, https://www.youtube.com/watch?v=QGs7ZOVHdFw; Bercot, "What the Early Christians Believed About Christ's Descent Into Hades," Scroll Publishing, accessed March 5, 2015, https://www.youtube.com/watch?v=KqCve1AxJlM.

6. Bible Hub, *naos*, accessed March 5, 2015, http://biblehub.com/greek/3485.htm.

7. Bible Hub, *hilasterion*, accessed March 5, 2015, http://biblehub.com/greek/2435.htm.

8. Doug Hamp, "The Second Coming of Jesus and the Battle of Armageddon, the Heavens Will Pass Away! (1 of 2)," accessed March 5, 2015, https://www.youtube.com/watch?v=LFejq-ViZTM.

9. Ibid.

11. Doug Hamp, "The Second Coming of Jesus and the Battle of Armageddon, the Heavens Will Pass Away! (2 of 2)," accessed March 5, 2015, https://www.youtube.com/watch?v=uZ_xGPjapSY.

Chapter 19: Everybody Loves a Wedding

1. Charles R. Swindoll, *Insights on John* (Grand Rapids, MI: Zondervan, 2010), p. 153.

2. Ray Vander Laan, "Joy of Living Water," That the World May Know, accessed May 25, 2015, https://www.thattheworldmayknow.com/joy-of-living-water.

3. Ibid.

4. Bible Hub, "Isaiah 12," accessed March 13, 2015, http://biblehub.com/interlinear/isaiah/12.htm.

5. Bible Hub, *skénoó*, accessed March 5, 2015, http://biblehub.com/greek/4637.htm.

6. Mark Biltz, "The Birth of the Messiah Revealed in Scripture," accessed March 5, 2015, https://www.youtube.com/watch?v=3w3MNZQXlrs.

7. Ray Vander Laan, "Original Setting of the Christmas Story," That the World May Know, accessed December 12, 2015, http://v2.followtherabbi.

com/uploads/assets/audio/originalsettingofthechr_378.mp3. For a wonderful teaching describing why the shepherds of Luke 2 would not have been in the fields during the winter, listen to Ray Vander Laan's teaching on the original setting of the Christmas story.

8. Doug Hamp, "The Millennium: Heaven on Earth? (Part 1 of 2)," accessed March 5, 2015, https://www.youtube.com/watch?v=jIixFhdIXgU; Hamp, "The Millennium: Heaven on Earth? (Part 2 of 2)," accessed March 5, 2015, https://www.youtube.com/watch?v=XzVuE2wGzCs.

9. Vander Laan, "Joy of Living Water."

10. Ray Vander Laan, "I Led You Like a Bride," accessed May 25, 2015, https://www.youtube.com/watch?v=zdTsybH_f64.

11. Remember the point made in chapter 13 of this book—that John 12:37-43 states Jesus is the Lord of hosts, or *Yahweh Sabaoth*, of Isaiah 6:1-10.

12. Dr. Larry Crabb, *Finding God* (Grand Rapids, MI: Zondervan, 1993), p. 18.

13. C.S. Lewis, *Mere Christianity* (New York: Collier Books, 1960), p. 106.

Connect with Phil Baker:

www.reclaimingthefaith.blogspot.com